You may be skeptical when you hear the word *cure,* but what you hold in your hands will forever change your thinking about addiction and recovery. *RATIONAL RECOVERY: THE NEW CURE FOR SUBSTANCE ADDICTION* lives up to its promise by introducing the Addictive Voice Recognition Technique—the revolutionary approach to overcoming alcohol and drug dependence. Here are just some of the discoveries you will make with

RATIONAL RECOVERY:

- You **can** take care of your problem *yourself.*
- Anyone—yes, *anyone*—can quit an addiction, for good: all you need to do is to decide to quit, then apply AVRT.
- How to apply AVRT—the process is carefully explained, step by step, with simple exercises to get you going.
- Recovery = secure abstinence.
- How to eliminate "white-knuckling," the struggle that can wear you down.
- How to unlearn traditional disease concepts of addiction that may be holding you back from recovery.
- With *RATIONAL RECOVERY,* there are no relapses, no enablers, no codependents, no triggers, no warning signs, and no "steps."
- You are a normal, healthy person who simply never drinks or uses drugs.
- The Abstinence Commitment Effect—the return of hope, health, and happiness—a direct result of following your own personal Big Plan.
- You *can* tame your Addictive Voice—forever!

RATIONAL RECOVERY

RATIONAL RECOVERY

THE NEW CURE FOR SUBSTANCE ADDICTION

Jack Trimpey

POCKET BOOKS
New York London Toronto Sydney Tokyo Singapore

The statements made by the author regarding certain products and services represent the views of the author alone, and do not constitute a recommendation or endorsement of any product or service by the publisher. The author and publisher disclaim any liability arising directly or indirectly from the use of this book, or of any productions mentioned herein.

Wherever they appear, Rational Recovery®, Addictive Voice Recognition Technique®, AVRT℠, RR℠, Beast℠, Addiction Diction℠, and Big Plan℠ are proprietary service marks of Rational Recovery Systems, Inc.

An *Original* Publication of POCKET BOOKS

POCKET BOOKS, a division of Simon & Schuster Inc.
1230 Avenue of the Americas, New York, NY 10020

ISBN: 0-671-52858-0

First Pocket Books trade paperback printing November 1996

10 9 8 7 6 5 4

POCKET and colophon are registered trademarks of Simon & Schuster Inc.

Cover design by Brigid Pearson
Cover photo by Rieder and Walsh/Photonica
Text design by Stanley S. Drate/Folio Graphics Co. Inc.

Printed in the U.S.A.

CONTENTS

PART III

A Rational Recovery World

ACKNOWLEDGMENTS

Although I am the author of this book, and I was once addicted to alcohol, the inspiration behind Rational Recovery—the movement, the people, and this book—is my wife, Lois. Rational Recovery (RR) sprang from our shared, personal experiences stemming from my own addiction to alcohol. For a decade, our hearts and minds have been joined in the very enjoyable project of creating a clearly marked map that can lead anyone out of the darkness of substance addiction.

The Rational Recovery movement has succeeded against long odds due to the courageous efforts of thousands of volunteers—RR Coordinators from almost every population center in America and in countries abroad. RR Coordinators are important people in any community—pioneers of our times—carrying on the age-old tradition of changing the way things are, trying to make the world better than it was. Having recovered from addiction themselves, they know a lot about it, and their voices are heard above popular mumblings of hopelessness and despair. Their chief reward is the kick they get from encouraging others to quit their addictions without making a big deal of it. Their understanding has been sharpened by their own sorrow, their sensitivity tempered by the pain they have felt, and their vision accustomed to the darkness faced by addicted people. They know.

RR Coordinators understand American values. They stand up for principles of individual liberty, personal responsibility, and self-reliance when those priceless traditions of freedom are threatened. They know that people are free only because they fight to be free and that the foundation of freedom is individual responsibility. Having accepted responsibility for acquiring, maintaining, and ending their own addictions, they have become the foremost experts in the entire field of addiction recovery. RR Coordinators are social reformers of the modern age, a time when the addiction recovery group movement is a defining feature of American society.

A number of professional people have helped Rational Recovery become known in the academic world. I thank Marc Galanter, M.D., Chief of Psychiatry at New York University Medical School at Bellevue Hospital, for his warm reception when Lois and I visited New York to assist in the design of a scientific study of Rational Recovery. Similarly, I thank Ceane Wills, Ph.D., and David Gastfriend, M.D., of Harvard University Medical School, for being the first to show interest in documenting the common reasons people decline to participate in the esteemed 12-step spiritual healing program of Alcoholics Anonymous. A good number of professional people, physicians, psychologists, social workers, counselors, nurses, and educators have also contributed to the growth of the Rational Recovery Self-Help Network during its early years.

Rational Recovery could not have been written were it not for the hundreds of men and women who have participated in our Addictive Voice Recognition Technique® [AVRT] programs since January 1991. From their stories and struggles, I learned many of the principles of AVRT. Nearly all of them had struggled for years with the traditional "disease" approach of Alcoholics Anonymous and Narcotics Anonymous, with tragic and painful results. Most had been in addiction treatment programs based on the 12-step program—some with multiple admissions to expensive treatment centers—and discovered that for them, addiction treatment is a hall of mirrors. They started over, this time by returning to many of their *original* beliefs about themselves and about addiction. To that foundation, they added the principles of AVRT contained in this book. Today the large majority, 70% of them, are abstinent and have built new lives by trusting their own intelligence, their own strengths, their own family values, and their own human nature.

I thank the State of California Department of Drug and Alcohol Programs, whose professional staff provided valuable education to the Rational Recovery movement by visiting and evaluating our program. Their close attention to the only viable alternative to 12-step, disease/treatment services in the state of California, and their willingness to inform the public about the nature and quality of Rational Recovery programming and its vital importance to the many who still suffer from addiction, will be repaid many times over as the winds of change fill their sails.

This book is dedicated to Margaret Sanger, founder of Planned Parenthood. Today, contraception and family planning are available to all American citizens largely due to her willingness to confront the religious zealots of her day who used their powerful positions in government and God's name to censor information on contraception and family planning. The result was needless suffering and death, as well as government destruction of personal liberty. Ms. Sanger, at considerable expense to herself and her own family, breathed life into the word *choice* at a time when giving knowledge of contraception was a crime. She understood what needed to be done, and she did it. As a social reformer, she set a standard that activists and reformers today can strive to match.

One day soon, concise information on planned abstinence from substances may also be available to all citizens. This book is a beginning, our effort to achieve that important goal.

RATIONAL RECOVERY

Introduction

Over a decade ago, I defeated my own twenty-year addiction to alcohol by stubbornly refusing to drink any more of it. I had struggled with alcohol dependence for many years, enjoying its pleasure and suffering its sting, convinced all the while that I was somehow "marked" to continue my folly. I thought I had a disease that caused me to drink against my own better judgment.

As a professional social worker in the 1970s and later, I actively promoted the popular belief that alcoholism is a *disease,* probably inherited, certainly incurable, and one that renders a person powerless over the choice to drink or not. I referred all of the problem drinkers ("alcoholics") I saw to the 12-step program of Alcoholics Anonymous (AA), which for many years has enjoyed a reputation as the only thing that really works. I noticed that very few who attended AA really stopped drinking, but I thought, "I understand their problem because I have it, too. I can see why they don't get better." I was strangely fascinated that "we alcoholics" continue to drink in spite of the well-known trajectory to despair that lies ahead. I did not suspect until much later that it was partly *because* of the popular disease concept that so many fulfill its sodden promise.

Since my early twenties, I had been a world-class drinker, far outdoing others I knew in the pursuit of alcoholic pleasures. I did not attend very many AA meetings myself, perhaps thirty in all, because AA's 12-step program made little sense to me. Also, I am not group-oriented. I am not inclined to talk about my personal problems in front of strangers. I began attending AA meetings in the late 1960s. I was in my late twenties, having a rip-roaring time getting drunk in the evenings and weekends, and sometimes I went to work recovering from hangovers. My tolerant boss once noted on a performance evaluation, "He comes to work with the residuals of the night before." Undeterred, I continued drinking with the idea of being more careful in the future. One late night I wrecked the family car while under the influence of alcohol. My wife, Lois, finally demanded that I do something about the problem, and she took me to an AA meeting held in a church basement. I went inside.

On a coffee table, illuminated by a candle, the Holy Bible was lying open. I listened as a group of gaunt, unshaven men told of their sad experiences in life and spoke reverently of "the program." Gesturing toward the 12-step creed hanging on the wall, one of them told me that I could survive the deadly disease of alcoholism by joining their "fellowship." I cringed a little, but I drew upon my humility (actually my fear of getting fired from my job and being divorced) to listen further.

They described their fellowship as "not religious but spiritual," but I immediately recognized that their program of twelve steps was distinctly and intensely religious (see "The Twelve Steps of AA" following). I found this puzzling because I have always viewed religion as something to be held out for the world to see, even to be proud of, certainly not to be hidden or disguised as something else. I wondered why they would say their program wasn't religious when it obviously was.

The 12 Steps of AA

STEP 1 ▶ We admitted we were powerless over alcohol—that our lives had become unmanageable.

STEP 2 ▶ We came to believe that a Power greater than ourselves could restore us to sanity.

STEP 3 ▶ We made a decision to turn our will and our lives over to the care of God, as we understand him.

STEP 4 ▶ We made a searching and fearless moral inventory of ourselves.

STEP 5 ▶ We admitted to God, to ourselves, and to another human being the exact nature of our wrongs.

STEP 6 ▶ We were entirely ready to have God remove all these defects of character.

STEP 7 ▶ We humbly asked him to remove these shortcomings.

STEP 8 ▶ We made a list of all the persons we had harmed, and became willing to make amends to them all.

STEP 9 ▶ We made direct amends to such people wherever possible, except when to do so would injure them or others.

STEP 10 ▶ We continued to take personal inventory and when we were wrong promptly admitted it.

STEP 11 ▶ We sought through prayer and meditation to improve our conscious contact with God as we understand him, praying only for knowledge of his will and the power to carry that out.

STEP 12 ▶ Having had a spiritual awakening as a result of these steps, we tried to carry this message to others, and to practice these principles in all our affairs.

Those present were mostly quite unlike me, but there was one man there, Bob, whom I knew. Bob worked at a boy's home where I worked part-time. I had always considered him a gentle, caring soul, a loner who was often absent from work. He would return in a few days—sometimes a week or so—and would not discuss or explain his whereabouts. Bob had been drinking episodically for most of his adult years and was a long-term member of AA. The home's administrator accepted his marginal dependability, probably in exchange for low wages and no complaints. He was kind, sincere, and well-liked by the boys under his care.

Bob spoke to me about his own lifelong struggle to remain sober. He seemed to avoid answering my many questions about the 12-step program and said, almost wistfully, "Here, read this book. We call it "The Big Book." It tells us all we need to know in order to live with our disease." I watched him intently throughout that meeting—not because I wanted to be like him, but because I was afraid that perhaps I *was* like him. He seemed hopeless about himself, about life, even about his future, but he spoke reverently of the program he had studied carefully for many years even while his "disease" progressed.

This was not adding up. I thought I had come to a meeting of former drinkers who would explain to me how they quit drinking. I fully expected that they would inspire me to knock it off, to help me grin and bear the difficulties of quitting, and perhaps to offer me some encouragement when I felt tempted to drink. I already sensed that sooner or later my drinking would have to come to a halt. Later, of course, sounded much better than sooner. I later learned that "halt" had another meaning in AA, that the letters *h-a-l-t* stood for *hungry, angry, lonely,* and *tired*—four daily-occurring conditions under which the Fellowship predicts people will drink alcohol unless they are "working a good program."

My perception that AA was religious was confirmed when I read "The Big Book." As a well-churched person, I had read that kind of material for many years. I commented on this at a meeting, and someone explained that religions are not geared to handle alcoholism, that alcoholic priests and ministers come to AA because they need more than their religions can provide. Someone else chimed in to reassure everyone that AA is nevertheless compatible with all religions, ". . . and in fact, AA has salvaged many from alcoholism and sent them back to become upstanding members of their churches."

I accepted this explanation, not only because I had more pressing concerns than to debate the matter, but because I did not feel like challenging this group of sincere, well-meaning people who, it would seem, knew more about alcoholism than I did and who agreed with each other on absolutely everything. "Take what you like and leave the rest," they said, so that is what I did.

I eventually left the religious 12 steps, each of them, but took the disease concept as my own. The disease idea clicked profoundly within me. The moment I thought of drinking as a symptom of a disease I had probably inherited, it felt as if a great responsibility had been lifted from my shoulders. My guts settled down, and I could suddenly see my own behavior in a different light. No longer did it seem that I was behaving stupidly and irresponsibly, no longer did I sense an urgent need to quit drinking alcohol, and no longer did it make sense for me to damn myself for my behavior. I was simply doing what we alcoholics do. We eat to live and live to drink, knowing that tomorrow we may die.

I remember sitting alone in a Detroit bar one evening, my first drink, a double martini, before me. I felt pleasantly excited as I looked at it, but then I had second thoughts. "This stuff is ruining me," I thought. The good feelings left, and the drink and I just sat there in silence, seeming to look at each other. Then I thought about my many attempts to quit drinking, and I recalled the AA meetings I had attended. "I am one of them," I thought, "even though their program is not for me." I wondered if I, too, would be pulled to the bottom by an inherent problem I did not understand. It seemed like such a mysterious condition that could hold my life in check by its threat of imminent downfall, without warning, at any time. I wondered if I would finally become so desperate I would "snap" and accept the religious conversion they proposed and devote my life to the spiritual Fellowship. Alcoholism seemed preferable.

I thought more about Bob and tried to imagine my life in that mold. I decided I would rather die. It did not feel bad to think this way, because the alternative to both AA and dying, as I understood it, was perfectly acceptable—to continue to drink and do what comes naturally. I looked at my hand and imagined it moving to the glass, taking it to my lips, and sipping it down, and then I thought about the future. I saw myself in the proverbial gutter, then in the literal gutter along a street in downtown Detroit. I thought, "Is that what's going to happen to me?"

I felt afraid for a moment and then quickly took the drink and drank it down. Then I thought, "So this is how we are. A disease that makes us powerless over the desire to drink alcohol." The alcohol took effect, and I thought, "Well, there are worse diseases than this!" I still remember chuckling as I thought that, and I quietly lifted off into what I called "the home zone"—the lingering warmth of alcohol that displaces one's nagging awareness of life's problems. As I got more intoxicated, I pondered questions about God and felt sublime.

Drinking that drink seemed to prove my powerlessness; it was just one more example of my powerlessness to act in a responsible way. I believed that my desire to drink was irresistible, and that my own moment-by-moment drinking behavior was a *symptom* of something unknown and beyond my control. I sincerely believed it would take something besides my own critical judgment and self-control to take care of the problem.

I explained all this to Lois, and she was not impressed. She insisted that I simply quit drinking altogether, but I suddenly recalled from my recovery group meetings that *alcoholics cannot be understood by their families* until they, too, come to believe that alcoholism is a disease resulting in loss of personal control. So I was able to accept my wife as an outsider to the secret society—those who really know what alcoholism is all about—as someone who would *unrealistically* expect me to quit drinking, as if I didn't have the disease. Very subtly, I was being drawn close to the Fellowship by my desire to continue drinking alcohol. I said I would start attending AA meetings again. She said she was encouraged by that, but she would not accept going to meetings as a substitute for abstinence. I thought she just didn't understand.

Although I expected that something would eventually have to intervene or rescue me, I could not imagine anything that could prevent me—or even *deter* me—from drinking. As a child growing up in the Methodist Church, I learned to worship and pray to God, but not to expect favors from God. My God cannot be manipulated, does no favors, doesn't disappoint, and doesn't get even. Aloof from human affairs, my God is simply recognized, honored, or worshipped in a spiritual way. He's just there, and that's that.

As AA understands Him, however, God was going to live my life for me, take control of me, provide character repairs, and miraculously keep me sober. This was out of the question. I would live free or die.

When I explained my personal beliefs to the group, they told me to read "The Big Book." I reread it, and I was once again insulted by its sophomoric fundamentalism and even more concerned that AA claimed to surpass the great religions of the world in its ability to contend with addiction.

I got the message clearly: If I didn't surrender my critical judgment, my personal beliefs, and my *self* to the Fellowship of AA, I was doomed to drink myself to jail, to asylums, to hospitals, and to death. "Anything can be your Higher Power. Try nature," one AAer said. So I tried nature as my HP. But my appreciation of nature in those days was *heightened* by a few drinks—I drank to brighten the sunrise and to beautify the sunset. "Try wisdom," another AAer coached. So I tried wisdom as my HP, and I found that I did not have the wisdom to know wisdom from folly. "Then," they said, "let the AA group be your Higher Power," and I looked around the room and saw a group of people I would not choose as friends who were willing to pose as my God. They finally said, "Well then, you can be your own Higher Power." I then knew that something had happened to them and they were no longer thinking for themselves, that their spiritual program was more important to them than common sense, or my problem. I tried a number of HP's, theirs and mine, and they all turned out to be flops at keeping me sober.

"You just want to drink. You aren't ready to quit," they finally said. I knew I wanted to quit, but I also knew they were right. They told me that if I didn't turn my life over to a Higher Power, I would continue to drink. When I suggested I would quit on my own, they said that would be impossible, and even if I did quit for a while, I could not be happy and would eventually relapse. "You are in denial," they said, "which is a symptom of your disease."

Part of me wanted to agree with them. That "part of me" was never discussed in AA. It was simply called an incurable disease. I loved my disease for reasons I did not know, so I accepted that I was crazy to think I could stop drinking all on my own.

I tried a number of different AA groups in different cities, seeking one with a different flavor. There was one called "We Agnostics," to which the mainstream groups sent their "intellectuals, atheists, and agnostics." There, members found support since they were with their own kind, a subspecies of alcoholic seemingly unfit for the regular simple program of spiritual nourishment. Few noticed or seemed to care that there was no written program to replace the standard 12-step program, and that an entire chapter of "The Big Book" was devoted to predicting the demise of agnostics, atheists, and intellectuals. Several ersatz versions of the 12 steps were circulated, with objectionable words and phrases whited out or paraphrased. There was some effort to use current psychological theories to bolster the down-home religious concepts such as taking moral inventories and making amends, but in the final analysis, these maverick groups were identical to the main groups. They were convinced that they suffered a disease that made them different from others, and they believed that if they did not attend recovery group meetings, they would inevitably fall off the wagon.

I quit AA and continued to drink for many more years, as they predicted. I thought they were crazy on the one hand, but quite right on the other. I continued with my career as a social worker, fairly steadily during the days, and often drank during evenings and weekends. As a social worker, I was well placed to search for special programs that might be more relevant, and I did check around, but AA was the only game in town. I attended meetings sporadically with the idea that maybe something, either AA or I, might have changed.

Neither ever did. Looking back, I can see that many of my perceptions were shaped by society at large, which has embraced a philosophy of addiction that *fosters* addiction. I also see that my original, natural viewpoint, before my exposure to professional education and 12-step meeting attendance, was right on target: Anyone can quit now for good, and I had better bite the bullet and get my recovery over with. I had learned the value of individual responsibility as a child, but as an adult I surrendered to a highly gratifying belief that I drank for hidden causes and would need outside help of some kind to stop.

Finally, around 1982, when I had had enough (problems, not alcohol), I decided that either AA was essentially right or AA was essentially wrong. If AA was correct, I reasoned, I would soon die. If AA was dead wrong, as I had long suspected, then I was solely responsible to take control and quit drinking altogether. I finally picked a time, and when that time came, I did it.

Quitting for good was much easier than I thought. When I decided I would no longer drink, I resumed my life—as a person who simply does not drink alcohol. The first couple of months were the most difficult, with much yearning to drink and some irritability, but I did not become like an adolescent, as predicted by experts who believe that addicted people do not grow and mature. Few besides my family even noticed. Because normal behavior is so unremarkable, even *they* soon began taking my abstinence for granted.

Before long, I was feeling much better and enjoying life. For a couple of years, however, I noticed that I still felt insecure about the possibility of relapse. Occasionally, Lois would imagine I was off somewhere drinking. I wondered, "What if AA is right? What if it is true that I cannot do it on my own? Maybe I'm just a dry drunk, biding my time until my next downfall?" I considered returning to AA for a "tune-up," to see if I could fit in sober, as a way to reinforce my plan to stay sober.

I didn't return to AA because it finally dawned on me that Lois had been right all along, that I had made myself physically dependent on alcohol by drinking so much of it, that I had sustained my addiction by avoiding my own responsibility to stop, and that I had continued drinking in spite of the bad consequences because I accepted the *nonsensical* idea that I was powerless to do otherwise. My attachment to my "disease-of-relapse" (as alcoholism is often referred to) was simply a respectable way of planning to drink in the future.

When it finally sank in after two years that I would never drink under any circumstances and that I could predict this with a high level of confidence, my addiction was over. I could finally see myself as a normal, healthy human being who simply doesn't drink alcohol. At first I thought I had accomplished something very special, that I had beat the high odds against me.

I now know that self-recovery such as mine is commonplace. According to research, fully 40% to 70% of those who recover from serious addictions do so without getting help of any kind, including attending self-help and support groups. People do it all the time, but they are dismissed as "not really alcoholic." To follow this logic, no one is an "alcoholic" until they attend their first AA meeting.

A Consumer Movement Begins

Working at a county mental health clinic, I came across many people who wanted to quit drinking but nevertheless continued. I found that they were facing the same dilemmas I had faced; they continued to drink in spite of the negative consequences, in spite of their better judgment, and in spite of their many attempts to get help from professionals, from treatment programs, and from the recovery group movement.

They struggled within themselves, relapsed, and usually got worse. On the one hand, they wanted to stop drinking; on the other hand, they didn't. Even though they rejected much of what the 12-step program offered, they also accepted many of its essential concepts. Specifically, they came to believe, just as I had, that they were suffering from an inherited, incurable, progressive *disease* called "alcoholism." They believed that their disease set them apart from others and that recovery is an extremely difficult, life-consuming undertaking. They also believed that recovery is a mysterious process and that remaining sober is dependent upon moral betterment, serious self-searching, personal growth, spiritual growth, belief in God, prayer, and religion.

They *tried* to accept the simple 12-step program of powerlessness and surrender, which was presented to them as not only the *best,* but the *only* way to get better. Try as they might, they were unable to do so. Given the limited choice between the 12-step "recovering" lifestyle and their addictions, they simply preferred their addictions and chose to *accept* addiction as a way of life. And just as I had, they continued drinking.

Those unfortunates were not sicker than those who did well in 12-step programs; they were in the wrong program. Their misfortune was that AA was the only game in town. I tried to find services for them that were not based on the "disease thinking" and religious concepts of AA, searching more energetically for them than I had for myself. This isn't because I am selfless or altruistic; addicted people often don't look very far for help.

One day, I called every hospital within two hundred miles asking what services existed for people who did not want to participate in a 12-step program. I found none. The people I spoke to said, "No other program works. AA is broad enough for all people. People who don't want to participate in a 12-step program aren't really motivated. Some people have to get worse before they get better."

Lois and I talked often about the 12-step monopoly, sometimes late into the night, and our fascination and interest grew. In 1985, we decided to work together during our free time (Lois was a high school teacher) to create a new organization, patterned after AA but emphasizing abstinence through self-reliance and common sense. We settled on the name "Rational Recovery." We ran a few ads in magazines and newspapers, and soon we started hearing from addicted people and their relatives from all over the nation who were undertaking the same search. They, too, had found that all roads to help lead to the 12-step program of AA—it was the only recovery game throughout America.

I decided to go to bat for people who simply wanted to recover from their addictions by using their own natural abilities. In 1986, I started several Rational Recovery self-help groups in the Central Valley of California, and people attended in increasing numbers.

I found there was a complete absence of self-help literature that did not promote the "disease thinking" of AA, so to give participants something to work with, I wrote a series of essays for the group. Many of them noticed that my material contradicted most of what was set forth in *The Big Book*. One evening, Lois suggested the essays could be organized into a small book called *The Small Book*, and within two years *The Small Book* became a groundbreaking publication in the addictions field.

1985 to 1989 were crazy years for Lois and me, since we lived at considerable distances from our jobs. Rational Recovery gained momentum, triggering excited responses and volunteerism from all over the nation. People were desperate for a viable alternative, and wherever the RR banner was hoisted, people turned out to find out what it was. We sensed that our lives had taken a major turn and that we would likely devote our careers to Rational Recovery. We made the difficult decision to mortgage our home, lease it to a family, and purchase a thirty-six-foot motor home. We parked it halfway between our places of employment so that we would have more hours during the day to work on RR. We also knew that the motor home would eventually become a field office for RR, in which we could travel to any community to set up new local RR projects.

By 1989, Rational Recovery had sixty groups nationwide. I resigned from my county mental health position to devote full time to managing this young, fast-growing organization. Six months later, Lois left teaching after several years. We had bet the family farm on an unknown venture, believing that people would pull together to create an entirely new addiction recovery system, a *rational* recovery system.

We immediately set out on a national motor-home tour, calling ahead to contacts in twenty cities, coast to coast. When we arrived in each city, public meetings had been arranged by our advance people. We got to work, explaining our new approach to recovery based on a technique we called "Addictive Voice Recognition" and some simple concepts of self-acceptance. We announced that something big was happening and that it was no longer necessary to go to AA. Many local newspapers reported on our whirlwind tour, and soon the major media picked up on our activities.

Within two months of our return to California, a story on Rational Recovery appeared on the front page of *The New York Times*. The story quickly hit the newswire in most American cities. For two months, the telephone in our home rang nonstop, even throughout the night. Thousands of people, from all walks of life, called in—the drunk and the sober, families of addicted people, professional people, publishers, journalists, reporters, and editors of many publications. Some began by saying they had been getting a busy signal for over a week, but didn't give up because they knew why the phone was tied up. Their statements, once they got through, were unforgettable. Here are a few that we heard over and over.

"It's about time!" "Hooray!" "I knew this would happen, but I didn't know just when!" "I've been thinking for years about doing this myself, but I didn't really think it could be done." "Congratulations! You're finally here!" "Is this what I think it is?" "This means I'm not crazy!" "You don't know how important this is!" "How can I help?"

We did know how important our work was, because we had been in the belly of the beast ourselves. And we needed help—lots of it—to move forward. The help was there, the program took shape, and today there are Rational Recovery Self-Help Network (RRSN) groups, free of charge, in hundreds of cities in the United States and abroad. A new movement had begun, and informed consumers created a new market for recovery services.

The literature behind Rational Recovery is a critical link in the overall program. *The Small Book* went through three self-published revisions before it was finally published by Delacorte Press in 1992. Clearly, RR is an evolving organization, and the program is flexible to accommodate what we learn along the way. *The Small Book* was titled as a counterpoint to *The Big Book* of Alcoholics Anonymous, and the Rational Recovery Self-Help Network (RRSN) was from its inception an imitation of the 12-step recovery movement. I have described RR many times as the second party in addiction care, and I have urged people to take sides on matters pertaining to addiction and recovery.

The Small Book sets forth concepts of Addictive Voice Recognition Technique, or AVRT, provides a backdrop of psychological self-help material, and presents what is probably the first step-by-step critique of the 12-step program of AA in print. It has been used for six years as a central reference for RRSN participants, and it is widely used to define and characterize Rational Recovery. The *Small Book* continues to be recognized as a groundbreaking publication in the addictions field and is a valuable guide for people emerging from AA and addiction "treatment."

The book you are reading, however, is not a revision of *The Small Book*. The book you are reading is intended to become the *primary, essential* reading for addicted people. AVRT is clearly explained in this book.

Origins of AVRT

Although I discovered and named the Addictive Voice Recognition Technique, or AVRT, I did not invent it, nor did I synthesize it from existing theories and practices in the fields of psychology or addiction treatment. AVRT was taught to me in a very direct way by the hundreds of clients who have come through the program. By 1989, after several years of Rational Recovery organizational development, I had only a basic understanding of the technique as presented in *The Small Book*. But by 1991, I noticed that I was rapidly gaining new insights into AVRT beyond the personal understanding that had helped me defeat my own addiction. Participants gave amazing descriptions of their own Addictive Voices. Soon their behavior in the program became understandable within a concrete, multidimensional, dynamic vision of the human brain. When participants were presented with this structural model of addiction, they usually felt greatly relieved to learn that they weren't congenitally defective or diseased. They were also encouraged to understand finally, in a simple way, why they had persisted with drinking in spite of everything. They gained hope and confidence in their ability to *control* their addictive behavior and voluntarily end their addictions. I began to take notes, and the discipline of AVRT emerged. So far, I have found no other written material that summarizes the vivid thinking and feelings of addicted people—other than the book that is in your hands.

Rational Recovery, now over a decade old, is a pioneering effort to bring order to the chaotic addictions field. Along the way, we have learned many things we did not expect to learn, such as the surprising potency of AVRT, which has shaped our program.

Of a group of 250 persons who enrolled in AVRT: The Course between 1991 and 1993, 65% remain abstinent today. All had extensive unsuccessful experiences in AA and about 90% had multiple prior admissions to 12-step treatment programs. A study of Rational Recovery self-help groups by New York University Medical School at Bellevue Hospital conducted by Marc Galanter, M.D. ("Rational Recovery: An Alternative to AA for Addiction," *The American Journal of Drug and Alcohol Abuse,* 19:4, 1993, pp. 499–510), found that 74% of those who attended for four months were abstinent. Approximately 300 early responses to a questionnaire at the back of *The Small Book* immediately following publication of the book found 91% abstinent, not surprising for a self-selected population, but nevertheless an indicator that something very good is going on.

Studies have recently been done by major universities to identify the reasons why people leave AA, to determine the characteristics of people who do well in Rational Recovery, and to discover which elements of RR account for its effectiveness. Hospitals and other health care institutions, recognizing their 12-step bias, have been licensed by Rational Recovery Systems, Inc., to include AVRT in their programs and to offer Rational Recovery by name to the public. *The Chicago Tribune* reported on an RR-licensed hospital in which 80% of inpatients who were offered the choice between AA and RR elected RR.

We have been shocked to find that the state of affairs in the addictions field is far worse than we originally thought. Several sections of *Rational Recovery* discuss the problems in American-style addiction care, but I will briefly cite some statistics here to give a sense of the problem.

Although it is generally believed that the recovery group movement and addiction treatment programs are helping large numbers of people to defeat their addictions, this is not so. First, the recovery group movement population is ever-changing and anonymous, making research extremely difficult. This permits sustained, exaggerated claims of success by its enthusiastic members and supporters. But according to an issue of the *Harvard Medical School Mental Health Review* in 1990, no more than 10% of those who have a drinking problem ever go to AA. But what about those who do make the effort to go to AA meetings? We find from AA itself, in its 1989 triennial membership survey, that at least 50%, and as many as 81%, drop out within the first month, and only 5% of those who start attending meetings continue for one year. Those who continue as members most often do not remain sober for long, although longer periods of attendance are associated with longer periods of sobriety. Charles Bufe, in his *AA: Cult or Cure?* estimates that AA's overall success rate, for its members, is less than 5%.

Considering that America has placed its trust almost entirely in Alcoholics Anonymous, and considering that our courts, hospitals, and social agencies routinely mandate AA as part of their important work with substance abusers, it would seem cause for public alarm that so few who attend AA remain in the program or stay sober for long. This problem is urgent because people exposed to the program are routinely told that 12-step meeting attendance is essential to recovery. Nevertheless, we hear constant optimism about the recovery group movement and addiction treatment. "Addiction is a treatable condition!" they say. Is it? "Treatment works!" they say. Does it?

Rational Recovery makes these questions moot for you. RR is not part of the recovery group movement, and you will administer your own cure. As the saying goes, if you want something done right, do it yourself.

PART I

1

What Is AVRT?

Since AVRT wastes no time in getting to the point, I will demonstrate AVRT by presenting a transcript drawn from a conversation with a woman I'll call Virginia, who telephoned the Rational Recovery office in 1994. The conversations presented in this book are composites of actual dialogue; nothing has been embellished or invented.

Yes, Virginia, There Is a Cure for Alcoholism

"I just got out of a hospital rehab program. I guess it didn't do me any good," she said. "I only stayed sober for ten days."

I asked, "Why did you go into the program?"

"Because I'm an alcoholic," she said. "I got real bad, and I needed help drying out. I hate living my life this way, but nothing works. I've been in two other rehabs in the last three years, and I've been to a lot of support meetings, but I always go back to drinking."

Notice that she portrays herself as a victim, inexplicably drinking in spite of receiving much treatment, and she describes how painful her life is.

"So, what's your plan this time?" I asked.

"That's why I'm calling you now. I still need help," she answered.

I pressed a little. "Let me ask again. **What is your plan concerning the future use of alcohol?**"

She was perplexed. "Plan?"

"Yes, Virginia," I responded. "What is your plan? Are you going to drink some more? Or, are you going to quit drinking?" I waited as her wheels turned.

In American-style recovery, the idea of planning to quit drinking is considered unrealistic, most often a sign of the disease of alcoholism.

Finally, she answered, "I don't have a plan, one way or the other."

I asked, "Does that seem strange to you?"

"I'm not sure what you mean," she said.

I proceeded to draw a rather bizarre picture. "I mean, Virginia, you have been in three expensive hospital rehabs in the last three years, and you say you hate living in the chains of addiction. But when I ask what your plan is for the future use of alcohol, you come up blank. Isn't that odd?

Although the lack of any plan to quit drinking is a chief characteristic of addiction, addicted people do not perceive that a plan to quit would be of any help.

Annoyed, she said, "Well, if I knew that, I wouldn't have a problem, would I?"

Pressing further, I said, "Of course not, which is exactly why I ask this blunt question. You have a serious addiction to alcohol that you say is ruining your life. You placed this call to find a way to end that addiction, didn't you?"

"Well, I think so," she said, "but you are making it sound like I can just wish this problem away and go on as if I weren't an alcoholic."

Notice the antagonism toward anyone who would suggest that one simply quit drinking. You will be learning much more about this common reaction.

I continued, "What did you learn last month during your hospital rehab?"

"Learn?" she asked, puzzled. "Oh, I learned that I will never really recover from my alcoholism because it is a chronic disease. I will have to go to meetings for the rest of my life, and relapse is a *normal* part of recovery. I can spot signs of relapse, especially denial, by looking for feedback from others. If I don't go to meetings, I am probably in the process of relapse. I still have a lot to do with getting my Higher Power together, and I have trouble with step one, which is the powerless step. I still have some trouble with that, and there're still some problems with my personal inventory that I will have to work out. I have no serenity, and my spiritual life is way down. I had post-acute withdrawal symptoms in the hospital, but I couldn't figure out what they were because I felt normal. Life seems impossible when I look very far ahead, and that's what scares me, so I try to go one day at a time. I read *The Big Book* over and over, because they say I will eventually understand the meaning of the steps. There, is that what you mean by what I learned?"

She is fully involved with the formalities of treatment, and she is articulate in discussing her inner life with others. It is common for people "in recovery" to become self-involved, preoccupied with spiritual and psychological matters, and to speak of themselves as if they are subjects navigating an obstacle course.

I leveled with Virginia. "Yes. You just told me that you have no plan to recover from alcoholism. You plan to flounder with your addiction for years to come, experimenting with Higher Power ideas, playing games with the powerless idea, trying to prove to yourself that you're a decent person, and going to meetings that bore you stiff. And, very importantly, Virginia, you plan to relapse any time you feel like it."

A long silence ensued. Finally, she quietly said, "That is perfectly correct."

You may wonder why she didn't become angry at this confrontation. This is because she is of two minds about addiction and recovery. On the one hand, she wants to keep drinking, but on the other, she wants to solve her problem. Moreover, I didn't suggest she actually quit, but only described how she flounders in recovery.

She continued, "And I feel like killing myself when I think of it."

"Have you been thinking of getting rid of yourself for quite a while?"

This was a safe guess on my part. Suicidal ideas are a very common occurrence among addicted people, although they rarely take action on those ideas.

"Yes," she whispered.

"But, obviously, you do something else instead. What do you do each and every time you think of killing yourself because of your drinking problem?"

"I get drunk."

Suicidal ideas serve an important purpose of justifying drinking.

"And you have no plan to stop drinking. Isn't that strange, Virginia? Did anyone in the hospital suggest you stop drinking alcohol?"

"Yes, the pharmacist said I shouldn't mix alcohol with my antidepressants."

"So at least *someone* besides me thinks you can choose not to drink alcohol. But what do you think? Would you like to make a plan to stop drinking, for good?"

Annoyed once again, she said, "It's not realistic for me just to say I won't drink anymore. This thing has destroyed others in my family—my father, and two brothers. It is a disease that runs in the family, and that's part of what's going on with me. You don't seem to understand. Have you ever been addicted to anything?"

Addicted people will manipulate never-addicted people, skillfully and endlessly, and they will reject counsel they don't like if it comes from a never-addicted person.

"Yes, booze, for many years. And I also used to believe the same nonsense you've been telling me for the last few minutes. I thought I had a disease that was making me drink, and I thought I was destined to drink forever. But I finally cured myself by quitting drinking."

She retorted, "Thinking there's a cure is denial! Alcoholism is incurable."

There is a pamphlet from Hazelden Publications, an AA-oriented publisher, titled, "Don't Tell Me I Don't Have a Disease!" A picture shows a man with an insistent expression, as if his life depended on believing alcoholism is a disease. People in addiction treatment are taught that challenging the disease concept is dangerous and can result in death.

"Oh yes, Virginia," I explained. "There is a cure for alcoholism, and it's as old as the hills."

"A cure? You said a *cure* for the disease of alcoholism? The counselors at the hospital say we can only arrest it. Isn't the idea of a cure dangerous thinking?"

"Well, if you think that 'cure' means you can keep drinking, perhaps."

Virginia finally asked, "**So, what's the cure?**"

"**Abstinence**," I replied.

"Anyone can be a dry drunk," she said, now sounding well rehearsed.

To discourage people from making a commitment to permanent abstinence, which would result in immediate and complete recovery, the recovery group movement predicts that people who take that approach will disintegrate or explode. "Dry drunk" is a fictitious condition that is said to afflict alcoholics who merely quit drinking and fail to surrender to the 12-step way of life. This condition, called "addictive disease," is inferred from any irregularity or imperfection that may be noticed in newly abstinent people, and it is said to be progressive and fatal. Dry drunks, it is said, almost invariably relapse, and if they don't relapse, they can never be happy. The dry drunk concept steers people away from the most obvious, effective, risk-free, and wholesome solution to any substance addiction—an immediate commitment to permanent abstinence.

I interrupted, "Hold on. Let me ask you, what would your life be like if you never drank again?"

"I can't think of what that would be like," she said.

"Won't," I corrected. "You won't, because you plan to drink forever. But go ahead, Virginia, take a peek. What would you be doing today if you hadn't been drinking for the last few years?"

"I would be in business as a graphics designer in Europe, where my ex-boyfriend lives. He would have me, but not in this condition." She recounted how her fiancé finally gave up on their relationship because of her repeated relapses.

"So today is just an outcome of your past drinking, and you

can see that your future, likewise, will be an outcome of any further drinking. But, do you *want* anything better than what's going on now?"

"Yes, very much. That's why I called."

"Then, how about making a plan to never drink again?"

She hesitated, "I can't. It makes me feel too anxious. I just can't."

She knows I'm not kidding, and she realizes that she is capable of quitting anytime she chooses. If this weren't so, she would not feel anxious or take my suggestion seriously.

"Very good, Virginia," I said. "You are actually doing very well at what we do in Rational Recovery. Right now, you are *feeling* your addiction. And you are having conflicting thoughts about the use of alcohol. You are *ambivalent* about drinking, something *all* addicted people have in common. On the one hand, you would like to stop drinking and get on with your life, but on the other hand, you are terrified of giving up alcohol. That part of you wants to drink forever."

Virginia senses she is understanding something for the first time, something extremely important. This early insight will grow rapidly, build on itself, and result in lifetime abstinence.

"Yes!" she exclaimed. "You've hit it on the head again! At one level, I *do* want to flounder with this addiction forever, playing the recovery game and relapsing from time to time, but I *also* want to get this behind me and get on with my life. I'm sick and tired of being sick and tired. Right now, I have a strong desire to quit drinking for good. But I'm afraid to feel it too much. I may be in denial—denying that my disease is chronic and incurable and progressive. If I relapse again, my hopes will be dashed, and I'll be more depressed than ever. But I *do* feel both ways. And I *do* want to get better. Right now!"

She recognizes that she is of two minds. There is the voice that wants to get better, and there is the voice of her addiction, which wants her to languish in recovery. Most people who call Rational Recovery face the same dilemma, and they are usually excited at the prospect of an actual, immediate cure *from the ravages of addiction. So I made Virginia an offer she would not likely refuse.*

"Okay," I said, "you're on. If you want to kick your addiction for good, here's the game plan. Ready?"

"Okay, go ahead."

"Think right now about the idea of never drinking again. Are you open to that?"

"I'm open to that."

"Fine. But there's another voice in your head, and it is saying something else. What does it say?"

Virginia paused and said, "A voice says, 'You can't do that. You know you'll drink again. You're doomed to a life of drinking. It can't be any different.' "

I explained, "What you are hearing in your head is what we call the Addictive Voice. It is the part of your own thinking that argues incessantly for more drinking. It tells you how impossible it is for you to decide simply to quit drinking once and for all. Get it?"

"Like there are two of me?" she asked.

"Almost. There is only one of you, but you are of two minds about quitting. You may plan never to drink again, but your Addictive Voice has different plans. You can learn to recognize your own Addictive Voice as not-quite-you. Those thoughts are yours, for sure, but they aren't *you*."

"Oh, *that* voice! You mean the one that is telling me right now to have a drink once we hang up?"

"You're doing it, Virginia! You are now practicing what we call Addictive Voice Recognition Technique, after only a few minutes of talking about it. In Rational Recovery we call it 'AVRT,' for short. The letters almost spell out the word *avert*. You can completely recover from your addiction in a relatively short time by doing what you just did."

Some people have a profound insight after as little explanation as this. Once, after I appeared on a radio talk show, a man called me to say that he had heard my explanation of the Addictive Voice while driving to a business meeting at a hotel. He had struggled with his addiction for many years and was so struck by his insight that he pulled off the highway to think it over. He realized he was rushing to appear at the hotel so he wouldn't be late, but he also knew he would wait half an hour in the cocktail lounge, having a drink before the meeting. On the phone, he exclaimed, "I can see that it's like there are two of me, each arriving early for two totally different reasons. I could never see this before, and I can also see that my drinking days are finally over!" Others, such as Virginia, are skeptical about the insight until they understand it better.

I continued, "Now, tell me what you think of AVRT so far."

Virginia paused, then said, "Well, I can see it could give me some control, some of the time, but I doubt that it would last for long. I can probably use AVRT to do better at times, but no one's perfect. I really doubt that I can *always* resist the desire to drink."

"Let me suggest, Virginia," I said, "that just now you heard your Addictive Voice, but failed to recognize it."

"I don't think so," she said.

"Here is what I heard your Addictive Voice say: 'AVRT is neat, but I will still drink any old time I really feel like it.' Do you see how your thinking predicts you will drink whenever you feel like it?"

"Now that you point it out, yes. I do see. I'm setting myself up so I can drink."

I said, "Let's say 'it'—your Addictive Voice—is setting you up to drink. It disguises itself as you, and you end up doing its bidding. In a sense, you have an enemy voice within you, a voice that overrides your own better judgment."

Virginia said, "This is already starting to make more sense than thinking I have a disease. This Addictive Voice, as you call it, is a real, uh . . ."

"Beast. We call it the Beast, because it behaves like one and doesn't care about anything but booze. It doesn't care about you or anything you value, including your relationship with your fiancé, your career, your health, or even your life. It will tell you that life is so rotten that you may as well commit suicide, gambling that you will drink instead of going to the trouble of killing yourself. But it's easy to recognize, Virginia, and once it is exposed, it is defeated. I have no trouble hearing your Addictive Voice now on the phone, and with a little practice, it will be just as easy for you."

Feelings of hopelessness are part of any addiction. They can lead to serious depression. AVRT offers immediate hope and a sense of personal control that some find exhilarating. Like others who learn about AVRT, Virginia responds to this with some very good feelings.

"I get it!" she said. "This feels like a terrific breakthrough! Right now I have a feeling of hope I haven't had for years. I actually feel like *I can do something to help myself*. Why haven't I heard of this before? I mean, with all the treatment I've had. . . . Why isn't this information given in regular treatment programs?"

I told her, "Things are changing. Rational Recovery has been around for over a decade, and is well known by the professional and treatment communities, but most people haven't heard of RR or AVRT yet. RR is a well-kept secret because the 12-step program dominates almost every addiction treatment program and crowds out all other points of view. AA seems to help some who *choose* it and appreciate its good points, but it probably harms even more people who, like you, are forced into it by lack of choice. As in your case, many people become very discouraged and depressed when they find the 12-step program is against their values or does not work for them."

Virginia asked, "You know what this means?"

"What?"

"This means I'm not crazy. The more treatment I got, the more confused I got. What I'm seeing now is so simple, it seems like I have always known it. Maybe I have, but I didn't trust myself."

Virginia enjoys feeling vindicated from the negativism of 12-step recovery. Being able to reject disease/treatment concepts is very important to recovery from addiction.

"I'll bet that feels good," I said.

"It's like a great weight has been lifted," Virginia said. "I have hope. You can't imagine."

"Oh, yes I can. I was there, too."

Virginia has been abstinent since that call nearly two years ago. She went on to read this book in an earlier version. She has made a lasting commitment to abstinence, and her life is much improved. She went to Europe, as she dreamed of doing, and now functions as a normal person who simply never drinks alcohol or uses drugs, not even at the sidewalk cafés of Paris! Her boyfriend, she says, appreciates her more than ever.

Virginia is one example of how seriously addicted people may finally accept responsibility and take charge of their lives.

2

An Overview of AVRT and Rational Recovery

Addictive Voice Recognition Technique (AVRT) is the name Rational Recovery has given to a very simple thinking skill that permits anyone to recover immediately and completely from addiction to alcohol or drugs. AVRT is also a description of how human beings naturally recover from substance abuse, alcohol or drug dependence, or "addiction." For eons, people have been figuring out AVRT on their own, but they have not named it. This special knowledge has been around for as long as people have felt the sting of substance pleasure, yet it has never been set down as educational material.

AVRT is a forgotten heritage in America, where it has been replaced by an opposite concept. We had it, but lost it. Rational Recovery has rediscovered this special knowledge, named it, and registered the name with the United States Patent and Trademarks Office. We have done this to keep it simple, to keep it separate from influences that would make it more or less than it is. Even though AVRT is as old as the hills, it is brand-new to contemporary America—in fact, revolutionary. After hearing a brief explanation of AVRT—a doctor from Pittsburgh, Pennsylvania, recently said, "People just *quit* their addictions? What a radical idea!"

Do You Have a Drinking or Drug Problem?

Nearly every self-help book on addiction I've read has a section that helps the reader to decide if he or she really has a drinking problem or drug addiction. Often there are checklists with questions like "Do you drink more than you intended? Do you have blackouts? Do others complain about your drinking? Have you lost a job because of drinking or drug use?" and "Do you hide how much you drink?" These books are usually written by persons who have no personal experience with substance addiction, or by people who believe in addictive disease. By asking such questions, they are setting you up to be told that, *in their opinions,* you have a problem. They believe addicted people are pathetic dumbbells who cannot understand the link between their drinking/drugging and their serious life problems and don't know what to do about it.

I strongly prefer to make the opposite assumptions: If you aren't sure you have a drinking problem, you probably don't; and if you do have a drinking problem, you are acutely aware of it—whether you are sober as a stone or drunk as a skunk. I also believe that if you know you have a problem with drinking or drug use, you know perfectly well what to do about it. Therefore, I will not use pages in this book or your time in reading them to teach you once again what a drinking or drug problem is. It's different for everyone, and it would be arrogant for me to say you have a problem with alcohol or drugs if you think not.

It is fair at this early moment, though, to say that if you *suspect* you have a drinking or drug problem, you probably do. Here's why. Your suspicion is probably based on your own experience of the drawbacks of drinking or drugging, yet you plan to continue with it. That is a problem. Moreover, you are engaged in an extended inner debate about what to do—to drink less or at certain times, to drink or use different beverages or substances, or to quit some or all of them for a while or forever. The presence of that ambivalence or indecision, while continuing to drink or use, fits our definition of *addiction.* AVRT, if you choose it, ends that inner debate and allows you to resume your life as a normal person who simply never drinks or uses drugs.

Does this talk about abstinence sound scary? I'm sure it does. Ideas of moderation or controlled drinking/using probably flood your thinking as you read this page. These ideas feel more comfortable because *you are doing nothing different about the problem*—the same problem, incidentally, that has led you to pick up this book. You may want to classify yourself as one who need not abstain, using a convenient handle such as "social drinker," "problem drinker," or "party person." But follow your suspicions, and you may find yourself. Follow your intuition, and you may recover without much ado.

Unfortunately, your body is unlikely to change in its relationship to alcohol or drugs, and predicting the future may be more of a wish fulfillment than a realistic plan. Your continued efforts to get away with the indulgence of drinking or using may be compared to shooting craps. You can continue to roll the dice or walk away from the game. When you are ready, AVRT will make quitting much easier than it may now appear.

Detox—The Short of It

Very few people need medical attention for alcohol withdrawal. Those who do need medical help with detoxification need it very badly, because they may have seizures and delirium tremens (DTs) and may die without prompt medical attention. If you are dependent on alcohol, make a plan now for detoxification, a plan that you know is safe. You probably know how to get off alcohol, because you have done it many times before. If you're unsure, consult your doctor.

It's a good idea to let someone know you are self-detoxing, in case you get sick. If you get shaky or nauseated, it's helpful to have someone around for moral support and to watch over you. Drink fluids such as Gatorade, AllSport, or other thirst-quenchers for athletes. They may take the edge off by helping balance your blood chemistry. Chicken broth is a soothing remedy. Thiamin tablets taken as directed on the container also help. Eat small amounts of food, sleep. You may know of other things that will help, but there is no way to avoid discomfort.

Remember that during detox you are *choosing* discomfort—

yes, sickness!—over the deep pleasure of alcohol or drugs. It cannot be otherwise. The discomfort will be no worse than a bad case of the flu and probably more like a mild case. You will feel bad in order to feel better. Think of other things, read if you can, watch TV. Stick around home unless you know you will not get sick away from home and suddenly decide to get a quick fix. Don't drive while detoxing. You may not be sharp and might get into an accident, and a police officer will smell alcohol on your breath, even the next day.

If you have ever had serious withdrawal symptoms, seek medical attention before you quit. If you have been drinking over a pint of liquor every day for more than a month, and especially if you are over forty, consult with a physician about withdrawal. If you notice symptoms such as feeling very weak and shaky on your feet, poor balance, fast heartbeat, strange visions, or hearing things, see your physician or go to an emergency room. If you detox at home, it is good if someone stays with you during the first day. If you are taking more than the prescribed amount of Valium or other prescribed medication, see the doctor who prescribed it. If you are an opiate user (heroin, morphine, codeine) or if you use cocaine, just stop and suffer for a few days. If you are in reasonably good health, you won't die, but you will have to pay back some of the pleasure you borrowed against the future by taking drugs.

I have been challenged on this position by recovering people who insist that withdrawal is a horrendous experience that I don't understand because I was addicted to alcohol and not opiates and who point out that some people have died during opiate withdrawal. I respond that I know from firsthand experience that acute withdrawal from alcohol can be very painful, certainly painful enough to justify drinking; any such justification, however, is nevertheless the Addictive Voice. Because opiate withdrawal is accompanied by elevated blood pressure, persons suffering from hypertension may die from a stroke. So, if you are in doubt, consult a physician. Let him or her know that you will be using AVRT as your recovery program if you do not wish to be referred for addiction treatment.

If You Quit, You Will Quit Now

Sounds like an order, doesn't it? But this is an example of your sensitivity to the idea of abstinence. Actually, "You will quit now" is only a statement, because events occur only in the present moment—the "now." AVRT is a *now* approach to complete recovery that frees you, your time, and your resources from the costly process of solving personal problems first and recovering later.

Freedom from addiction feels good. Your journey to recovery will be a short one, for this entire book can be read in a few hours. It will be an exciting ride, with many good feelings along the way. You will be challenged to use your own mind to *take control of yourself,* to take back your life from addiction, and to feel good as a fully recovered person.

Read *Rational Recovery* carefully, and enjoy the many insights you will take from it. The book is divided into three parts. Part I presents some background information. Part II is vivid instruction on AVRT; and Part III presents information for families and persons interested in the field of addiction.

If you find some of what you are about to read awkward, annoying, or even threatening, rejoice in the awareness that you are unlocking the prison that has held you captive for many years. You may have called that prison "freedom," your freedom to drink and do as you choose, but behind the door of AVRT lie many pleasant surprises. Any change in thinking or behavior is difficult. Quitting an addiction, if that is what you choose, is one of the biggest life changes you can experience.

The next few pages contain a "crash course" on AVRT—all you need to know in order to recover completely from your substance addiction. Get a grip and read on.

The Crash Course on AVRT

The following 200-word description of AVRT may be enough for you to break through and end your own substance addiction, right now!

> Observe your thoughts and feelings, positive and negative, about drinking or using. Thoughts and feelings that support

> continued use are called the Addictive Voice (AV); those that support abstinence are *you*. When you recognize and understand your AV, it becomes not-you, but "it," an easily defeated enemy that has been causing you to drink. All it wants is pleasure. "I want a drink" becomes "It wants a drink." Think to yourself, "I will never drink again," and listen for *its* reaction. Your negative thoughts and feelings are your AV talking back to you. Now, think, "I will drink/use whenever I please." Your pleasant feelings are also the AV, which is in control. Recovery is not a process; it is an event. The magic word is "Never," as in, "I will never drink/use again." Recognition defeats short-term desire, and abstinence soon becomes effortless. Complete separation of "you" from "it" leads to complete recovery and hope for a better life. The only time you can drink is now, and the only time you can quit for good is right now. "I will never drink/use again" becomes "I never drink now." It's not hard; anyone can do it.

Are you starting to get it? AVRT is a piercing insight into the nature of addiction that places you in complete control over the decision to drink or use drugs. Some people figure it out on their own, others learn by reading, as you are here, others learn better in group discussions, and others learn through skilled, personal instruction at Rational Recovery Centers.

AVRT is like the Heimlich maneuver, a first-aid technique that has saved thousands from choking to death. It can save your life, it is extremely simple, it is based on common sense, and it replaces a common error that makes the problem worse. (Prior to the Heimlich maneuver, the standard first aid was to pound a choking person on the back, driving the obstruction deeper. Similarly, the recovery group movement often has the effect of aggravating addictions and preventing prompt recovery.) AVRT, however, is first aid you give to yourself!

Although AVRT is very, very simple, you have to know what you're doing, and learning it can be tricky at first. This is because your Addictive Voice is determined that you will keep drinking or using, so it can survive. It is therefore ruthless in its pursuit of alcohol or drugs, but it can also be quite subtle, forceful, seductive, persistent, and patient, and it has many other qualities.

Few realize that most people recover completely from substance addictions on their own, without getting help. You probably know some yourself, friends, relatives, or neighbors who finally quit for good when they had enough, without making a big deal of it. AVRT is how they did it. Afterward, some say, "It was getting the best of me, so I just quit. I finally knew I had enough and quit for good." Others say, "It wasn't easy at first. I still wanted to do it, but I overcame it. When I wanted to do it, I thought about the bad times." Many say, "I went cold turkey and white-knuckled for a while, and then it was gone." White-knuckling is an RR term for the anxiety caused by struggling with the beast instead of recognizing the AV.

Although these people were seriously addicted, they somehow turned themselves around. If you will notice the use of the pronouns "I" and "it" in their comments, you will see that they were doing something along the lines of AVRT. When you have read further, ask anyone you know who *independently* quit an addiction, "How did you do it?" If you listen carefully, you will very likely hear echoes of AVRT.

It does help, however, to know what you're dealing with. The Addictive Voice is a tough character, and it is determined to keep you addicted. It is also subtle; it has been causing you troubles without your knowing it. But when it is exposed to you through AVRT, it collapses, and you will prevail.

ACTION

Bullets for Your Beast

The following bulleted points fit together as a perfect defense against future drinking or fixing.

- Make a safe plan for detox. You are responsible to protect yourself against acute withdrawal symptoms. If you are in doubt, consult with your physician.
- Clear your mind of everything you "know" about substance addic-

tion. Focus only on your own behavior and the consequences you experience from drinking or drugging. Forget for now about the recovery group movement, the disease concept of addiction, brain chemistry, lousy recovery statistics, and nonsense jargon like *denial, relapse, triggers, enabler, alcoholic, addict,* and other recovery group movement concepts.

- Focus on the obvious. If you're doing something harmful to yourself, wouldn't it be good to stop it? If you have trouble drinking moderately, wouldn't it be good to quit altogether?
- Right now, experiment with the idea of *never* drinking or using again. Think of the pros and the cons. Listen to your own thoughts about quitting for good, and notice the mixture of feelings you have.
- Notice that you feel *both* ways about quitting. On the one hand you want to quit, but on the other hand, you would like to continue drinking or drugging as much as you want, forever. You are *ambivalent,* feeling both ways.
- Your Addictive Voice (AV) is your body talking to you, in thoughts and feelings, telling you to drink or use drugs. It is the *sole cause* of your substance addiction.
- Your AV is the *expression* of your appetite or desire for alcohol or drugs. That appetite originates in the biological, animal side of human nature, so we call it your "Beast."
- Your Beast expresses itself through conscious thoughts, mental images, and feelings, but it cannot act on its own. It is a dumb thing that knows only one answer to any question, one solution to any problem, one action for every occasion. You are human, much more intelligent and versatile, and therefore you have an enormous advantage over it.
- Recognize that your Beast is *ruthless.* It cares for nothing you love. It wants only one thing—the pleasure of alcohol or drugs. It will exploit any tragedy, take advantage of any good fortune, to get you to drink or to use.
- Notice how clever and convincing your AV sounds, how *it seems to be you.* It can use your name, has access to everything you know, uses reason very well, and remembers only the good times drinking or drugging. *You,* of course, have many other memories, and you can reason far better than it can.

- Notice that when you think about the possibility of drinking or drugging, you feel anxious, knowing the likely consequences, but you also feel pleasantly aroused, anticipating that familiar pleasure. That pleasant feeling is your AV. Remember, your Beast has feelings just as you do. It will be jealous of people who drink or use without problems, it will resent people who interfere with its supply, and it will feel excited when you consider drinking or using. It likes the disease idea because then you can call your decision to drink or use a "relapse." Regardless of its disguise or how pleasant it feels, it is your deadly enemy, so treat it as such.
- Use Addiction Diction: Your Beast must use pronouns to get what it wants, and its favorite pronoun is "I." If you hear "I want a drink," recognize that "it," your enemy, wants a drink. When doing AVRT, stay in the first person pronoun "I," as in "I am in control. It wants a drink, but I don't drink." This will force the AV to use the second person pronoun "you," and it will say something like, "You can handle it. You've been good now for six days, and you can have just a little, just this once." Rejoice! You are in control. You have forced your adversary to come to you, using the pronoun "you," arguing, begging, and pleading. Sometimes, it will even speak for both parties, you and it, by saying, "We need something. Let's go downtown and get some." Have no mercy. Be at least as cruel to it as it has been to you. Abstain.
- Pick a time to quit. No matter when you decide to quit, it will be "now," so now, right here as you're reading, is a perfectly good time to quit for good.
- Go ahead with your Big Plan, your plan to give up your addiction forever. Do it alone, following the instructions below, and don't share it with anyone. Ain't nobody's business but your own.

How to Make a Big Plan

- Halfhearted or experimental plans to quit for good won't do the trick. It's all or nothing. It's up to you to learn how to make a Big Plan that will endure for eternity. Think about the meaning of each of these five words, "I will never drink/drug again."
- Feel the discomfort. That is your Beast, frightened of you. It knows

you are capable of destroying it, just as you know it is capable of destroying you. When you think of never drinking, your Beast will generate strong feelings that may include anxiety, depression, anger, grief, and a desire to be left alone. These feelings are common in early sobriety, but they fade with time.

- Think about why you are quitting for good—no new problems caused by drinking or using, a better life, better marriage, education, health, money, whatever you hope for. Feel the hope. That is you at your best.
- Now, say the words slowly to yourself, with as much meaning as you can, "I will never drink/use again." Mean it! Trust that you will always be able to recognize the inner longing to drink or use as your deadly enemy. Be willing to let your "old friend" suffer and die.
- Look at your hands, which are necessary to consume alcohol or drugs. Understand they are under your complete control at all times. Your Beast has no power over you; it is a quadriplegic that must appeal to you in order to convince you to drink or use. Wiggle your index finger. Now challenge your Beast to do the same. Get it?
- Listen for the echo. When you state your Big Plan, you will almost certainly hear some serious commotion in your head. It may be angry commotion, or sadness, or fear, or bald cynicism like "Oh, sure. A likely story. What a lie. What a lot of crap this AVRT is." That is your Beast in action, defending itself against the worst thing possible. You are the one threatening it, in effect, with death. Fortunately, it is not you. You will survive, but *it* is certainly upset! Too bad.
- Now, complete your Big Plan by saying it again, with meaning, and add, ". . . and I will never change my mind." Your Beast will get the message. Humans naturally dominate Beasts, within or without.

You Now Have a Big Plan

- From here on, your task is simple, but crucial. All you do is listen for and *recognize* any thinking or feeling that even remotely suggests that you will drink alcohol or use drugs again. The "R" in

AVRT stands for recognition—not "removal," "refutation," or "reasoning with." Just recognize your Beast's feelings and thinking, and they will fall silent. It is only when you engage in dialogue with the AV, or attempt to reason or argue with it, that you will have "white knuckles." You will be surprised and fascinated at how much of your thinking is actually your Addictive Voice. You may be stunned to discover how much recovery movement concepts have become part of your Addictive Voice, paving the way for more drinking or using.

- Learn the potent technique of "Shifting," fully described in a later chapter, and discover that you can voluntarily control your feelings in the presence of alcohol or drugs. Any leftover feelings of powerlessness over addiction will vanish forever!
- When you have stopped drinking or using for a few days, you may feel uncomfortable, restless, or irritable. That is not a physical craving, but only "Beast activity." This is not mysterious, nor is it a symptom of addictive disease, the "dry drunk." Your Beast is plenty upset at what you have done.
- Notice how you feel about your Big Plan. This is big stuff. You are doing something that will change your life forever. You will be able to move forward, feeling the good and the bad in life without the anchor of addiction pulling you down. How does it feel?
- In Rational Recovery, we call the good feelings following your Big Plan the Abstinence Commitment Effect (ACE). Many people feel quite uplifted, even exhilarated, to have conquered an addiction. If you feel good now, trust your feelings!
- Do not accept that such feelings are "a pink cloud." Those good feelings are you! Trust them! The ACE is not just a peak experience that fades away. It unfolds for many years to come. A decade from now, you may still feel the pleasant effects of your Big Plan. I still do.
- Many people appreciate AVRT as if it were a subroutine in a BASIC computer program:

    1. I never drink.
    2. "(anything thinking or feeling that supports drinking)"
    3. Go to 1.

- In the short run, you will probably discover that some of your pet hang-ups, the ones that seemed to cause you to drink or use, don't even exist. They were simply well-worn paths to the bottle or needle that no longer have a purpose. Because a Big Plan changes the way your future looks, depression is a problem that commonly fades away. With the understanding that there is no possibility of any further drinking or drugging, social anxiety, problems related to anger, and irritability may also be expected to diminish during your early months of lifetime abstinence.

- Don't count time. Counting time since the last drink or use is Beast activity. If you're never going to drink or use again, why count time?
- Stay alert for new Beast activity, which may be sudden or gradual. The Beast doesn't give up easily, and it is a strong opponent. When you feel the struggle within you, it is only your old enemy having a hard time with its new master—you.
- Knowing this builds great confidence that your addiction is over once and for all. Your Beast activity will taper off, and within a matter of weeks or months abstinence will be effortless.
- Your Beast will never really die or completely disappear. It cannot forget the past pleasure and will wait patiently for any opportunity—sometimes sudden, sometimes subtly planned, sometimes in unusual circumstances—to drink or use again. Years or decades from now, your Beast will still occasionally wake up. This is harmless and means absolutely nothing, except that you are in good health and your Beast is trying to do its job. With your Big Plan, Addiction Diction, Shifting, and knowledge of the Structural Model, you are secure. You cannot fail to recognize your AV because there is nothing more conspicuous to a formerly addicted person than ideas of indulging once again. Be as confident as you can be. After all, you won!
- Don't congratulate yourself for abstinence, or expect others to do so. Is it really remarkable or cause for celebration that you have been acting responsibly?
- No one will know that you are completely recovered for quite a while. It is for you to know and them to find out. Some will never believe you, but so what?
- If you are considering recovery group meetings to decrease the chances of relapse, think again. If you are never going to drink/use again, what is your purpose in attending recovery group meetings?

Is there a chance you will drink? If you think so, you are hearing your AV. Strangely, your interest in meetings is probably your AV, suggesting that you can't know what you will or won't do in the future, that you don't know right from wrong because of a mysterious disease, and that somewhere out there is a drink or a fix with your name on it—unless you scurry off to a meeting. Subtle, eh? If you have trouble thinking this through, read the rest of *Rational Recovery,* go to an RR meeting, or call or e-mail RR!

- Don't hang around with recovery groupers. Form new relationships based on common interests (passions!) rather than common problems.
- The bottom line is this: Part of you may be deeply skeptical of AVRT, Rational Recovery, the people behind RR, or of the whole idea of sudden self-recovery. When you doubt AVRT, you are only doubting yourself and your own ability to quit your addiction, right now and for all time. You may think, "It can't be this simple." And that, of course, is your Addictive Voice, loud and clear!

By now, you may be getting the hang of AVRT. You may see that complete recovery may very well be within your reach, and within a short time. Congratulations. You have noticed the obvious. Notice how *that* feels!

ACTION

Questions

Now, take a moment to reflect. Look at your substance problem both ways—as you did before AVRT, and after AVRT. After just a few pages of reading, new possibilities are before you. Ask yourself some questions, such as:

1. What would my life really be like if I didn't drink or use at all?
2. Is drinking/using really as important as I have made it seem?
3. What if I quit for good, with a Big Plan, and still have big problems?

4. Is there some disease or physical condition that has been compelling me to drink?
5. Should I get treatment for my addiction?
6. Do I need more support in order to remain sober?
7. Do I really want to change?
8. Do I really want to give up the pleasure of drinking/using?
9. Have I already gone over the edge, so there's no use in trying?
10. Is AVRT something I want to do immediately, or sometime later when conditions are more appropriate?
11. Is there any evidence that AVRT works?
12. Is AVRT just a put-on? Can it really be that easy?
13. Why total abstinence, when moderation would work?
14. Why a lifetime commitment, when it is easier to abstain for limited periods?
15. Can I really know for sure that my drinking or using days are over?

What AVRT Is Not

AVRT is not a form of addiction treatment; it is an attractive *alternative* to addiction treatment. *Rational Recovery* is unlike any other recovery book because it gives addicted people clear, direct instructions that if followed will result in lifetime abstinence. Addiction treatment is an *indirect* approach that assumes that your drinking or drug use is a symptom of some hidden cause. The treatment intends to correct or remove the cause, following which you inexplicably become sober.

AVRT is not therapy or counseling, but it makes those services possible, if you need them. Whatever problems you have are your own, and AVRT makes no attempt to make you a happier, better-adjusted, more successful, or more self-accepting person. Those are your responsibilities, also. The outcome of AVRT, however, is nearly always improvement in all areas of life. After all, one is no longer burdened by the yoke of addiction.

AVRT is not a philosophy any more than a recipe for bread is a philosophy. Follow the directions and you get bread. AVRT fits well with most philosophies because it isn't one itself.

Likewise, because AVRT is not religious or spiritual, it dovetails perfectly with any of the great religions. Christians, both Protestant and Catholic, Jews, Buddhists, Muslims, humanists, atheists, agnostics, or people from any persuasion will find no contradiction of AVRT in their beliefs. Indeed, descriptions of AVRT-like concepts are common in the scriptures of the great religions.

AVRT strengthens the foundations of Rational Recovery by going beyond any particular philosophy, any psychological theory, or any combination of counseling, therapy, or health care. Except for beliefs and values pertaining to your own drinking or use of nonprescribed drugs, your religious views, your psychological understandings, and your beliefs about health and nutrition will have little, if any, actual bearing on your recovery from substance addiction. AVRT is not a design for living nor a plan for self-improvement; it is a method to achieve secure abstinence and that is all it is. Because the focus of AVRT is narrow, it can reach far more people than more elaborate systems of thought can. I doubt that any legitimate religion would suggest that human beings, addicted or not, are incapable of independently abstaining from alcohol or drugs. Many religions encourage abstinence, and AVRT is a tool to that end.

AVRT is not part of the recovery group movement. In fact, AVRT replaces the recovery group movement with individual self-recovery. When you have a fuller understanding of AVRT, you may see that the recovery group movement is itself an expression of the AV. To use an extreme example, imagine attending a meeting that begins, "What is your plan for the future use of alcohol or drugs?" If you say, "I will continue to drink, but moderately," the leader would say, "That is fine, but we can't help you with that goal." If you say, "I will never drink or use again," he would say, "If that is so, then why are you here?" This is not an example of how the Rational Recovery Self-Help Network conducts meetings, however. RR Coordinators know that people have much to discuss and much to learn, and people are welcome to participate in order to become oriented in AVRT.

Because our concepts of addiction and recovery are far removed from the popular recovery group movement, people often fail to realize that RR groups are not really support groups, and that once the basics of AVRT are known, attending recovery groups has little to do with whether one will continue to drink or use. For example, we prefer the expression "self-help group" over "support group," which denotes dependency.

AVRT relentlessly challenges the ideas of addictive disease, addiction treatment, powerlessness, alcoholism, codependency, triggers, sponsors, warning signs of relapse, family alcoholism disease, one-day-at-a-time sobriety, enablement, surrender of control, dependency on higher powers, and endless "recovering," because these are *deadly* ideas to large numbers of addicted people. During a time of special vulnerability, when one is desperate for *anything* that will help, the 12 steps may "take," and become a part of one's *Addictive Voice.* To people who are struggling with an addiction, they are seductive ideas—subtle, inviting, and appealing. For many, they are ideas that remain in place until thoroughly debunked. Remember, the AV is any thinking that supports the idea that you will drink or use. All of the above qualify in spades.

Likewise, many mental health practitioners persuade addicted people that the secrets of recovery may be discovered by indirect, therapeutic means. This is a variation of the disease concept of alcoholism, in which the drinking appears to be a symptom of yet another problem, some emotional insecurity, or some inner disorder. "Treat the real problem," they say, "and the symptom of drinking will go away." This kind of thinking is tenacious. In the past, I occasionally presented addiction as if it were a mental health problem, which it is not. I have also implied that learning to feel better is a way to ensure sobriety, on the (false) assumption that happy folks are less inclined to return to drinking. *Rational Recovery* sets the record straight on these and quite a few other matters.

Rational Recovery from addiction is a natural and healthy process; once learned, AVRT becomes automatic and effortless. People who overcome addictions are living examples of triumph over adversity.

3

An Adjustment of Attitude

This book is ridiculous. It can't be this simple.

—Your Beast

Rational Recovery headquarters in Lotus, California, is a very busy place. Word is getting around that something new is happening. People call for a wide range of information, including meeting information, how to start an RR group, the recommended readings, upcoming conferences, lectures, workshops, and so on.

Most who call are calling for themselves, and they want *whatever it is* that RR has. Quite often they are desperate. After only a few months of answering the RR phone, Lois and I recognized that we had opened a Pandora's box, that across the nation people were discouraged by their experiences in the recovery group movement and addiction treatment. We began to see distinct patterns in the statements people made, and it became clear that many were being systematically intimidated, misguided, and harmed. They told of "slogan therapy," in which very reasonable questions were dismissed with snappy comments like "Take the cotton out of your ears and put it in your mouth" and "Fake it 'til you make it." Many found themselves bewildered by "denial hazing," in which cherished beliefs were viewed as disease symptoms and all signs of self-confidence, self-reliance, and self-esteem were regarded as "sick." Distraught family members told of being diagnosed as "codependent" and were in a quandary because they felt responsible for "enabling" a family member's substance addiction. We began calling their troubles *recovery group disorders* and *addiction treatment disorders.* Many people troubled by 12-step programs are relieved just to hear that there is a name for their predicament. They say, "This means I'm not crazy!"

Addiction produces a combination of *desperation for help and contempt for oneself* that permits spectacular abuses. AA has a proprietary interest in all chemically dependent people, and you are one of them. Its methods for gaining and retaining members are sometimes subtle, but often delivered with authority borrowed from our social institutions.

I believe it is unwise to become entangled with 12-step activities. Churches are far more appropriate for the ends they espouse. Therefore, I have listed several suggestions for you to consider. Remember that these suggestions are not advice, and you know far better than anyone what is best for you.

ACTION

Some Suggested Dos and Don'ts

1. **Never say you are "an alcoholic" or "an addict,"** no matter how much you drink, how long you've been drinking excessively, how much your parents or grandparents drank, no matter what physical illnesses you may have as a result of drinking, and no matter how many doctors, psychologists, social workers, and nurses tell you that you are "an alcoholic," or "an addict." Just say, "No, I am not an alcoholic. You are mistaken if you think I am an alcoholic. If you keep calling me an alcoholic, I will take some action to stop you." Do not put in writing that you are an "alcoholic" or suffering from "alcoholism," because "alcoholics" are a special class of people discriminated against by courts, insurance companies, and employers and viewed negatively by the public. Admitting or stating that you are an "alcoholic" is like testing positive for HIV—you can't rid yourself of the stigma,

and it invites the most extraordinary kind of discrimination and social and institutional abuse. [Labeling yourself is also detrimental to your recovery from addiction.]

2. **Avoid being referred to agencies** that may label you ''alcoholic'' in their records. Ask agency employees about this. Request that your counselor or physician use the acceptable terms *excessive drinking, heavy drinking, drinking problem, problem drinking, alcohol dependence, alcohol abuse, drug abuse, self-medication,* or *drug dependence,* instead of the expressions *alcoholism, alcoholic, or addict,* in any records. If it is suggested that your request indicates that you are ''in denial,'' discontinue contacts with that service provider. Ask about that agency's reporting obligations. Try to prevent your name from becoming part of any database compiled by government-controlled agencies. Individuals in that database comprise a special class of people who are treated differently. Your employer has access to your diagnosis if you receive insured care for ''alcoholism.'' As the health care field changes, it is in your interests to avoid being identified within the federal and state data systems as an ''alcoholic,'' a ''drug addict,'' or as one suffering from ''the disease of alcoholism.'' All of this can be avoided by quitting your addiction immediately and then seeing what problems you really need help with later.

3. **Never say you're out of control, or that your life is unmanageable.** If those things were really true, you would have to be locked up or assigned a guardian or conservator to manage your personal affairs. You chose to drink. No one else did. Even if you made irresponsible judgments while intoxicated, they were your lousy judgments and you were in control and therefore responsible for the consequences.

4. **Do not admit that you violated any law under the influence of alcohol or drugs.** Do not do it in an AA meeting, in an RR meeting, in a chemical dependency program, while talking with a chemical dependency counselor, or most especially, while attending an AA meeting in jail or in prison. Confessing crimes

while doing a fearless moral inventory has no relevance to overcoming alcohol or drug dependence, will probably be used against you, and may result in charges being brought against you. If you are required to attend AA meetings, remain silent about your past, refuse to do fearless moral inventories, and avoid personal entanglements with a sponsor. In order to abstain from alcohol or drugs, Addictive Voice Recognition Technique (AVRT) will allow you to remain sober as a stone without submitting to Higher Powers, sponsors, and other 12-step program expectations or requirements.

5. **Never incriminate yourself** if you are asked by an authority figure if you have been drinking. People who ask rarely have your interests at heart, even chemical dependency counselors and other professionals from the addictions field. Telling on yourself is usually unwise and may lead to consequences far more painful than your drinking or drugging.

   A man recently called Lois and explained that after over a year of abstinence he had taken just one drink. He immediately regretted doing it, resolved he would drink no further, and did not. But his probation officer somehow came to suspect that he had been drinking and referred him to a chemical dependency counselor. The counselor spoke with him in a very friendly, supportive way, almost pleading for him to admit he had taken a drink. "Just once, you've got to trust someone," the counselor said. "This is really for your own good, and nothing bad is going to happen if you did drink. You will be glad later if you'll only level with me now. Now, just tell me, did you have just one drink?"

   The caller could hardly contain himself on the phone as he told Lois, "I told him. I knew better, but something happened inside me—maybe it was because I was brought up in a good family to be honest. But I told him I had one drink the week before. For this, I have been sent back into treatment, which means attending 12-step meetings every single day for the next three months, and I must show up for two counseling sessions a week with a counselor I detest." The caller cried because he had worked so hard to succeed after release from prison and was finally making it. He explained that he would certainly lose his job, the most important thing in his life since his release, not because he had been drinking, but because his treatment schedule conflicted with his work hours. The alternative to treatment and AA meetings? Return to prison.

This caller is one of hundreds of thousands of people locked into the American addiction treatment gulag, where a warm, helping hand is also the one that can turn the key on a prison cell.

6. **Do not admit to alcoholic "blackouts,"** even though you may have had memory lapses while intoxicated. If you do admit to blackouts, you may be accused of saying or doing things you cannot deny because of your admitted blackouts.

7. **Do not reveal highly personal information at AA meetings.** Although the meetings are anonymous in the sense that people do not use last names, they are not confidential. No group process is really confidential. One man wrote in a letter, "After my first treatment program through the Veterans Administration, I chose a man for a sponsor who practically blackmailed me with information I had given him by confessing my 'sins.' When he felt I was not complying with the program enough, he made the information public, which caused serious damage in my social life, in my work, and in my personal relationships. Now I'm back in AA, and it's scary, since I am seeing similar things happen to others." Telling other people about your mistakes does not relieve guilt or contribute to your recovery from alcohol or drug dependence. Confession, the flip side of "denial," may gain you the momentary acceptance of group members, but that is not something you need. Instead of confessing guilt, stop damning yourself, give yourself less to damn yourself about by abstaining, and concentrate on your own self-acceptance rather than the acceptance of others.

8. **Seriously consider going to jail if you are convicted of drunk driving.** If offered a substance abuse diversion (SAD) program that requires AA attendance, you are free to decline. State

your reasons for refusing, if you do. If you are intimidated or forced to accept 12-step involvement against your wishes, call the Rational Recovery Political and Legal Action Network at the Rational Recovery national office (see Appendix C). There is dignity in defending your First Amendment rights and in paying the price for a stupid act. If you choose jail over a SAD program, it's over when it's over, and you are then free to drink responsibly if you so choose (remember, RR is an *abstinence* program designed for *addicted* people, not for the occasional drinker who got caught), or free to work on your addiction on your own terms or using AVRT. An impending jail sentence is severely intimidating for most people, and under those circumstances AA may seem to be a program of attraction rather than promotion. By taking the so-called ''easy way out'' and appearing to believe yourself that you are diseased with alcoholism, your life may be forever changed. Your treatment can follow you for many years, even though you are not addicted to a substance, have been abstinent for years, or are committed to permanent abstinence. By identifying yourself as an ''alcoholic,'' you will be subject to the endless moral and legal authority of the institutional 12-step recovery movement. It's important to remember that in today's computerized world, it's easy to get into a government database—and practically impossible to get out. You can easily be labeled—*for life.* The saying ''Once an alcoholic, always an alcoholic'' takes on new meaning here.

9. **Discuss these issues with your attorney** if you are mandated to AA or if you believe that you are being denied your constitutional rights. Many people feel strongly that the religious aspect of AA results in an infringement or violation of the First Amendment freedom of religion clause. Others feel that their Fifth Amendment rights are violated because mandated 12-step participation requires confession of guilt. Still others have pointed out that the Eighth Amendment (cruel and unusual punishment) may be violated when recovery group disorders or addiction treatment disorders result from forced 12-step participation. Clearly, AA-refuseniks are not provided equal ''treatment'' (in ei-

ther sense of the word) under the law as required by the Fourteenth Amendment.

10. **Read *Rational Recovery*** and *The Small Book* as well as the bimonthly *Journal of Rational Recovery* to supplement your decision to remain sober on your own. Get a copy of *The Rational Recovery Catalog* (call 1-800-303-CURE; or write Lotus Press, Box 800, Lotus, CA 95651) for a wide range of literature, audiotapes, and videotapes to increase your understanding of Rational Recovery. Go to a Rational Recovery Center for intensive AVRT, or attend Rational Recovery Self-Help Network (RRSN) meetings in your area. If these are not available in your area, call Rational Recovery for information on how to start a local RRSN project or how to bring an RR Center to your community. (See Appendices for addresses and phone numbers.)

11. **Stop drinking or taking drugs.** It's risky business. In the amounts you probably use, it isn't good for you and will probably cause you more trouble than good.

Rational Recovery in the Post-treatment Era

The implications of AVRT are awesome—for the individual and for society at large. The emergence of AVRT within Rational Recovery has challenged the concept of addiction treatment in America and points toward a return to authentic, traditional, American values. As such, *Rational Recovery* is the first book for America's post-treatment era.

In its decade of existence, Rational Recovery has achieved some outstanding successes, considering its small size and limited resources. The media has been kind on one hand, but biased and unimpressed on the other; and the professions, in spite of their genuine interest and willingness to pitch in and help, ultimately have little to offer addicted people. Politicians are vexed with the problem of mass addiction, but cannot stray far from solutions based on the status quo. Hospitals have flown the Rational Recovery banner and opened their doors to a new kind of patient—the one who wants the shortest route to recovery, AVRT. But the character of addiction care will not change much until the public demands a better mousetrap. Ultimately, the marketplace rules and will determine the shape of addiction services.

Rational Recovery has the very best product in the addictions field, AVRT. While many still receive expensive addiction "treatment," the post-recovery era has quietly begun in a number of American and Canadian cities. In 1995, Rational Recovery Systems, Inc., began establishing locally owned and operated Rational Recovery Centers. The centers, staffed by formerly addicted people who teach the same method they used in their own recovery, provide skilled instruction on AVRT in a brief format called AVRT: The Course. The cost of AVRT: The Course demonstrates once and for all that addiction care can be very inexpensive, very effective, and mercifully brief.

An RR Center is a unique resource in any community. It is a place people can go to quit a substance addiction without becoming part of a government database, without being expected to tell stories on themselves, without leaving behind volumes of records containing confidential information, without undertaking moral, psychological, or spiritual improvements, and without a prescription to attend recovery group meetings. In fact, no records are kept at the RR Centers, because collecting and recording background information would drive the cost of AVRT up and because background information has nothing to do with drinking or drugging in the first place. Attending recovery groups after learning AVRT is not discouraged, but it would be fair to ask what the purpose of attending meetings would be if one is not going to drink or use drugs in the future. Many who complete AVRT: The Course are referred to other organizations for help with problems other than their addictions.

Although addiction treatment may be passé in areas having an RR Center, treatment of *legitimate* mental health and medical problems, when they persist, will continue to be immensely important everywhere.

Why would one enroll in AVRT: The Course after reading

this book? Because learning styles differ. For example, some people figure out how to work on automobiles, sew, ski, play tennis, or cook by sitting down, experimenting, and doing it. Others read books about those subjects and create their own self-study programs. Some learn much better by hearing the subject discussed, rather than by reading, and others do best with "hands-on" instruction, with or without reading, and they enroll in formal training. People who enroll in formal training programs usually do quite well, because the material is presented clearly by skilled instructors. If, after reading this book, you choose to go to an RR Center and enroll in AVRT: The Course, that doesn't mean you are not motivated, or that you have a worse problem than someone who reads it once and never drinks again. It means that you are serious about solving your problem with addiction and are determined to do it by using AVRT.

AVRT: The Course is an unprecedented program in which people attend classes for several weeks to learn *the skill of abstinence* and nothing else. It is brief, inexpensive, and upbeat. Some may wonder if RR Centers are only for those who can afford the modest charge for services. That is a matter beyond the control of Rational Recovery, but it is fair to wonder why any agency now spending public funds on addiction treatment would not immediately enroll their addicted clients in AVRT: The Course and pocket the difference as a savings of public funds.

4

The Recovery Hall of Mirrors: Let's Shatter the Illusions

If you have been to an amusement park and seen a "house of funny mirrors," you know that reality can be distorted so that things aren't what they seem. Little things look big, large things appear small, and common objects are distorted beyond recognition. In this chapter, I will present some common, popular ideas about addiction and recovery that can be troublesome—if you believe they are true.

***Illusion* 1** ▸ The Grand Illusion: Recovery from substance addiction has something to do with attending meetings where people talk about themselves.

People who decide to attend their first recovery group meeting have already considered quitting their addictions, but they choose to attend the meeting instead of quitting for good. This is the nature of addiction. AA literature states, "The only requirement for membership is a sincere desire to quit drinking/using," acknowledging that quitting is essential and if a newcomer has not considered quitting, then now is the time to do so. But the very next message to the newcomer says you can't quit for good on your own, but only one day at a time while you build a new philosophy of life, one meeting at a time. The stage is quickly set in recovery groups for endless procrastination of the vital decision to quit one's addiction unconditionally and forever. That crucial decision becomes lost in endless discussion of spiritual and psychological matters, all of which seems to prove that quitting for good is a lost cause.

It is commonly believed that abstinence is a result of solving psychological, moral, emotional, and spiritual problems, and that social support is indispensable to becoming and remaining sober. This misshapen idea is the focus of several very strong lenses—the mass media, government funding sources, the health care professions, the courts, and the recovery group movement itself.

You can witness this illusion through the looking glass of your television set when you see shadow-forms of anonymous people speaking in disguised voices. They tell how their lives were salvaged from addiction through membership in the recovery group movement, but they cannot explain how they quit drinking and take no credit for remaining sober. Instead, they credit the recovery group movement for their new lease on life, sometimes exclaiming, "Don't ask us how it works; it just works." They do not believe it is likely or even possible for addicted people to recover without joining their organization, and they are noticeably eager to welcome new members.

Mystery, secrecy, and personal anonymity describe the means America has chosen to remedy one of its most serious social problems. Although the recovery group movement seems to grow in response to an epidemic of mass addiction, let's consider the possibility that the reverse is actually happening: that mass addiction may be a natural outcome of the recovery group movement's assumptions about human beings and its visions of addiction and recovery.

Nine out of ten who enter the recovery group movement simply pass through and leave with vivid memories of what they saw. Many of them who are not taken in by the ruse go on to quit their addictions, but many others become troubled, even enchanted, by the images they saw while passing through.

Some stay in the recovery group movement because they like

the images, but many others stay because they are desperate for anything less frightening or disappointing than their own lives. Many have forgotten that they once searched for a way out and have become accustomed to their special way of looking at things. Fascinated with the marvelous illusions cast by a wavy looking glass, they strive to convince others that their visions are true, assuming that those who cannot see the illusions they see are blind.

Each illusion below is followed by an explanation that, I believe, corrects it back to reality.

***Illusion* 2 ▸** "Chemical dependence," "addiction," and "substance abuse" mean the same thing, and may be used interchangeably.

"Chemical dependency" is an *individual liberty with known risks* such as organic disease, mental deterioration, psychiatric syndromes, social ostracism, violence, divorce, unemployment, arrests, and imprisonment. Most often, chemical dependence is a *benign* state in which people use substances for personal reasons, including pleasure, often in the presence of painful and harmful side effects.

Some people *choose* to remain chemically dependent and can think of no good reason to change their behavior. They truly want to devote their personal resources to sustaining their supply of the substance. Within their experience, chemical use and abuse is meaningful and fulfilling, and sometimes even moral, ethical, and appropriate. They defy efforts to infringe on their freedom to treat their bodies as disposable containers. Their motto, which Rational Recovery accepts, may be construed as "Live free *and* die."

Human beings depend upon many chemicals, including oxygen, but it would be odd to describe human beings as "oxygen addicts." Many people depend upon prescribed or over-the-counter drugs to lead more healthful and comfortable lives. Others use substances for the pleasurable effect they produce; these include caffeine and other stimulants, tobacco, sugar, fat, herbs, alcohol, marijuana, opiates, and miscellaneous substances called "street drugs."

All substances taken in sufficient amounts, including oxygen, have negative side effects to offset their benefits, and it is correct to say that people would not suffer a drug's side effects if they did not use it. A "side" effect, however, is secondary to a substance's primary effect, which in the case of alcohol and drugs is *pleasure.* One way to limit side effects of substances is to limit or prohibit people's access to the substances. A more effective way is to enable people to limit or prohibit their own use of the substances.

It is vitally important that consumers of a substance be *educated* about its side effects. People who drink heavily, eat lots of sugar, take drugs for enjoyment, eat fatty foods, smoke cigarettes, or drink a pot of coffee or tea each morning are not *necessarily* addicted. If they are aware of the negative side effects, they may freely choose these dependencies for reasons that are entirely personal.

An "addiction," however, is a different thing altogether. **An addiction exists *only* when an individual continues to use an intoxicant against his or her own better judgment.** Addiction exists only in the presence of *ambivalence,* when the desire to use a substance is accompanied by a desire to minimize personal harm by reducing or quitting the use of the substance. Addiction is characterized by a subjective experience of "loss of control," which is actually the *reversal of intent.* Reversal of intent results in an impaired ability to stand by earlier decisions not to drink or use, to predict the amount or types of substances to be consumed during any drinking or using session, and to predict the behavioral outcomes of drinking or using.

When asked if he or she is addicted, an addicted person might honestly say, "Yes. I want to quit, but I can't." A chemically dependent person might honestly say, or might learn to say, "No. I like what I am doing, and it's nobody's business but my own." Either of them may learn to lie skillfully in order to conceal their drinking or using from others.

The term "substance abuse" is always someone else's opinion about the use of intoxicating substances; substance abuse can never be proved. It is an expression of disapproval intended to discourage or prohibit others from persisting in the use of the substance. Use of the expression rarely has the desired effect.

It is easy to conclude that someone who carries cigarettes, smokes frequently, and becomes uncomfortable when out of cigarettes is dependent on nicotine, but that does not establish that he or she is abusing nicotine or would like to quit smoking. Even if asked, he or she might not answer honestly. The same is true of alcohol, heroin, cocaine, marijuana, and a host of other pleasure-producing substances. To a cigar smoker, the idea of abusing a Havana cigar is absurd, and to a marijuana smoker, the idea of substance "abuse" is ludicrous.

It helps to understand that the foundation of knowledge for contemporary addiction care did not arise from careful consideration, but from common usage within the recovery group movement. See Appendix A.

This leads to the next illusion.

Illusion 3 ▸ The state of addiction may be objectively determined or shown.

This very serious error is made when *chemical dependency* is confused with *substance abuse* and *substance addiction.*

American society sincerely believes that the use of freely chosen intoxicants constitutes substance abuse, that all chemically dependent people are addicted, and that the judgment of society on such people is best encapsulated in the concept of addiction treatment. In this scheme, the absence of a desire to quit intoxicating oneself is regarded as a symptom of a disease that not only causes one to drink or use other drugs, but also to *deny* that one really wants to quit drinking or using, or deny that there is sufficient reason to quit. In this state of disease-and-denial, citizens are deprived of credible status, consigned to second-class citizenship, and very often forced into addiction treatment programs that, ironically, presume that they have a sincere desire to quit drinking or using. Consequently, our addiction treatment industry has become an American gulag that runs parallel to the former Soviet Union's past misuse of psychiatry to enforce the will of a government upon its citizens.

In Rational Recovery, we deny that substance abusers deny. Instead, they lie. There's a big difference between lying and what

Sigmund Freud called "denial." Denial is a defense mechanism that results in not knowing that something obvious is so. This is rare, and the term "denial" is in general misuse today. For example, you know what your problems are, and you know that they are largely caused, directly or indirectly, by your drinking or drug use. You also have a good idea of how often you drink or use and about how much. Denial presumes that you are unaware that your use of alcohol or drugs is causing you problems. Granted, you may lie a lot, but if you plan to continue drinking or drugging in spite of your problems, wouldn't it be stupid to tell everyone? Would you tell your boss that you get drunk every night and plan to keep it up? Would you tell the policeman how many drinks you really had? Would you admit to your spouse how much you *really* love to drink or get loaded?

All addicted people know how much they love their substance of choice, all of them know that their addictions have a down side, and all of them wish they weren't as chemically dependent as they are. As your ability to recognize your Addictive Voice improves, you will see why "alcoholic denial" is an erroneous concept.

Recently a woman confided to me that one of her employees was a heavy drinker, wondering if he might be an "alcoholic." I told her that he was the only one who could possibly know, because addiction is known only to one who is drinking against his own better judgment. She was intrigued and pointed out that in our society it is assumed that the "alcoholic" is least likely to know that a problem exists. I added that self-intoxication is a basic freedom, an individual liberty, and that "alcoholic" is often a label given by one person to explain another person's use of alcohol. She then said, "Well, I hope he knows that if he continues to drink as he does, he will be fired." She had not warned him, assuming he was probably "in denial" and not really responsible for his decisions. I suggested that she give him warning and give him a copy of *Rational Recovery.* Then, if he continued to drink excessively, he would have to choose to quit or continue drinking. She said, "Yes. Then, if he continues to drink and gets fired, that is the cost of his freedom to drink." She was quickly able to see that he is a victim of nothing, that he is just as responsible for his behavior as anyone else and should be treated accordingly. The employee, too, should be protected against sudden dismissal for reasons that may be unclear to him.

The term "denial" implies, among other things, that addicted people are morons who cannot figure out that they are drinking or drugging themselves into trouble. It is used to describe people who do not know they are addicted. No such persons exist, for addiction is known *only* to the addicted person. Remember, addiction is drinking or drugging against one's *own* better judgment, not against someone else's judgment.

The American Society for Addiction Medicine (ASAM) is an enclave of physicians whose chemical dependencies brought them before the judgment of others, peers who told them they were finished unless they repented. To save their careers, the doctors fled into "treatment," asserting they were suffering a disease characterized by "denial," a cardinal symptom of that disease. It is pleasing to believe that physicians who will once again practice medicine were only suffering from a disease and that they have received treatment. It is much more pleasing than to understand that they willfully intoxicated themselves with disregard for the public safety. The same is true with airline pilots who once flew passenger planes under the influence of alcohol or drugs. While the disease model makes for an enchanting rehabilitation of one's public image, the public may be better served by making abstinence, rather than treatment, a condition of continued employment of "substance abusers" in sensitive positions.

In the history of Rational Recovery, the condition of "denial" has never been observed. This seems odd, considering that ASAM recently described alcoholism as a condition virtually *defined* by the presence of "denial" symptoms.

When I conduct professional workshops, I usually explain that I have never seen an addicted person who is in "denial" and then ask the audience for an example of the phenomenon. The response is always the same—stunned silence, followed by widely differing explanations of the term. Recently, one psychologist told of a man convicted of drunk driving, mandated into treatment after the second arrest, and now in "denial." He is angry at the policeman who was "out to get him."

"If he hadn't been drinking, he wouldn't have been arrested," the psychologist said. I asked him what his client is denying, and he explained that the client is placing the responsibility for his arrest on the policeman, instead of accepting responsibility himself. I replied, "Isn't it a policeman's responsibility to arrest people suspected of drunk driving? Aren't policemen really out to get drunk drivers and aren't they intended to watch for suspicious drivers and arrest them?" The psychologist concurred, adding, "But you're turning this thing around. The policeman isn't responsible for drunk driving. The driver is!" I assured him, "But your client has *admitted* drinking and driving. He only says that the policeman is responsible for his arrest, a man who in all probability really *was* out to get him. That's what they're paid to do. This man has admitted drinking and driving but believes he has a getting-caught problem; you say he has a drinking problem and is in denial. Why is your client suddenly 'sick' because he admits to acting stupidly but is angry at the cop responsible for his arrest?

The psychologist answered, "Alcoholics cannot comprehend that they are causing their own difficulties by drinking, so they blame others when they get in trouble. That's denial, and that is what he was doing."

I finally said, "Should he be thankful for being arrested?"

The psychologist answered, "Yes. He's not a first-time offender, and he must undergo treatment. Many people later feel grateful toward the ones who intervened and brought them into treatment."

I said, "I hope your client holds out against your denial talk, because you are trying to convince him he is not responsible for his drinking, and he says he is. The judge wants him to abstain or not drive at all, but no one will sit down with your client and help him decide whether he would rather drink or drive. To avoid going to jail, he will soon start lying in order to make it through the ordeal of mandated treatment. If abstinence is all you want, why don't you just ask him if that would be agreeable?"

The psychologist said he would think it over, and later in the workshop he said he was starting to see how he might start viewing his client as a normal human being who made some serious errors and might do well to choose abstinence.

The disease-model "treatment community" perceives that all chemically dependent people are addicted and don't know it; that their presumed ignorance is a symptom of a disease for which they are not personally responsible. (They forget so soon that, during their years of inappropriate drug use, they knew all along *exactly* what they were doing.) This illusion, above all others, has brought us the American treatment tragedy in which chemically dependent people who are exercising the fundamental freedom to intoxicate themselves are coerced into treatment programs that forcefully impose a belief system that makes recovery *from addiction* impossible.

Chemically dependent newcomers to recovery support groups are often smugly told, "You're in denial. You may continue to drink, but you won't be able to enjoy it." Here, a chemically dependent person is told by *others* that he or she is addicted, against the *group's* better judgment. Later, he or she may experience uneasy feelings concerning continued use, but that uneasiness is not, *per se,* the result of going against one's own better judgment. More likely, the person feels uncomfortable as a result of going against *others'* judgment, especially when they are *predicting* "Betcha can't have just one."

The reason to drink or not to drink is thus *externalized*—taken away from the chemically dependent person. This sets up an oppositional relationship between newcomer and group that continues until the person finally surrenders under the *illusion* that he or she is powerless to exercise better judgment over the desire to drink or use drugs, when actually that person has been exerting his or her own free will against the judgment of others. The treatment in store is likewise externalized in sponsors, Higher Powers, and ancient philosophical dilemmas. Addiction treatment is often a disguise for those who would deprive us of our *freedom* to make bad decisions. Such people feel justified to *intervene* in the lives of others, pass *judgment* on others' behavior, and to "treat" others' desire for pleasure, "for their own good."

Few "do-good" movements in American history have achieved such social prominence as the recovery group movement, which is often referred to as the American treatment tragedy. The recovery group movement is only a replay of the American prohibition tragedy, but the toll in suffering, in lives, in money, and in threats to our constitutional freedoms is much larger this time. Like a retrovirus, the disease/treatment mentality has penetrated the protective membrane between church and state, resulting in the release of enormous sums of money for addiction treatment that is little more than religion and pop psychology disguised as scientific health care. This social service is provided by agencies that spread the illusions, misconceptions, and bad advice we may call the *collective* Addictive Voice, the root cause of mass addiction.

Let's imagine that a homeless, skid-row drunk comes to us panhandling for money. We give her a dollar, convinced that we have just purchased another drink. Suppose, also, that she hasn't had money for a fix since yesterday, and she is able to communicate easily. Let's talk with her and see if she's addicted and in need of treatment.

US: Gee, aren't you cold?

HER: Yes. I get chilled to the bone sleeping under the bridge.

US: Isn't there a shelter down the street?

HER: I'd rather not go there. Too crowded, too much noise to sleep. Sometimes I eat there.

US: We gave you money for food, but you could eat there?

HER: Allergies. Milk and beans make me sick.

US: You look sick. You been drinking a lot?

HER: Not a lot. Keeps me going on a cold day.

US: You know, it doesn't have to be this way.

HER: Yeah, I think about that. But this is what I do. Sure gets me down sometimes.

US: You could get help.

HER: With what?

US: Help with your drinking.

HER: Thanks, but I can do that just fine, all by myself. I need other help, but not that.

US: Would you be here on the streets if you didn't drink?

HER: Maybe not, but here I am.

US: What have you done to help yourself with your drinking problem?

HER: Who said it's a problem?

US: Look what it's doing to you!

HER: You mean look what *I'm* doing to me!

US: Have you ever tried to get help?

HER: Don't need none. I'll take care of myself.

US: You don't really want to be homeless like this, do you?

HER: No. Got any suggestions?

US: If you get some help and quit drinking, you can build a new life.

HER: No, I mean, do you know where I can stay tonight?

US: How about up the street, at the shelter?

HER: I told you, beans make me sick, and they keep talking like you. Thanks for the dollar. Bye.

This woman is exercising an individual liberty to use alcohol for its distinct pleasurable effect. Although she is risking her life each evening as she slumbers exposed to the elements under the influence of alcohol, she is not necessarily *addicted* to alcohol. She is physically dependent on alcohol and whatever is given to her, including the dollar we gave her, public assistance with food, medical care for hypothermia and liver disease, and possibly burial at government expense. Although she sustains her chemical dependency from the largesse of society, we might look askance at spending public funds to treat a hypothetical disease when she is exercising an individual liberty. It is entirely possible that she might change her mind, even later the same day, and say, "I really do want some help. I don't want to live this way any longer. I'd rather die than sleep outside." With this statement, the woman is stating that she is addicted, not just chemically dependent. Then is when we might turn to her and ask a most compassionate yet blunt question: "What, then, is your plan for the future use of alcohol?"

When we first met her on the street, it would have been easy for us to identify her remarks about accepting life on the streets as a symptom of "alcoholic denial," but what would that be saying about her? Would she be helped in any way by our label?

Chemical dependency is usually a most unattractive lifestyle that naturally leads to a desire to give up using the substance. To browbeat her with our opinions of what's best for her and label her as a diseased person may confer upon us a sense of competence or moral goodness, but it is doubtful that she will appreciate it or benefit in any way. The dollar we gave her is a symbol that she is calling the shots, not we, and that the dangers and inconveniences of street life are the cost of her freedom. For her, drinking alcohol *is* the most meaningful activity; if and when she gets ready to quit, she will probably, according to statistics, do so without getting outside help or receiving addiction treatment for her intemperance.

The impulse to regard chemical dependence as a mental illness justifying incarceration has been tried and abandoned because of the implications to a free society. We may strongly disagree with this woman's judgment that she is really free, and we may believe that what she calls freedom is a prison in which she will needlessly die, but the judgment is hers until she may be declared mentally incompetent. Her prison is better than ours.

Illusion 4 ▸ Sin Equals Disease.

In recent years, "addiction" has become an extremely popular term for describing a wide range of behaviors formerly called "sins." Many would agree that defining sin is best left to religious communities, but the convergence of religion and science in the 12-step recovery movement has brought us full circle to a most pernicious mind trap called "addictive disease."

This expression, which means the disease of sin, is a subtle fusion of opposite meanings that can go unnoticed by even sophisticated intellects. Like a faulty rivet that sends the ship to the bottom of the sea, the disease concept of addiction is the fatal flaw in our addiction care system. The "sin" of intemperance has been misidentified as a disease, calling forth a practice called "treatment," which, if understood as "exorcism," might well be suited for combating sin, but which is only marginally useful in the treatment of disease.

Sin may or may not be objectively definable, but it was decided once and for all by the nation's founders that *within American society,* sin shall be a matter of personal conscience, subjectively determined or even ignored altogether. This feature of the U.S. Constitution radically changed the course of human history by snatching liberty and governance from the hands of religion and placing them before each individual citizen. The Salem witch trials, which predate the founding of the nation by over a century, show us that when the state is permitted to define sin, tyranny is a natural outcome. (Also natural is the human tendency to confuse the subjective with the objective, which has happened in the field of American-style addiction care.)

The common meaning of "sin" in America is "an offense against God or against religious law, or a state of separation from God." Among the religious denominations, ones with more liberal theologies trust the person's subjective relationship to God as the final guidance in matters of personal conduct. As a general rule, the more fundamentalist a religion is and the more it relies upon the objective content of scriptures, the more objectively "sin" is defined. The dynamic interplay of theology and politics is one of the most admirable aspects of the U.S. Constitution, which has been called "the great American experiment." Because of the separation of church and state, we have become a great nation—not so much in the economic sense, but in our ethical stance among nations. That priceless separation insists that while laws may regulate behavior, sin cannot be objectively defined, and government has no business combating sin.

The 12-step recovery group movement, however, has vaulted over the U.S. Constitution by disguising itself as a treatment program for a disease epidemic. Sin-disease has infected the American consciousness to such an extent that the government has undertaken to stamp it out. Once again, our courts are hearing cases pertaining to sin, and sentences are being handed out requiring religious indoctrination. A great, government-supported industry, the treatment community, wages war on sin. This is reminiscent of the Salem witch trials in that expert witnesses *divine* the presence of sin, and sentencing is predicated on sin. (Of course, I am referring here to the drunk-driver and other diversion programs that "diagnose" addiction and offer 12-step indoctrinations as an alternative to imprisonment or harsher penalties.)

***Illusion* 5** ▸ Addiction is a disease. Many addicted people do not like to drink or use, but are compelled to do so, even though it makes them feel bad.

Try explaining this to a child. I did once, even though I knew better. While we were driving through a city, he noticed a drunk slumped in a doorway and asked, "What's wrong with that man?" I said, "He's drunk," and the child had no more questions. But I teased a little and said, "I think he lives in that doorway. We could probably see him there tomorrow." The boy, about twelve years old, said, "Really? Kind of stupid, if you ask me." I responded, "He does that because he has the disease of alcoholism. Have you studied about addictive disease in school?" He said, "Yeah," and then he turned and looked at me with a wry smile and added, "It's not a regular disease, though."

Straight-faced, I answered, "Of course it's a real disease. Alcoholism is inherited. it is an illness of your brain that makes you powerless to quit drinking. No matter how hard you try not to drink, something comes over you and you drink and drink." The boy said, "Temptation. That's what comes over an alcoholic. We talked about this after class, my buddies and me. One of my buddies' dad's an alcoholic, or at least he gets drunk all the time. He gets rough, too. But he wouldn't be so crazy if he wouldn't drink booze. His dad isn't crazy, and he isn't sick, either. He's just a mean drunk, but he goes for weeks sometimes with nothing to drink. He's an okay guy when he's sober, but then temptation gets the best of him and he starts it up again. He doesn't have to go out and buy booze when he's doing okay without drinking." I confessed I was just kidding, and I told him I was one of the many who also disagree with the disease idea. I commended him for thinking for himself and not getting taken in by everything said by adults.

If you don't accept the disease concept, hold your ground, continue to demand clear, convincing evidence, and trust your own common sense. If you aren't sure, consider the discussion below. If you do accept the disease concept of addiction, pay attention to what the concept of addictive disease *means* to you. If the disease concept relieves you of any responsibility to abstain, or explains away your past misbehavior, you may be listening to your Addictive Voice. If you don't care one way or the other about the disease concept, you have probably thought it through and discovered the truth, that it really doesn't matter a whit as far as your life is concerned. Either way, you had better quit drinking or using drugs.

Regardless of your beliefs on this matter, remember that the disease concept of addiction is an article of faith and your opinion is just as credible as the opinion of any scientist, physician, counselor, or other expert. The experts are divided, having the same doubts and confusion as the general public. Remember, also, that the addictive disease idea has been around for hundreds of years, but it became accepted only through strenuous propaganda efforts by the recovery group movement.

One organization, The National Council on Alcoholism, was founded in the 1950s for the sole purpose of disseminating the disease concept to the public. (Despite its title, it is neither a governmental nor a scientific organization, but a nonprofit publicity arm for the recovery group movement.)

In the absence of supporting evidence, the disease concept gains acceptance on other grounds.

1. **Authority.** Doctors say it's so, and they should know. The American Medical Association says alcoholism and drug addiction are diseases. People in recovery, the survivors themselves, say they have a disease.
2. **Intimidation.** It is vital to the survival of alcoholics and drug addicts to accept that they have a disease, so that they may receive life-saving treatment. Challenging the disease idea is dangerous, resulting in suffering and death for others.
3. **Discrimination.** Employment in certain jobs and holding public office requires endorsement of the disease concept of addiction. One may receive leniency in court and be granted early parole from prison by admitting to addictive

disease. Community programs based on the disease model are more favorably reviewed and funded than if based on other concepts.

4. **Desperation.** Addicted people are told that unless they come to believe they suffer from addictive disease and label themselves accordingly, they will die. Typically, they are under great stress, seeking anything that will help. Family members are told that addiction is a family disease that will destroy them all unless they admit they have it and get treatment.
5. **Financial gain.** The profit motive accounts for much of the enthusiasm for the disease concept of addiction. Addiction is an incurable, insurable disease. The addiction treatment industry is an expansion of the 12-step recovery group movement into the money economy. The service called *addiction treatment* usually amounts to little more than an expensive introduction to AA by professionals who nearly always belong to AA themselves.
6. **Secondary gains.** The disease concept relieves you of personal responsibility for acquiring, maintaining, and ending the addiction and absolves guilt stemming from your antisocial behavior.
6. **Coercive logic.** Refusal to admit you are diseased is seen as proof that you have the disease. Even if you quit drinking or drugging, you still have the disease, according to the recovery group movement.
7. **Media feeding habits.** The stories of people in recovery make for juicy press and great talk shows. The disease model presents addicted people as victims, *different* from others, so that the public is spared the discomfort of wondering about themselves or others they know who drink too much. Audiences love to hear stories of affliction, past degeneracy, psychological intrigue, and miraculous healing by faith and spiritual awakening.

To counter the biases listed above, here is some background information.

Substance addiction *causes* diseases such as liver disease,

heart disease, neurological disease, digestive tract disease, diseases of the skin, and also aggravates a much larger number of other legitimate diseases. These are side effects of the substance or drug, but there is no known disease that causes one to drink or use drugs.

There is not even a tiny shred of evidence that substance addiction is, or is caused by, a disease, even if "disease" is meant to include psychological or developmental disorders. Research recently compiled in the *Harvard Medical School Mental Health Review* shows, "For the great majority of alcoholics there is no good evidence that they began abusing alcohol because they were anxious, depressed, insecure, poorly brought up, dependent on their mothers, raised in unhappy families, subjected to child abuse, or emotionally unstable during childhood or adolescence. . . . Abstinent adults resemble the general population in their psychiatric symptoms." Rational Recovery has been saying this for over a decade.

Conversely, and very importantly, addiction is not a *symptom* of any disease. Addiction is merely a *fact*—a state of being. People who drink heavily or use drugs a lot are not *necessarily* included among the addicted, even though *most* of them may in fact be addicted. This discrepancy sets up endless illusions in the recovery hall of mirrors.

Addiction to alcohol or drugs is a devotion to *pleasure* produced by the substance, an ineffable self-indulgence that ultimately becomes a condition of chemically enhanced stupidity. Pleasure seeking, sometimes called "hedonism," is a natural human trait signifying health. Addiction, however, goes further than hedonism into a zone I call "hyperhedonism," a *surpassing* devotion to the specific pleasure given by certain substances. Because there is no disease, there is no "treatment" and no "cure" in the medical sense of these words. But in the broader sense, there is a perfect, guaranteed, immediate cure available to any addicted person—planned, permanent abstinence.

Illusion 6 ▸ Substance addiction is a "treatable" disease.

The term "addiction treatment," when used throughout this book, means outside help, most often professional, based on the assumption that addiction is a symptom of something—a disease, brain chemistry, psychological problems, spiritual deficits, poverty, cultural influences, childhood deprivations and traumas, or perhaps the position of certain stars at the time of one's birth. Addiction treatment involves changing or compensating for those circumstances so that the symptom—drinking or drugging—may subside.

Addiction treatment is a mind-boggling concept because it may consist of anything and is defined entirely by itself. For example, when a doctor learns that a patient drinks too much, the treatment may be to prescribe treatment. But the doctor will not know what condition will be treated, nor can the doctor find out what the treatment consists of. If he or she asks a treatment specialist what the treatment is, the answer might be group therapy, family counseling, and support group attendance. If the doctor asks what the group therapy consists of, the answer will likely be working to overcome denial, gain self-esteem, admit powerlessness, heal relationships, learn social skills, or other *therapeutic goals*. These treatments, consisting of indoctrinations and exhortations, are for conditions *other* than substance abuse, which is known only by the behavior of self-intoxication. If the doctor persists and asks what conditions are being treated, the answer will be "addiction," a *symptom* of conditions not observed by the physician. The actual treatment for substance abuse or addiction, of course, is *abstinence,* which could have been prescribed from the start with comments like "It's time for you to stop drinking/using for good"—and with far better chances of success.

America has an abundance of excellent treatments for a wide range of human problems. Here are some examples:

1. **Medical treatment.** We enjoy the most sophisticated medical services in the world.
2. **Psychiatric treatment.** Enormous advances have revolutionized treatment of mental illness and mental diseases. With medication, many people are freed from the torment of mental disease and from confinement. Drugs for de-

pression, anxiety, and hyperactivity can restore people to happy lives.

3. **Psychological treatment.** American psychology has helped in the humane treatment of the mentally ill and in aiding people to seek a better life. Psychological testing has helped quantify human behavior for better understanding, and refined counseling methods bring relief from debilitating behavioral and emotional conditions.
4. **Psychosocial treatment.** The field of social work helps people overcome life problems by modifying the environment and empowering people to solve personal, family, and relationship problems.
5. **Osteopathy and chiropractice treatment.** Using a holistic theoretical perspective, health problems are effectively treated, pain is relieved, health restored.
6. **Specialty treatments.** They include physical therapy, occupational therapy, art therapy, nutritional therapy, respiratory therapy, speech therapy, massage therapy, acupuncture, reflexology, herbal therapy, homeopathic medicine, and scores of exotic practices that add immeasurably to health, vitalization, and comfort.

All these treatments produce desirable results. ***But there is no treatment for addiction any more than there would be a treatment for dancing.***

Those who know best, the formerly addicted people "in recovery" in AA, have long said therapy doesn't work. AA came into existence in the 1930s, when all of the professions *admitted* they were powerless to dissuade people from self-intoxication. The foremost experts of the time on the subject of substance addiction, Carl Jung (from the field of psychology) and Robert Silkworth (from the medical profession), said that counseling and psychotherapy may help with problems other than addiction, but are of little value in combating addiction itself. In 1990, *The Harvard Medical School Mental Health Review* restated what has been known from the start:

> It is useless to try to solve some other psychological or social problem first and hope that drinking will then stop. What-

> ever the original cause of drinking, it eventually comes to dominate the alcoholic's life, and continuing use makes any kind of therapy impossible. Psychotherapy can hardly help them while they continue to drink, because alcohol prevents insight. Even for temporarily sober alcoholics, psychotherapy alone is not enough.

The addiction treatment industry has careened out of control for decades in spite of repeated warnings by noted authors, health professionals, and researchers. Here is the introductory paragraph of a large scientific study done at Kansas City Veteran's Hospital in 1975:

> The widespread acceptance of alcoholism as a disease has affected not only the thinking of helping professions but the perspective of governments. The health professions define the treatment of alcoholism as their competence and governments accept responsibility for supporting the professional effort in terms of ever increasing treatment investment. Humanitarian and political pressures have created a demand that more be done, and all has been carried forward on this tide—new clinics and hospitals, new government agencies, new training courses, and newly certificated professionals, and pressure groups which further urge on the tide.

The study showed that addicted people (and their families) who received no treatment for anything but were merely advised to quit drinking *did better* one year later than people who received extensive addiction treatment. Over twenty years have passed, and neither the methods nor the outcomes of treatment have changed. The nation has forged ahead with the false promise of addiction treatment, and the result has been a free fall into the socio-medical behemoth alternately called the recovery group movement and the addiction treatment industry.

The disease concept is *attractive* to addicted people because it shields them against immediate responsibility to quit drinking or drugging, and because it produces a causal pathway in their thinking that supports future drinking. The "disease of relapse," as alcoholism and addiction are sometimes called, is a highly *gratifying* concept among addicted people because they have a shared, passionate wish to continue drinking or using drugs. A secondary attraction of disease thinking among addicted people is found in the mitigation of guilt and responsibility for preposterous personal behavior. In victimhood comes perverse dignity. "If I have a disease, then how can I blame myself? For that matter, how can anyone else?" A disease/treatment promotion circular published by the State of California shouts, "Alcoholism is nothing to hide!" Granted, addiction becomes very difficult to hide, and that's why most people eventually quit or seek help, but to lure one out of hiding with the bait of a contrived *medical diagnosis* requiring treatment drawn from old-time religion seems disingenuous. Ironically, the nature of treatment has become a paramount reason people give for *not* getting help, for resigning themselves to addiction and its subsequent problems.

Defenders of the 12 steps routinely cite the American Medical Association as having evidence that "alcoholism" is a disease. This is not so. Here are the facts:

The American Medical Association is less than forthright. Alcoholism is not even listed as a disease in their diagnostic manual. *Alcoholism* is a folk expression for *alcohol dependence*, which doesn't even sound like a disease. At the 1987 conference of AMA, the following statement was recorded: "The American Medical Association *endorses the proposition* that drug dependencies, including alcoholism, are diseases."

This "definition" was derived by a voice vote and is not a definition at all. It is a mere "endorsement" of a "proposition"—that is, an *opinion*. A democratically achieved consensus of opinion within the AMA, which represents less than half of the physicians in the United States, must not be interpreted or represented as a finding of hard science. Yet billions of dollars are rained on the problem of addictive disease. If you tell your physician about this, he or she will very likely admit that the disease concept has always sounded fishy, but that he or she doesn't specialize in addictions.

Alas, there is no evidence for a disease, nor any lab test for diagnosing "alcoholism." AA founder Bill Wilson said, "We [of

AA] have never called alcoholism a disease because it is not a disease entity." Wilson was right. RR is right. The American Psychiatric Association, which conflicts with AMA on this issue, is also right. They use the terms "alcohol dependence" and "alcohol abuse," which are preferred over the folk expression, "alcoholism."

At a recent workshop I gave, one person cited the World Health Organization as an endorser of the disease-treatment model. I asked, "What organization is WHO a part of? Do you know?" He wasn't sure, but someone said, "The United Nations." There were some chuckles, but the point was made. People who cite intimidating authorities as proof of addictive disease have no proof of their own, and the authorities they cite aren't credible on the subject. The United Nations is a *political* organization, and WHO is not in a position to know one way or the other if addiction is a disease, because it is not a scientific organization. It is merely a service organization with a international political agenda.

Illusion 7 ▸ Addicted and chemically dependent people need "treatment."

Says who? Treatment for what? And of what would that treatment consist? Some chemically dependent people develop serious withdrawal symptoms that do require life-saving treatment. The long-term dependence is not treated, but rather the immediate symptoms of withdrawal. How may one's desire for and pursuit of pleasure be "treated"? Perhaps a better question follows:

What is to stop anyone from quitting the use of a substance? Whatever appears as the answer to this question is the sound of the Addictive Voice. The recovery group movement generates mountains of explanations of why people continue their chemical dependencies or cannot summarily give them up. An entire subculture has grown up around the idea of personal powerlessness, exotic causation, unwholesome introspection, and endless not-quite-recovering.

The Addictive Voice, which shifts immediate personal responsibility to desist from self-intoxication *away* from the individual, reverberates loudly in the corridors of our social institutions, yet we attribute the rise of addiction to ever more remote causes, some even beyond our national borders. The homeless alcoholic woman we met earlier, however, has figured out that she is *perfectly* free to quit her alcohol dependence at any moment and that help with this isn't helpful, but annoying.

The preamble to the U.S. Constitution guarantees ". . . life, liberty, and the pursuit of happiness." Do we think the Founding Fathers, most mourning the loss of loved ones in the Revolutionary War, were concerned about the *cost* of freedom? Self-intoxication, whether the laws of the land reflect it or not, is a fundamental freedom. After all, whose life is it? The ugly results of self-intoxication are the *cost* of that freedom and a complex of related freedoms. How better to hold a slave than to "treat" his desire for freedom? As a concept, the *treatment of desire* not only clashes with uniquely American concepts of freedom, but also places an expanding shroud of social oppression on large segments of society, including our chemically dependent and addicted masses.

If I drink every minute of every day, am I not making a *choice* to do so? If I am free to do this, am I not free to stop it? If I can think of no good reason to stop drinking, why should I stop? Whose life is it, anyway? Remember, addiction is intoxicating oneself *against one's own better judgment*. If I am willing to accept the risks involved, how can I be "addicted" or otherwise diagnosed? Who will render this *opinion*, and, very importantly, what's in it for them? If you let your eyes follow the bouncing dollar, you may notice that addiction treatment benefits those who treat far more than those who are treated.

Use of the word "treatment" bears scrutiny by all. It implies that a disease exists, one that is genetic, pernicious, progressive, incurable, and lifelong. In addiction treatment, people are diagnosed, and this information is coded and recorded. Sufferers are fundamentally different from others in subtle ways that are best understood by other sufferers. It is expected that sufferers will socially segregate themselves so that they mingle largely with their own kind. They are prone to sudden relapses; thus they are poor risks for certain kinds of responsibilities, including employment and citizenship. The social implications of "addictive disease" can be far more disabling than the social stigma of habitual drunkenness.

Addiction begins not with intoxication, but with awareness of pain and a desire for a better way of life. It continues with a sense of ambivalence, being "of two minds," and it ends with reclaiming one's self from the grip of pleasure.

Illusion 8 ▸ Addiction runs a progressive course counter to a person's wishes, and if not "treated," it progresses toward death. (Substitute "malignant tumor" to sense the illusion.)

Drinking or drugging by an addicted person is *willful* behavior that truly reflects the addicted person's momentary desire. While addicted, a person may experience occasional or frequent *reversal of intent,* wherein a decision not to drink may yield to a decision to drink. But to say that one is not in control, out of control, or that some force other than self has intervened to move one's voluntary muscles is an unnecessary leap in logic. In addition to wanting to drink or use, one may *also* desire to avoid the consequences of the addiction, but the behavior, nevertheless, is chosen in spite of the known risks involved. Addicted people are not victims of any predisposition, malady, disease, or inherited deficiency. Instead, they are facing the same responsibilities as any other citizen but making consistently poor decisions in dealing with them. Addictions may result in death from acute intoxication, from diseases caused by addiction, or from dangerous behavior resulting from impaired judgment. But the consequences of addiction, even death, are best attributed to the individual rather than to circumstance at birth.

As you become more involved with AVRT, you will learn to regard your Addictive Voice as "not self." This does not change the reality described in the above paragraph. The logic of AVRT is *contrived* for the singular purpose of achieving lifetime abstinence and does not conform to other systems of thought. AVRT is a self-taught thinking skill that allows you to make your mind up about drinking and make your decision stick.

Illusion 9 ▸ Treatment works!

Probably *less than a third* of all people who stop their addictions get help of any kind. Eminent researcher George Vaillant, M.D., found in his forty-year study, *The Natural History of Alcoholism,* that a majority had overcome their alcohol problems on their own and that relapse was progressively less likely the longer one abstained. Many veterans of the Vietnam conflict returned to the United States addicted to heroin, but upon resuming civilian life, 90% of them quit using altogether without getting "treatment." (Sixty-four percent had used narcotics before entering the military.) Some say they had "spontaneous remissions" from the disease of addiction, but we may more realistically conclude that their better judgment took over when it was no longer appropriate to self-intoxicate. Even those who do get help do not often attribute their abstinence to the help they got.

Glowing reports of addiction treatment outcomes usually reflect the percentage of those who completed the program, often months or years long, overlooking the dropout rate, which often runs as high as 80%. In recent years, abstinence is less often considered a success statistic, substituting other factors such as self-esteem, fewer violations of the law, and subjective reports of well-being.

People who get treatment appear to do *less* well than people who get better on their own. A 1977 study by the Kansas City Veterans Administration Medical Center found that a control group given only a twenty-minute advice-to-quit session did significantly better one year later on abstinence and other measures than the experimental group that received the full range of intensive inpatient and outpatient services, individual, group, and family counseling, and many, many AA meetings. Independent researcher Chad Emrick, Ph.D., conducted a meta-analysis of scores of research of treatment outcomes and found an insignificant .02 correlation between treatment and abstinent outcome. The single-digit abstinence rates of the recovery movement cannot compete with self-recovery.

The Harvard Mental Health Newsletter recently stated, "Most recovery from addictions is not the result of treatment. According to the best controlled studies, expensive, elaborate treatment does not have an unequivocal advantage over brief counseling or no treatment at all. Of those who continue with AA following treatment, 71% continue to drink." Astoundingly, the newsletter continues, ". . . only 10% of all alcohol abusers are ever treated at all, but as many as 40% recover spontaneously." This suggests that no treatment is over fifty times more effective than treatment! If no treatment were only "just as effective" as treatment, addiction treatment should be abolished. No explanation, especially the idea that the self-recovered didn't really have significant addictions, can hide for long the fact that *addiction treatment* is a bogus practice that would best be abolished. These figures are a smoking gun in the American treatment tragedy.

Stopping an addiction is not as difficult as most people make it out to be; the struggle is shortly over. Staying stopped is also easy, because sobriety is self-reinforcing. When people take personal responsibility to quit their addictions, they get better regardless of how serious or long-standing the addiction. Addiction treatment is an underestimation of people's ability to quit on their own. Treatment doesn't work—people do!

Illusion 10 ▸ Some substances are more "addictive" than others, and some addictions are stronger than others, making them more difficult to overcome.

The Latin roots of the word *addict*, are *ad*, meaning "toward" or, "yes," and *dict*, meaning "say." People may become *dependent* on a wide range of substances by choosing to take them for their effects. Substances do not addict people; *people* do, by continuing to "say yes" against their better judgment, which says "no."

Addiction is a state of being, a fact that is neither severe, strong, nor serious. The *results* of some addictions, however, may be more devastating than others, but that does not mean that the addiction itself is stronger or more difficult to overcome. Interesting research by George Vaillant shows that abstinence is a more common outcome among men who were most "seriously" or "severely" addicted. Research on Rational Recovery groups by the New York University Medical School showed no difference in abstinence outcome among participants who were addicted to alcohol versus cocaine. It is often said that tobacco is more addictive than heroin, and that crack is the most addictive of all. To those who use those "most addictive" substances, this means, "Now you've done it. You're hooked. There's no turning back." To any addicted person, the most serious addiction in the universe is the one he or she has; other addictions are irrelevant.

We have declared war on external substances rather than upon the ignorance of addicted people. Rational Recovery's structural model of addiction, presented Chapter 10, finds the cause of addiction within each addicted individual and identifies human consciousness as the battlefield for each individual's war on addiction.

Illusion 11 ▸ There is something "wrong" with chemically dependent and addicted people.

It has been said that anything worth doing is worth doing in excess. Some may disagree with this wisdom on philosophical grounds, but that is hardly a good reason to say there is something *wrong* with people who are devoted to certain pleasures. If a person often chooses extremely risky behavior, such as rock climbing, highway speeding, or promiscuous sex, does it add anything to our understanding to say he or she is "addicted"? All we can confidently say is that those people are willing to take risks for something they find pleasurable or meaningful. These examples, incidentally, are not addictions in the sense that the word is used in Rational Recovery, for they do not involve the use of substances. Not long ago the term "addiction" always implied "to drugs."

Is there an addictive personality? Hardly. If you have ever observed a group of people in a treatment program, you will have seen enough human diversity to *overwhelm* any such assumption. Addicted people have little in common except their common pleasure of self-intoxication—and the suffering resulting from it. Addiction treatment focuses on the wide spectrum of human imperfection including *irrelevant* issues such as character flaws, health and nutritional problems, genealogy, emotional disturbances, spiritual deficiencies, psychiatric symptoms, relationship problems, family conflicts, and psychological maladjustments. Unwholesome introspection, guided by recovery group norms or "treatment specialists," occurs during a time of special vulnerability when a person is usually desperate from some self-induced life crisis. The tragic result is that the addicted person concludes that the life crisis is the result not of chemically enhanced stupidity, but of deep-seated, long-standing, or inherent personal defects.

George, for example, loved to drink cognac and got into trouble with his family because of it. He lost a job because he appeared for work late, then moved into his parents' home to save money while looking for a new job. At his father's insistence, he started attending recovery group meetings. "I think my downfall really began at those meetings and not when I started drinking too much and lost my job," he says several years later. "It seemed everything about me was wrong, like there was something seriously wrong with me that I had never suspected. The more I looked for answers, the more confused I got. Finally, I got fed up and quit going. I always had trouble fitting in with groups of people, and dropping out made me feel like a failure. By then, I was drinking more than before I started going." George's experience created an *addiction treatment disorder,* in which he learned to see his substance addiction is a symptom of other imperfections, conditions he could not realistically change. He became doubtful of his own thought processes and became depressed. He then drank more, thinking he was sick and alcohol was medicine. This, of course, leads to the next illusion.

***Illusion* 12** ▸ If an addicted person becomes better adjusted, more self-accepting, more fulfilled, more emotionally mature, and happier in life, he or she will become less inclined to drink or use.

If this really happens, so much the better. However, there are difficulties that make this picture an illusion. First, you will probably always have problems, personal hang-ups, and occasional miseries, and it is unlikely that you will be "fulfilled" during your lifetime. This can put off secure abstinence for a very long time. Second, even if you did achieve that happier, more fulfilled state, what would really stop you from drinking beside your own decision to not drink? Third, this illusion sets up conditions for abstinence, which automatically creates conditions for drunkenness.

In addiction treatment, your original problem—drinking or using drugs—is defined as a symptom of something else over which you are powerless. Recovery revolves around a commitment, not to abstinence, but to a plan for general self-improvement. The long, long road to recovery loops through support groups, inpatient detoxification, outpatient programs, and other publicly funded formats. In none of these programs will the treatment expect that you immediately quit forever, but only for one day at a time. If your addiction were abruptly ended, how could the next treatment session be justified?

Addiction treatment *teaches* relapse by implying that you will continue to intoxicate yourself until treatment of the root causes finally takes effect. It is a *bargain* that promises a payoff—a happier life, fewer problems, better friends, and better feelings all around—in exchange for your loss of that precious stuff. When things go bad, the deal is off, and back to the stuff you go. But if you win the lottery or have some other windfall of good fortune, your reasons for quitting are also removed, and back to the stuff you go. If there is no change for better or worse, there is no reason to consider quitting or remaining abstinent. Your addiction exists on its own, separate from all else. It's just there, it's all yours, and it will continue until *you* decide to end it.

In AVRT, you will take a direct moral hit for becoming addicted, for maintaining the addiction against your own better (moral) judgment, and for ending the addiction, immediately, all on your own, and forever. There is no sterile robe of "disease victim" to protect you or explain away your future drinking. When you get started, you may even feel sick inside, but you will also understand those feelings and the meaning of abstinence. Some of those bad feelings will be regret or remorse for your past behavior, and some will be grief for the loss of substance pleasure. There is no compensation due to you for any of this, even though hope for a better life may motivate your decision to abstain. Although your original family may have been imperfect, and you may have been mistreated, and society may have given you a rotten deal in some ways, you are not owed an apology or compensation, nor are you excused in any way for becoming addicted, for remaining addicted, or for any of your behavior associated with your addiction. AVRT is entirely uninterested in your personal problems and life's troubles. In fact, there is no guarantee that your life will not become much worse following your decision to abstain. As an abstinent person, you may consider yourself just like anyone else, taking the hard knocks of life, finding out that life can be lonely at times, and taking risks to gain the good in life. When you feel your history of addiction is a handicap in remaining abstinent, or that you need more than your own resources to remain abstinent, you are simply hearing your Addictive Voice.

In spite of all the hocus-pocus, you know you drink or use—good times or bad—because that is what you *want* to do. You are already "treatment wise." Stay that way.

Once you are securely abstinent, some form of treatment of your other problems may be a very good idea. You may then get your money's worth because you will be seeking help for problems that others can help with. You will be seeking help for the same legitimate reasons that others do.

But who's to say that you will need help with your personal problems? Having defeated a serious addiction, you may wisely conclude that you also have what it takes to tackle other problems unhampered by routine self-intoxication.

Illusion 13 ▸ There is no cure for alcoholism or drug addiction. Once an addict, always an addict.

Here we see the permanent loss of freedom that comes with "treatment." The authentic self is lost to a new self-identity as a "recovering" person, struggling endlessly against the inevitable. The idea of a "cure" to addiction is ridiculed, scolded, scorned, and denied by virtually every chemical dependency counselor in

America. They insist that addiction, whether to alcohol or other drugs, is hereditary, progressive, incurable, and, if one does not admit all of the above, fatal. To many people, the very idea of a "cure" is regarded as *dangerous* to people who suffer from addictions. Moreover, if an addicted person believes there is a "cure" or thinks he or she is "cured," that person is said to be "in denial," a symptom of the incurable disease, addiction.

There is no disease of addiction, and therefore no "treatment," but there certainly is a *cure,* if by that we mean a "fix" for the problem, a return to health and independent living. You are reading it. AVRT makes your last drink your *final* fix, freeing you from the prison of addiction. Those who have been in treatment may take back their lives from recovery.

Let me summarize the above points using the concepts of Rational Recovery:

"Denial" is a self-canceling concept because it obliterates the *self* as a viable entity in the struggle against addiction. The disease model of addiction is a fiction of convenience for addicted people, for those who "treat" addictions, and for people who wish to avoid the consequences of their addictions. Addiction treatment insulates addicted people from personal responsibility to change, while AVRT, as education, places responsibility squarely upon the addicted individual.

With AVRT, you are placed in the position of student. The knowledge you seek will not be revealed to you by a shaft of light from above, but through your own intelligence. Whether or not others care about you, love you, support you, or encourage you to succeed, you will be tested, and you will either pass or fail. The test will be in the form of real life experience when your Addictive Voice acts up. If you recognize it, you will pass, and if you fail to recognize it, you will drink or use. AVRT is a single-room schoolhouse with enough room for any addicted person regardless of intelligence, disabilities, previous education, religion, race, type of addiction, length of addiction, or other conditions.

There is more dignity in "stupidity" than in "disease," because you can *do something* about stupidity. With disease comes loss of responsibility, and with the loss of responsibility comes the loss of freedom. In Rational Recovery, addiction is self-admitted stupidity—acting against your own better judgment. By taking a direct hit of personal and moral responsibility, you may take dramatic, decisive action to end your addiction and in doing so be free from addiction as well as from an oppressive "recovering" lifestyle. You can live down stupidity; you can't live down the disease.

A list of further illusions in the recovery hall of mirrors could fill this entire book. *Rational Recovery* redefines both addiction and recovery in a way that appeals to your intelligence, your individualism, and your American heritage of freedom. *Rational Recovery* sets forth AVRT as a natural avenue to permanent abstinence that anyone can use to completely recover from addiction. It was developed by a formerly addicted person (me) based on years of experience helping addicted people.

My career is a vote for the integrity of addicted people who take responsibility for (1) acquiring, (2) maintaining, and (3) ending their substance addictions. Addiction to alcohol or drugs is not a symptom of unhappiness or some mysterious disease, nor is it a way that people cope with life's difficulties. So, quit first, and quit for good. Maybe your life will be better, and maybe it won't, but at least you'll be in a position to know what your problems really are. AVRT bets that you'll *know* what's best to do about them.

Phase: Tightening Your Focus on AVRT

- **AVRT is *education,* not treatment.** You use your own intelligence, and take personal responsibility. Recovery as education is a revolutionary concept in a society beset with ''addictive disease.''
- **You will not label yourself ''alcoholic'' or ''addict.''** You will not strive to become a better person. Stay who you are, warts and all. When you are consistently sober, you will tend to behave in ways that please you and others.
- When your addiction is stopped, you will have problems just like everyone else. How you solve them is nobody's business but your own. Although *treatment of addictions* is a pernicious illusion, there are many treatable other conditions, both psychological and medical, for which you may wisely decide to get professional help.
- In AVRT, there are no steps, sponsors, Higher Powers, counselors, therapists, psychological theories, sharing, group support, personal issues, enablers, triggers, codependents, warning signs of relapse, or religious teachings. No one is in denial.
- AVRT does not focus on your personal problems, your imperfections, your personality, or your past. Like a laser beam, it focuses *only* on your addiction.
- AVRT shows you exactly how to handle your desire to drink or use drugs. AVRT exposes your Addictive Voice, so you can recognize it

as the *sole cause* of your addiction. When you learn the technique of recognizing your Addictive Voice, you will, in effect, be *unable* to drink or use drugs.

- Once learned, AVRT is effortless. No white-knuckling. No agony.
- AVRT does not recommend or suggest that you join 12-step groups, support groups, or get counseling, treatment, or other long-term therapy. Nutrition, fitness, and health are not conditions of abstinence. All of these activities are fine if you choose them freely, but not as a condition of remaining perfectly abstinent.
- Medical treatment of the physical symptoms of addiction is often vital, so don't hesitate to see a doctor!
- AVRT can be mastered from reading alone. *Rational Recovery* is a complete self-help course in itself. Participation in Rational Recovery self-help groups, where AVRT is the central focus, can give you additional ammunition against the Addictive Voice. AVRT: The Course is a series of intensive AVRT sessions conducted by a certified AVRT specialist.
- When you have learned AVRT, you are completely recovered—a normal human being who doesn't drink. You do not need to attend groups. Stay home, work on your problems in your own way, and enjoy yourself. Groups don't keep you sober, you do!
- AVRT is your *guarantee* that you will remain sober for the rest of your life. Are you ready?
- How long will it take you to completely end your addiction? When you say it's over, it's over.

ACTION

Conceptual Checkout

Read through the following list of sentences. Reading it will help you form an organized foundation for your work in AVRT. If any of these concepts are not immediately clear, don't get hung up on them. Just read on and come back later. Remember, there are two forces working against you: your Addictive Voice, and society at large, which strongly supports the AV. That is why some of these ideas feel awkward at first.

1. There is no evidence proving the addictive disease theory.
2. Chemical dependence is an individual liberty with known, predictable risks.
3. Addiction, an unwanted chemical dependence, may only be subjectively identified. Addiction exists only in the presence of two competing mind-sets: one, the Addictive Voice, which intends to continue the addiction forever, and the other, the self, which intends to reduce or eliminate the problems the addiction causes. The essence of AVRT is the separation of these entities or mind-sets and restoration of perfect, voluntary control to the self.
4. Self-intoxication is always voluntary, willful behavior with the sole purpose of pleasure.
5. Recovery is secure, planned abstinence.
6. Anyone can quit now for good.
7. Most addicted people recover on their own.
8. Abstinence is a learnable skill.
9. The mental skill supporting lifetime abstinence can be described and taught to persons who have not figured it out on their own.
10. The Addictive Voice is the cognitive-emotive (thinking-feeling) expression of one's desire for substance pleasure, the prelude to all drinking or drugging. The AV is any thinking or feeling that supports or suggests the use of alcohol or drugs, ever.
11. The AV is the sole cause of addiction.
12. Circumstances such as unhappiness, pain, emotional disturbance, irrational thinking, family functioning, spiritual deficiencies, rotten childhoods, lousy parents, developmental glitches, low frustration tolerance, low self-esteem, moral degeneracy, and one's genetic endowment are neither causes of substance addiction nor relevant to recovery, even when strongly believed to be so. They are reasons given to oneself and others to self-intoxicate, but have nothing to do with the real motivation for drinking or drugging, which is pleasure. When

these peripheral issues are used to justify drinking or drugging, we hear the sound of the Addictive Voice.

13. Addicted people are not really interested in finding relief from negative feelings or emotions: relief is a zero-sum condition, a return to a neutral state following distress. They may feel very bad as a prelude to self-intoxication, but nevertheless it is the specific pleasurable effect, the high produced by the substance, that is the overriding motivation. This is why medication of depression and anxiety so often fails. Addicted people typically continue the use of the offending substance while taking the prescribed medication. Even when the medication provides relief, the desire for alcohol or drug-induced pleasure continues.
14. When addicted people quit using the substance, they return to improved physical and mental health. The reasons they once gave for self-intoxication become understood as results and not causes of self-intoxication.
15. It is logically impossible for an addicted person to be "in denial." One may convincingly lie, but self-knowledge defines addiction.
16. Psychology, philosophy, spirituality, and religion are irrelevant to recovery. Accordingly, abstinent outcome is only incidental to involvements with those systems of thought. No matter how well-adjusted, spiritually fulfilled, or mentally healthy you may become, the permanent memory and associations of past pleasure will continue to activate your Addictive Voice.
17. The Addictive Voice is a natural function of a healthy human body, not to be associated with any disease process, and not to be feared.
18. Nutrition is irrelevant to abstinence.
19. No matter how depressed, anxious, disappointed, or angry one may become, the Addictive Voice is easily recognized.
20. Anyone who chooses to may *perfectly* dissociate from the Addictive Voice and become securely abstinent.
21. The decision to abstain permanently cannot be justified

through reason alone, but may be easily arrived at through intuition.

22. Making a commitment to lifetime abstinence creates *polar ambivalence,* that is, strong opposite feelings. These feelings are called the Abstinence Commitment Effect or ACE.

The Challenge

It is human to become addicted, and it is also human to defeat addiction. Faced with a challenge, human beings naturally rise to the occasion and pit their own competencies against adversity. AVRT is a *head game* that draws on your intelligence—yes, your IQ. Defeating your addiction doesn't depend on *how* intelligent you are, but on how *willing* you are to apply whatever intelligence you have. If you carefully read the following chapters on AVRT, you will pick up the basic rules of the game. You will find no evasions, no spiritual teachings, no leaps of faith, little advice on whether you should or shouldn't continue your addiction. Once you understand the rules and follow a very simple logic that anyone can follow, you will find yourself permanently sober. In fact, if you follow the logic of AVRT to its conclusion, you will find that consuming your drug of choice—or any intoxicant at all—will be just as difficult as refusing it has been in the past. It will be virtually impossible.

The Stage Is Set

What you have read so far in *Rational Recovery* sets the stage for AVRT: The Book Course, which follows next. You already know quite a bit about AVRT—what it is and some of its qualities. You've gotten some theory, some philosophy, some politics, and, I hope, some inspiration. You may already feel well along the way to recovery. Just one question: *Are you ready for this?*

PART II

AVRT: The Book Course

Important Instructions

NOTE **1** ▸ Do not read further in this book during any day in which you consume *any* amount of alcohol or other drugs. This is possible for any addicted person. To learn AVRT, you must hold your Addictive Voice in check. If you do drink or use drugs, you will not be able to hear your Addictive Voice or comprehend what you read. It helps to be mentally clear. If you have been drinking or using today, put the book down and return to it tomorrow. AVRT will still be here, and so will your addiction.

NOTE **2** ▸ *Word exchange* for users of drugs other than alcohol: *Rational Recovery* is written for both alcohol and drug addictions. Replace "alcohol" with the name(s) of your favorite stuff. The words "drink" and "use" are interchangeable.

6

Hello in There

Whatever this is, it won't work. It can't really be any different.

—Your Beast

Yes, you—the one with the drinking problem.

Do you understand that just reading this book could separate you from your precious stuff forever?

That is what you want, isn't it?

Oh? You're not sure? Very interesting.

Part of you wants to keep it up? To continue drinking? But part of you wants to quit? Seems as if you're not really sure. Maybe you haven't had enough to drink. To drink or not to drink; that is the question. Such suspense.

You know the reasons you want to quit the stuff. Your addiction is a horror show. It's scary, isn't it? It's scary because you have already stopped many times, and each time you go back to it. Then more bad things happen, and then you do it some more—to take away the pain, to get high, to forget. Sometimes it seems like everything is okay, but you know that sooner or later more bad things will happen. And you also understand that sooner or later you'll probably have to quit altogether for good. Or die the hard way.

But deep down you also know that you will drink again. You can't stop! Can you? Maybe you'll just have to die. But maybe it'll take a long time to die; you can make your addiction last a long time. Who knows? Maybe it won't be that bad. The booze does take the edge from pain. Maybe you can just wait it out and see how it goes. Maybe something will change, so that you can keep your addiction and get away with it. Besides, you're relatively young. Maybe you will grow out of it. Maybe they will come up with a new treatment for your problem. Then you wouldn't want it the way you do now. Then you could be normal. And you could drink as much as you want, any time you want, and not have to pay the piper. Maybe the best thing is to take it easy. Easy does it, as they say; don't make any rash decisions. Drinking has its pleasures, and they are hard to beat.

Well, if you haven't had enough to drink, get a bookmark. Place it in this page until you are ready to read further. Go back to your stuff and use it some more, as much as you want, for as long as you want. You are a free person, and you know the risks. Whatever you drink, snort, inject, smoke, or eat, enjoy it! You know how risky and expensive it is, so do it, and *enjoy it as much as you can.* This is not a joke or sarcasm. If you continue what you're doing, I really hope you get what you pay for and don't get hurt.

God, you love that stuff, don't you?

I will wait for you.

If you are ready to quit, though, turn the page and read on. The end is near.

7

I'm Still Here

You are ultimately alone in your struggle with your addiction. For our purposes, I hope you will feel alone, so that you will not be distracted from yourself. Your addiction is your own problem, and no one can really help you with it. It's completely up to you to decide whether you will continue drinking or using or quit altogether.

I understand some important things about you, even though I have not met you. *I know why you drink so much,* even though you may not be so sure at times. I have lived in the world of addiction, so I understand how frustrating it is to be addicted and how painful the consequences are. I also know exactly, in detail, how you can defeat even the worst substance addiction, and I can teach you here how to do it.

Although I am like you, having been addicted myself, we probably have little else in common. It is irrelevant whether I or anyone else cares about you, or cares whether you continue to drink or use drugs. The important question is whether *you* care.

8

I Know Why You Drink

This isn't the right time. Put the book down. Read it later—maybe.

—Your Beast

Why do you drink in spite of all the trouble? I'm sure you have given this some serious thought. Could it be that you never learned to control yourself like others? Could it be that you were born to drink? Could you have a disease that releases druglike substances into your brain? Are your brain cells out of whack? Do you drink or use to compensate for life's sorrows? Or do you just love to get drunk?

Why do you drink so much when you know the harm it causes you? (I know that question probably annoys you.) The simplest thing in the world would be to never drink, so why don't you just give it up? What is this *thing* that drives you on to drink some more? Even as the world closes in around you, you want to drink some more. From time to time you damn yourself, then you drink to kill the time at hand. You drink for its own sake—to drink.

Your addiction is a mystery to you. If it weren't a mystery, you would know how to stop it, and you *would* stop it. During dark moments, you may feel despair that you actually plan to continue your addiction. Your hope has flown away, leaving you alone to your bitter affair with the stuff of your desire. "Why this?" you ask, and you hear only hopeless answers. Our culture provides you with *many* hopeless answers that fuel your addiction.

Some say you were *born to lose*. From your ancestors came your doom. If you *could* have done better, you *would* have done better, they say. But you have a *disease* called "alcoholism" that has been written in tiny cipher on the damp parchment of your life, and it has caused your life to become little more than a pile of ashes. The disease of alcoholism makes you *powerless* over your addiction. That's the reason you drink as you do, and that's the way it is. Each time you lift a drink, you are peeking back through time, seeing your own unruly ancestors who also obeyed the call of the wild and drank as their ancestors did.

Your disease. No cure. It's forever. You'll always be an alcoholic. Alcoholism is a disease of relapse. When you're sober it's like waiting for the other shoe to drop. And when it does, pow! How low is the bottom? Have you hit bottom yet?

How can you know if you've hit bottom—other than to drink some more?

But wait a minute. Maybe you *don't* have a disease. Maybe you *learned* to drink. Right? But you know you *must* have a disease. If you don't believe you have a disease, you're in denial. Denial is a symptom of the disease of alcoholism. You never can tell when you're in denial. If you think you're better, that means you're really sick. Feeling good is a pink cloud that will fade into despair. It always does. Why try? You're powerless. Surrender. Let go. Admit your life is unmanageable. Latch on to someone who's been through it. Let someone else tell you what to do. Just don't take the first drink, take the cotton out of your ears and stick it in your mouth, and fake it till you make it.

But maybe it's better being drunk. You can't fake it, and you can't make it, either. Take the drink. Let go. Surrender to what comes naturally instead of what doesn't. Life sucks, so what's the point in living? At least there's one thing that feels right.

Does all this confusion sound familiar? If so, you must be from America, where they came up with this disease nonsense.

Addiction Is a Sign of Health

Your addiction is an orderly process that you can understand. When you understand *why* you became and remain addicted, you will be free to stop it. Although you *may* have inherited a disposition to drink to excess, as well as a body that can tolerate it, there is no genetic blemish that *compels* you to drink alcohol. If you inherited an ability to drink more than others, or even an appetite for alcohol to go with that ability, that is all you inherited.

Your appetite for alcohol is an appetite for pleasure. Appetites are a sign of health, and pleasure is the spice of life. To call your desire for pleasure a disease conceals the real reason you drink or use and makes it much more difficult to stop. If you believe you drink for reasons other than pleasure, you may spend much time and money trying to remove those reasons rather than simply quitting your addiction.

Suppose that you inherited a fine ability to play sports or create music, and you love engaging in that activity. Would that *compel* you to engage in either of those behaviors? Some might argue that musicians, composers, sports figures, and others with exceptional talents are compelled to fulfill their potentials, but that argument is more figurative than real. Likewise, you are free to drink or not drink, to play ball or not play ball, and to dance or not dance.

As stated earlier, I have an enormous capacity to drink alcohol. My wife, Lois, however, cannot consume more than two drinks without getting sick. She enjoys one alcoholic drink now and then, but rarely more. When she does, a red light comes on in her thinking, and her body tells her, "Stop! You've had enough. Any more is bad for you." If she continues to drink, she will become very ill. When I have had two drinks, I get an inner green light, and my body tells me, "Drink! It's good for you!" When I have had eight drinks, the green light still shines brightly, and my body says, "That's a good start! Drink more!" There seems no time when I get that red light. Perhaps the light changes, but the lenses are all green. Clearly, our bodies are quite different in the way alcohol is metabolized, and it is quite plausible that our difference in this is inherited.

Although I could think of my way of drinking as a symptom of a disease (I did for many years), I can also view it as stupidity—stupid behavior in a nonstupid person. Either way, I am free to drink or not. Either way, it makes no sense for me to drink any amount of alcohol; it's not good for me.

Many of our current attitudes toward addiction are deterministic, predicting addictive behavior when other options exist. The result is often more addiction than would otherwise be the case. You, for example, did not inherit your personal behavior nor the thinking that causes you to drink, although at times it may seem so. You did not inherit the problem; you inherited the *solution* to the problem, a human brain that can now defeat you or your addiction! The outcome is entirely up to you.

There is strange comfort in the disease idea. It seems to explain *why*. It helps you make sense from chaos. The disease concept also takes the heat off you. If you accept the disease idea, a great burden is lifted from your shoulders. The burden is *personal responsibility!*

In Rational Recovery, we are each responsible for acquiring, maintaining, and ending our addictions, and we are also responsible for our behavior and the consequences of our addictions.

If you call yourself an alcoholic, the burden of responsibility is lifted, but you are subject to the endless moral authority of the Fellowship of Alcoholics Anonymous. They think they have a disease and that you do, too. They have that in common. They also have many other beliefs in common. In the last analysis, they may need you more than you need them. Statistically speaking, you can probably do better on your own. If you want to quit your addiction, you had better be clear about why you drink or use as you do.

De-e-e-e-e-e-e-e-e-e-e-e-e-e-e-e-e-e-e-e-e-e-e-p Pleasure

You drink because you love to get drunk. You get high because you love the feeling. If you think you drink for any other reason, you are dangerously deluded. Alcohol gives you two things:

(1) the pleasurable high or buzz, and (2) it replaces the pain of withdrawal with pleasure. Both are pure pleasure.

"Oh," you say, "I drink to relax." That's pleasure. Or, "I drink when I'm bored." That's pleasure. "I drink socially, to have fun, and to be a part of what's happening." That's pleasure, too. You love to drink for the pleasurable effect of alcohol. If this doesn't add up in your thinking, then think a little more about it.

You may also think you drink to cope with life, to "get numb," or to drink away the pain of depression or grief. If so, get ready to put that absurd idea to rest. Alcohol *causes* depression, both directly as a depressant drug and indirectly in the outcomes of your drinking, which you then "relieve" by drinking more alcohol.

No one gets numb from alcohol. You get a pleasurable buzz, and that's what you're calling "numb." Your depression is a *front* for your pleasure-chasing addiction, and you have been taken in by your own Addictive Voice. In Rational Recovery, this is called an "addicto-depressive condition," in which you believe that alcohol is reducing rather than causing depression. For example, you say, "I drink because I am depressed," instead of, "I am depressed because I drink." Many physicians' waiting rooms are filled with depressed, addicted people who often convince the doctor that they are driven to drink by depression and therefore need another substance, more effective than alcohol, to combat those feelings. If you are one of them, a section later on describing the addicto-depressive condition may be vital to you.

You may feel that life is unfair and rotten, and you may sometimes believe that you will never get any good out of life, but the core belief supporting both your addiction and your depression is that life will be hollow, meaningless, and hellish without alcohol. Because such a belief cannot be disproved, and because the addicted lifestyle creates depressing circumstances besides, it easily becomes a fundamental viewpoint that strongly supports continued drinking, even while the drinking is the primary cause of the depression. And you may also feel depressed as hell about all the drinking you still plan to do. Pretty depressing, huh?

If you drink daily, you may have picked up the idea that you drink to feel "normal." Many maintenance drinkers conceal the pleasure of their intoxication—the buzz—by calling their "tolerance" for alcohol a *symptom* of the disease of alcoholism. It may feel somewhat better in the short run to think of your "maintenance drinking" as a symptomatic of some other vague problem, one that may need addiction treatment by compassionate, professional people. But this is only one way to look at maintenance drinking. If someone else, never addicted, could crawl into your skin and feel what you call "normal," that person would probably die either of laughter or acute intoxication. Obviously, what you are maintaining is not a "normal" feeling, but an endless drunk. You may walk a straight line, but you fail to notice that your feet are touching the floor.

Can you drink without feeling the effect? If you had a stiff drink right now, what sensations would you get? Would you get numb? I know better, and I think you do, too. But if you aren't sure of this point, here is what human beings feel when they consume alcohol. See if I am wrong on any of this.

First, if it is a cold beverage, you feel the cold going down, followed within minutes by a pleasant, warm feeling in the abdomen. Then there is a gentle relaxation that spreads throughout the body. With more drinks, you feel a sense of well-being, and you forget unpleasant realities. You feel "high," and the world looks much simpler and safer. What may recently have annoyed or upset you now seems trivial. You feel good all over, and you might want to do something that is stimulating or fun. Or, maybe you want to just sit still and quietly savor the relaxed feeling. With a little more alcohol, you feel confident around others and speak with ease. Your thoughts come smoothly and naturally, and you sense that others will accept you. If you are alone, you are comfortable, fascinated with your own thoughts and able to relax. With more alcohol, you feel a surge of euphoria. Even though nothing has happened, you feel *very* good. Your thinking slows down, but you feel a warm, sometimes buzzing sensation in various parts of your body, particularly your legs and abdomen. Your troubles are gone, there is no tomorrow, and you can just enjoy the deep pleasure of alcohol. You know that your senses are awakening, but you don't care. You get impulses to say or do things you wouldn't do sober, and you do them just for the hell of it. Anything can be funny, and you find that you are laughing deeply. You want more drinks, to keep the deep pleasure alive. You drink some more, enjoying the taste. A warm, sweet feeling closes in, and you seem to be slightly removed from your surroundings. You seem to float, and your actions seem more automatic than guided by thought. Your body throbs with pleasure. Your emotions take on a new dimension, as if you feel everything more deeply. You may cry, express pleasurable anger, or feel extremely intelligent. When you notice the wonderful feeling slipping away, you drink some more to keep the fire burning. But the high fades into an awkward sense of being out of control. You drink to chase the high, and you begin to feel irritable or aggressive. You may say or do preposterous things that offend people and require others to stop you. You may fight. You may fall. You then sleep, pass out, or continue drinking and doing things you may never remember. When you awaken the next day, you feel raw and fearful. You know you tied one on and don't feel well. You remember glimpses of the night before, and you hope that you didn't do anything that will catch up with you later. Sometimes it all comes back in a flood of confused images, and you cringe at what you did. You wish you were like other people who don't suffer such problems from drinking, and you know something is seriously wrong. You think of quitting, but you *know* you will drink again soon. You are ready to do it again because you know what deep pleasure is all about, and you will do it again and again as long as you are able. You are feeling the call of the wild. Your addiction is a fact of life, and you sense you will live with it until you die.

Now tell me, was I wrong in why you drink? Are you *really* drinking to "cope"?

The Way It Really Is

Few understand what it's really like to be addicted. This is because people who are "in recovery" tell only half the story, the bad part of addiction. I have been addicted, and I have talked to literally thousands of currently and formerly addicted people. I get a much different picture from my experience and theirs than from listening to stories by people in the recovery group movement.

Drinking alcohol feels good. So does smoking marijuana, shooting heroin, and sniffing cocaine. That is why we did it, to feel good all over. That is also the *only* reason we did it. This is not to say that we didn't give other reasons for our supreme self-indulgence, because we certainly did.

Here are some of the most common reasons addicted people give for drinking and drugging, followed by the *real* reasons (the Addictive Voice) in italics, and then a capsule summary of the situation.

1. TO RELAX AFTER A HARD DAY.

   After a hard day, I want to feel the pleasure of getting high.

   Instead of naturally relaxing, one chooses the pleasure of drinking or using and then reports that one can't relax without the drug.

2. TO FIT IN WITH THE CROWD.

   When I'm with others who are getting high, I want to feel the way they do, high as a kite. I envy others who are getting a buzz when I'm not.

   Instead of awkwardly fitting in or leaving, as others would, one chooses the pleasure of drinking or using and then reports that one cannot fit in or feel comfortable without the drug.

3. BECAUSE LIFE HAS SO FEW SIMPLE PLEASURES, SO LITTLE MEANING, SO FEW OPPORTUNITIES.

   Just pop the cap, or take a hit, and it's there. No hassle, no waiting, immediate. Ahhhh.

   Instead of seeking life's common rewards, as others do, one chooses the pleasure of drinking or using and then reports that one cannot compete for life's abundance without the drug.

4. BECAUSE I DO NOT HAVE ADVANTAGES SUCH AS AFFLUENCE, ROBUST HEALTH, THE RIGHT ETHNICITY, EDUCATION, OR SOCIAL CLASS, MY OPPORTUNITIES FOR PLEASURE ARE RESTRICTED TO THOSE ASSOCIATED WITH ALCOHOL AND DRUGS.

   Who needs those things anyway? The high life is the best life, regardless of other circumstances.

   Instead of pursuing goals and overcoming disadvantages, as others would, one chooses the pleasure of drinking or using and then reports that one is coping with life's problems by drinking or using drugs.

5. TO ENJOY CERTAIN ACTIVITIES.

   I yearn to get high so much that I can't enjoy simple pleasures.

   Instead of participating in the activity, one chooses the pleasure of drinking or using and then reports that one cannot enjoy the activity without the drug.

6. BECAUSE THERE'S NOTHING ELSE TO DO. BOREDOM.

   Although there are many things I could do, I will use this opportunity to get high.

   Instead of feeling the discomfort of boredom to the point of doing something to relieve it, one chooses the pleasure of drinking or using and then reports that one is unable to cope with boredom without the drug.

7. TO HELP ME CONCENTRATE.

   If I get high, I will be able to stop yearning and possibly concentrate.

   Instead of applying oneself to a task, one chooses the pleasure of drinking or using and then reports that one cannot concentrate without the drug.

8. TO COPE WITH LONELINESS.

   Being alone is a perfect opportunity to get high.

   Instead of writing a letter or calling someone, one chooses the pleasure of drinking or using and then reports that one cannot cope with loneliness without the drug.

9. TO RELIEVE DEPRESSION.

   I don't want relief from depression—which activity, psychotherapy, or medication might provide—nearly as much as I want to get high.

   Instead of pushing against the depression with activity or getting psychological or medical help, one chooses the pleasure of drinking or using and then reports to the doctor that one is medicating depression with the unprescribed drug. Whether or not medical treatment is effective, one continues drinking or using, nullifying the therapeutic effect.

10. TO MELLOW OUT WHEN I'M UPSET OR ANGRY.

    Because I'm upset, I will drink or use to feel pleasure. Just thinking about that pleasure reduces my anger, so by the time I actually drink, I am rarely angry.

    Instead of experiencing or expressing the feelings of anger and allowing them to dissipate, one decides to drink or use drugs. The mere anticipation of pleasure causes the anger to dissipate. Nevertheless, one later reports that one is coping with anger by drinking or using drugs.

11. TO COPE WITH TRAGEDY.

    When tragedy strikes, I won't feel intensely bad, but I will feel pleasure all over.

    Instead of experiencing intense, realistic grief over the loss, one chooses the pleasure of drinking or using and then reports that one was unable to cope with loss without the drug.

12. BECAUSE I CRAVE IT.

    Yes, and I must never be deprived of pleasure, any time I want it.

    Instead of experiencing the physical desire to drink or use or the physical discomfort of withdrawal, one chooses the pleasure of drinking or using and then reports that one is unable to tolerate those feelings.

13. TO PROVE I CAN HANDLE IT.

    I don't want to lose my right to experience deep, physical pleasure.

    Instead of acting on one's better judgment and quitting for good, one chooses the pleasure of drinking or using and then reports that one is acting in a responsible way.

14. BECAUSE I LOVE THE TASTE.

    And I love all of the other physical sensations that come from drinking. In fact, nonalcoholic drinks, although they taste fine, leave me cold.

    Instead of learning to abstain from alcohol, one chooses the pleasure of drinking or using and then reports the real truth, that one derives such exquisite pleasure from drinking or drugging that everything else is secondary.

Cell Aberration or Celebration?

To some extent, we believed our reasons because there was a kernel of truth in them. But addiction is not a disease, a cell aberration; rather it's a celebration of pleasure—with every drink or use. Substance pleasure overtakes common sense—in the same old-fashioned way that accidental pregnancies occur—but it also blocks natural bad feelings that say "stop." It is a state of hyperhedonism that culminates in chemically enhanced stupidity and mounting despair. When pain finally outweighs the pleasure, people are naturally inclined to quit their addictions.

How Do I Do It?

Addicted people are strongly inclined to wonder endlessly, "Why, why, why, do I do this, when I know the trouble it causes?" Why is fairly obvious—you love to get zonked. In the pages to come, you will gain a sufficient understanding of why you have *continued* your addiction, in spite of everything. That understanding will then give you footing to ask the most important question of all, "How do I guarantee to myself that my addiction is really over?"

9

Listen Carefully!

This is interesting so far. It might help other *people.*

—Your Beast

That's right, addicted one—*listen.* Listen inwardly and you will near a *voice* that tells you to drink. Yes, *that* voice—the one that says, "We need a little something to relax," or, "It's time to have some fun; break out the booze." When you think of the bad results from your excessive drinking, it says, "The good outweighs the bad. Just be a little more careful next time." When you've stopped for a few weeks or months because of the problems drinking was causing, it says, "You have done very well. Things weren't as bad as you thought. It will be okay to have a drink or two, now and then. But be careful this time, so you can protect your right to drink."

If you think of quitting for good, it says, "Stop for a while. But *never* say 'never.' " When you think it would be wonderful never to feel the need to drink anything, it reminds you of how empty you feel and tells you that you will *never* feel right without the use of alcohol. "Take one day at a time," it says. "A future without drinking is too bleak to contemplate." The voice of your addiction shows you pictures of what it wants—a special drink, a line of coke, a needle—and it creates feelings of excitement and pleasure in you as it prepares you to drink or use. When you sip your drink, it says, "Ah, yes! How good." When you plan a trip or a vacation, it shows you pictures of yourself drinking. It sees life as an extended drinking opportunity and promises to comfort you until death do you part. It warns you against betrayal: "You've tried to quit before and couldn't do it, so don't make any promises you can't keep. You'll only feel worse if you do."

Though your addiction promises you great pleasure and serenity, don't forget it will not hesitate to kill you or to destroy anything or everything you love. **The voice of your addiction, the AV with its sentences, images, and feelings, is always with you, and it is your own worst enemy.** The Beast is dumb. It is an enemy within you that survives by drinking and survives in order to drink. It fears anything or anyone that would threaten its supply of that very precious stuff. The AV is nearly as intelligent as you, and it creates countless reasons to continue drinking. It remains disguised as you, operates in hiding from others who would interfere with your drinking, and it maintains utmost secrecy from you. For example, if you are now thinking, "I don't have any voice that tells me to drink," you have just heard your Addictive Voice in action.

You suffer from the illusion that you are one person. But for our purposes there are *two* of you. "Two of me?" you say. "No way. What kind of nonsense is this?" Read on.

Yes, there are two of "you." On one hand, *you* want to quit. On the other hand, "you" don't want to quit; "you" want to drink as much as "you" want, any time "you" want, forever. At least it seems that "you" do. But deep down inside, *you do* want to quit. Don't *you?* If you think, "Yes. I really do want to quit," then that is really the inner voice of *you.* These two *voices* argue endlessly, and the other "you," your Addictive Voice, has been getting its way. That is why you drink against *your* better judgment. The Addictive Voice is the *only* reason you drink. More on that later.

An Enemy Within

Your goal is to become one—your own self, free from addiction and free to live as you choose. But first, you had better get apart from "it," the other "you." You surely understand that "it" is a serious enemy to your happiness. (If you had a convincing voice in your head telling you to hit yourself on the head with a hammer, that voice would obviously be your enemy.) Eventually, when you are separated by a safe distance from "it," you will be in control. You will have defeated your dependence on alcohol or any other drug. You will be fully recovered, ready to catch up on the important business of living. Like having fun, for a change.

ACTION

Naming

Start separating from your Addictive Voice now by naming it "Beast." Giving it this particular name, with a capital *B,* will help you stay on target as you get in position to destroy your Addictive Voice. If you feel discomfort with this, it is because your Beast doesn't want to be called what it is. All the more reason to do it. Take charge.

"Beast" fairly well describes the way your Addictive Voice operates. In *The Small Book,* the expression "Beast" was used as a metaphor, a figment of the imagination like Jack Frost or other fictional characters. But "Beast" is actually *more* than a metaphor. In a very real way, there *is* a beast within each human being (see Figure 1). It is a carryover from prehistoric times when humans *were* beasts. The beast within you is amazingly effective in getting what it wants for survival. It has been responsible for the survival of the human race for millions of years, in spite of extreme hardships such as famine and radical changes in the environment. It doesn't give up, and it will use as much of your human capacity as it can to learn, reason, plan ahead, and move about in order to satisfy its *survival appetites.*

Somehow, it matters not how, an appetite for alcohol or other drugs has gotten mixed in with your other "legitimate" appetites for food, oxygen, and sex. Your beast brain believes that alcohol is just as important to survival as oxygen. It believes that it abso-

The Two-Part Brain

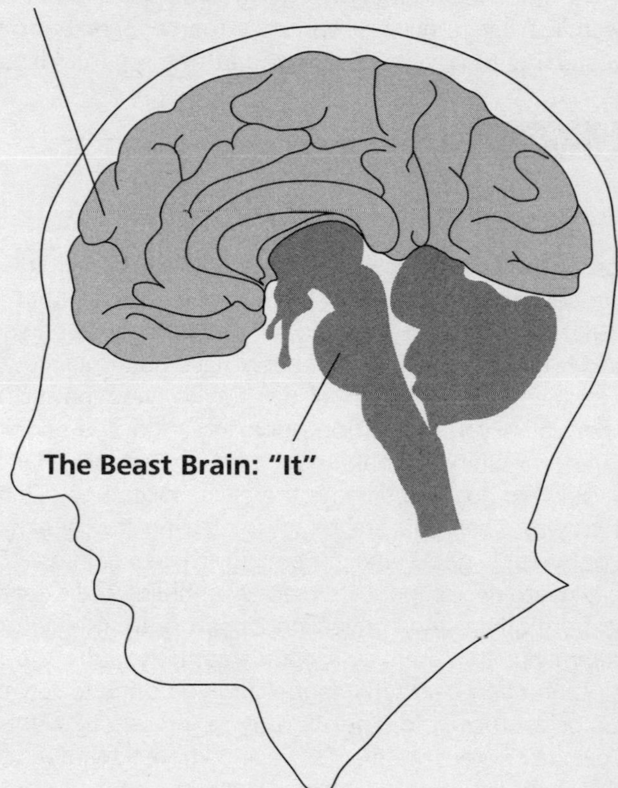

Figure 1. The Brain

lutely *must* have alcohol in order to survive. *Why* this is so is unimportant to your recovery.

Is this starting to register with you? Your beast brain has been directing your life as if alcohol were oxygen. And you've been going along with it, behaving like an animal, unable to *recognize* the many ways that your beast brain is expressing itself. Once again, you have been suffering the illusion that "it" is *you*. You have been *hearing* your beast voice for many years, but only now are you starting to *recognize* it as something *separate* from you.

ACTION

Start a List of Adjectives

In a notebook, list the adjectives that apply to your Beast. It is vital for you to understand your enemy. There is one adjective that I believe applies to the Beasts of all addicted people: *ruthless.* But if your Beast were only ruthless, you would probably have quit drinking long ago as your problems mounted. It is also *seductive,* very convincing in the way it persuades you to continue drinking. And it is *opportunistic,* seeing an opportunity to drink under any circumstances. Of course it is a *persistent* companion, always there—in success or failure, alone or in a crowd, when you are happy or feeling low, when you are excited or bored, in good times or bad, in sickness or in health, and—yes—until death do you part. It is *secretive,* hiding the extent of your drinking from others and concealing its nature from you. It is sometimes *commanding* in the way it demands that you drink, but it may be quite *caring* and *gentle* by suggesting you drink to feel better. It can even be *aristocratic* or *snobbish* by telling you that drinkers are special people who are more sensitive and know how to get the most out of life. Your list of adjectives will grow as you start applying the principles of AVRT.

Understanding the Nature of the Beast

Is this still an uncomfortable idea—that you "hear voices," are driven by primitive, beastlike desires, and that within you is a ruthless, antisocial nature that has been directing your life? Relax. Human begins *are* animals. True, we are a very special kind of animal. We think, enjoy beauty, music, art, and we have built a civilization that is a marvel even to us. But we appear to have evolved from other simpler creatures—beasts, if you will—that lived to survive. We have inherited much of the nature of those prehuman beasts in a primitive part of our brain called the "old brain," or *midbrain.* The "new brain," or *neocortex,* has evolved into a highly developed organ that makes human consciousness and civilization possible. *Everyone* thinks in voices and visual images, and everyone has an inner voice of survival that originates in the midbrain. Everyone has a thinking voice that says when to eat, when to go to bed, when to make love, when to go to the bathroom, and when to scratch one's nose.

The Addictive Voice is truly the voice of a beast. It cares for *nothing* but alcohol.

That is the definition of the Addictive Voice: any idea, feeling, or behavior that supports drinking alcohol. Its only love is that precious, precious stuff. It has no regard for you or anything you love. To your Beast, your body is only a machine to obtain alcohol; your life is only an extended *drinking* opportunity. When it is in control, you forget your love of other things, even your love of life itself, and you betray the people you love.

You face a worthy opponent that has already caused you great harm and that will struggle against you every inch of the way toward sobriety. It has remained hidden for many years, disguised as you. But in order to continue operating, it must remain hidden from you. As you read on, and during the weeks and months to come, you will learn more about how your Addictive Voice serves its master, your subcortical Beast.

But It's Only a Beast

Relax. Your subcortical Beast is no match for you.

Your midbrain is quite similar to the brain of a dog, a horse, or a tiger. There is a pecking order throughout the animal kingdom, where the smarter or larger creatures dominate the smaller, weaker, and less intelligent ones. Like most beasts, your Beast understands authority.

If you have ever been followed by a growling dog, you may have been aware that your choices were either to keep walking at the same pace, start running, or turn on the dog and face it down. Most often, a growling dog will cut and run when confronted by an advancing human many times its own size. But it does take some guts to confront a beast because of those rare exceptions when it may attack. Even though your dog-brain is unable to control or attack you physically, it will fluff itself up and pretend to be a winner. Soon you will understand that this is only a pose.

Your neocortex, on the other hand, is not only many times larger than your midbrain, but is also the most sophisticated organization of matter in the known universe. It can master both its physical and psychological environments. *Given the correct information,* the human neocortex (yes, *you*) is able to suppress *any* appetite, able to defeat *any* addiction, any time you choose. Anyone can hold one's breath until passing out. Children sometimes do this. Political activists often fast to death for values higher than food, and others become celibate as a means to obtain higher priorities and fulfillment. As you may have suspected, most addicted people, even when ardently attributing their success to something greater than themselves, stop using drugs of their own free will.

But all this sounds grim, doesn't it? Starving, passing out from no air, and having no more sex are serious deprivations. Your Beast reacts to ideas of abstinence from alcohol or other drugs in exactly the same way, as a *terrible* deprivation! Poor thing.

Your worst enemy is your Beast, *and vice versa!* It hides in the dark, damp recesses of your midbrain, and it cannot tolerate your seeing it for what it really is. As you learn AVRT, you will see your Beast, naked, in vivid detail. Only you can expose it, and when it is exposed, it is destroyed. When you have mastered AVRT, you may still have some troubles, but you will have the great advantage of being mentally clear as you solve them.

ACTION

Ask Yourself

Your Addictive Voice masquerades as you. For many years, you have *heard* it without *recognizing* it. Here are some questions that will help you target your Beast:

- Is it possible for you to drink without being aware that you are drinking?
- Is it possible for you to feel high without being aware that you are drinking?
- Can you have a drink without *deciding* to have a drink?
- Can you purchase alcohol without knowing how much it costs or knowing if you have enough money?
- Can you go into a liquor store without knowing where you are?
- Do you ever decide to drink because you are unhappy?
- Do you ever decide to drink because you are happy?
- Have you ever thought about owning a huge supply of alcohol?
- Do you become irritated when a drink is diluted or when your supply runs out?
- Do you ever look forward to drinking later in the day (or during the weekend, or later in the year)?

As you consider these questions, notice that you are always *conscious* of your decisions to drink and that your addiction is under your *voluntary* control. It is humanly impossible to drink without thinking of drinking.

Recall a time in the recent past when you quit drinking for a good reason, such as embarrassment, injury, fear of getting fired, an unusually painful hangover, or an angry spouse. You may have stayed stopped for several days, weeks, or months. But you fell off—that is, *jumped* off—the wagon. Now, remember starting up again. Maybe you were alone, or at a party, or at a bar. Concentrate on what you were thinking shortly before taking that first drink. Don't let yourself off easy here with the line, "I wasn't thinking anything. I just took a drink." That is impossible. No one but you made the decision. How did you change your mind? How long before you drank did you start thinking about it? What did you tell yourself to justify drinking?

Whatever it was that you thought to yourself, you were hearing the *sound* of your Beast, and it can be written down in one short sentence. Before reading further, write that sentence here or on another paper: ________________________________

Now, read on, and I will guess your reason to drink again.

Definition: Your Addictive Voice is *any thinking or feeling that supports any use of any alcohol or drugs in any amount—ever.* Therefore, whatever you wrote down is your Addictive Voice in print, in your own handwriting. Here are some possible reasons you may have accepted to justify your return to alcohol.

1. Screw it. Just do it.
2. It can't really be any different.
3. I am an alcoholic, and that's why I drink.
4. I want it, so I'll have some. To hell with it.
5. I'll be careful this time. Just a little won't hurt.
6. You've been good for five days now. You deserve a drink.
7. I haven't had anything for two weeks, and I still feel lousy. A drink will help me feel better. Sobriety sucks, anyhow.
8. Life sucks. There is only one thing that feels right. A drink.
9. I feel good. A drink will make this a perfect moment.
10. I'm in good health. My body can take it.
11. I'm in bad health. What's the use of quitting?
12. I *need* alcohol to regulate my body. My body *requires* it.
13. What will people think if I don't drink? They may think I have a drinking problem.
14. I can't stand this constant craving. I may as well get it over with and drink.
15. I can't go more than (three days, one month, etc.) without drinking. It's time to drink again.
16. Drinking enriches my life. It's one of life's few genuine pleasures.

17. I can't stand feeling so bored (stressed, depressed, anxious, angry, etc.). I need a drink right now.
18. This is a very special occasion. It wouldn't be right without having a drink.
19. I can't enjoy music, TV, food, parties, sex, traveling, or have fun without drinking.
20. I need something to relax after a hard day's work.

This is some of the language that your Addictive Voice uses to get you to drink. The list could go on and on, because the Addictive Voice is very *creative* in finding new reasons for drinking alcohol. One of the above reasons, or something close to it, was probably the one you wrote down as the reason you resumed drinking after not drinking for a while. But your AV is probably more creative than I am, and it may have found a reason I haven't thought of here.

Look again at the sentence you just wrote justifying your return to alcohol. Do *you* still stand behind that statement? If you do, you are failing to recognize your Addictive Voice. By now, you probably sense that your own thinking about the use of alcohol isn't logical or sensible. The thinking isn't really *you*. How many times has someone who knows you said, "When you drink, you aren't really yourself. It's like something else takes over." If you understand this, you are beginning to *separate* from you Addictive Voice; you are thinking *objectively* about your Beast, not as *you* but as "it."

Now, look again at the twenty Addictive Voice statements above. Note that fourteen of them use the pronoun *I*. Do you see the problem? Your Addictive Voice, which is your personal enemy, has taken control of the most important word in your vocabulary! It is masquerading as you, using your personal pronoun, *I*. Soon, as you learn more about AVRT, that will no longer be possible. You will be in control. At last.

That is what you want. *Isn't it?*

10

Surprise! You Have a Healthy Brain

You're the sickest thing on Earth. You'll never get better.

—Your Beast

Let's move beyond the disease model of addiction to a new vision of addiction. AVRT's *structural* model of addiction helps you to understand what's going on inside your head. This will give you a strong advantage at times when your Beast acts up and you feel vulnerable. When you catch on to what is happening between the structures of your brain, your addiction will no longer be a mystery to you. You will be able to see *why* you continued drinking in spite of it all.

Figure 2 shows a more detailed diagram of the human brain. It identifies the brain's anatomical structures and illustrates how brain tissues in different areas have different functions.

As you continue reading, refer to Figure 2. Become familiar with the way regions of the brain interact and notice there is no mention of brain chemistry. For frequent reference, place a paper clip on the illustrated page.

Your brain comes in two parts: a large neocortex ("new brain"), which is the *human* brain, and beneath the neocortex at the end of your spinal cord, the midbrain, which is basically the brain of a *beast*. Two brains. As I said earlier, there are two of you. I wasn't kidding.

Your beast brain is the organ of physical survival. It is like a

The Structural Model of Addiction

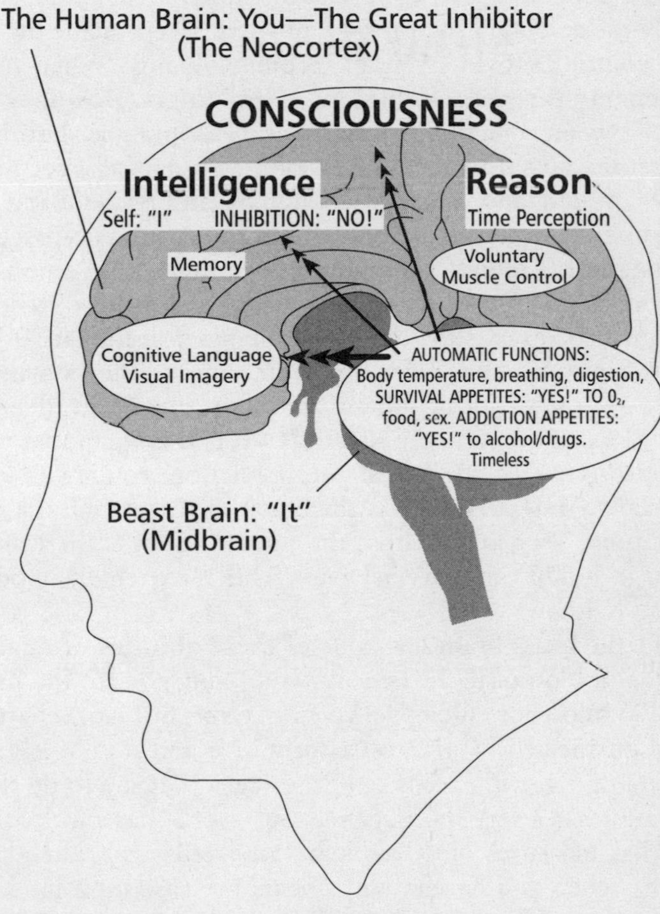

Figure 2

control panel that regulates bodily processes necessary for survival such as breathing, temperature regulation, release of hormones, digestion, heartbeat, and the biological drives and appetites for oxygen, food, sex, and—yes—alcohol and other drugs.

Your neocortex is *you.* Pure and simple. When you sleep, it is only the cerebral neocortex—you—that sleeps while the beast brain continues to do its thing, keeping you alive. When you are awake and hear yourself thinking, "I'm hungry. How long until dinner? I want something to eat," your beast brain is alerting you to what it wants. In your "mind's eye," you may also see mental images of food, and you may feel hungry and restless. You beast brain intends to survive, and it will prompt you to do practically *anything* to get food if you're hungry enough. The same is true with our most urgent survival appetite, which is for oxygen.

Your neocortex is the organ that makes you human. It is the organ of *consciousness.* This awesome object—the human neocortex—is the organ of self-awareness. It gives you identity, a sense of existence. It is the seat of "I." It is the organ that makes you *intelligent.* Yes, in spite of your addiction, you are an *intelligent* being. Your neocortex is the organ of reason and the organ of memory. Very importantly, the human brain is the center of language and of voluntary behavior. This is extremely important for you to know!

But the beast brain has *none* of these abilities or qualities. It is just a blob of flesh "beneath you"—*underneath* the human brain. While your Addictive Voice may be brilliant, charming, and sophisticated, your Beast is primitive and dumb. It can do nothing on its own except send messages that say to do this or do that. It has a very short agenda. Survive! It has a little laboratory that measures blood contents and tells you when you're hungry, when you haven't had a sexual release for a long time, when you are low on oxygen, and when you are out of booze. It can't talk, but instead it *uses* your language to enlist your voluntary muscles to get what it wants. You can *hear* it using your language centers, telling you in sentences what to do. You can *see* mental images, in color, in action, and in freeze-frame, telling you what it wants. You experience *feelings* of desire, hunger, craving, anger, and fear in connection to the necessities of life.

ACTION

Separating Your Self from Your Beast

Look at Figure 2 again and see the two organs—the neocortex, which is you, and the midbrain, which is the source of the Addictive Voice. Notice that the language center is within the neocortex. Language involves speaking with your mouth, thinking in words, sentences, and pictures. The midbrain has no language whatsoever, and in order to be ''heard,'' it must *use* your language center. In effect, the midbrain communicates with you to say what it wants, whether it is air, food, sex, or alcohol. With few exceptions, the midbrain is the organ of ''yes,'' and the neocortex is the organ of ''no,'' or inhibition. When you agree with what the midbrain wants, you take action. Very often, you disagree with what it wants. It will show you pictures and tell you to do stupid and inappropriate things. If it tells you, for example, to grab a fresh, moist strawberry from the grocery display and pop it into your mouth, you would probably quickly and intelligently intervene and say, ''No. Not now. Pay first. Then eat.'' If it is sexually attracted to someone, it may tell you to touch that person, but your neocortex may say, ''No, that could cause trouble. Maybe later, or not at all.''

The philosopher René Descartes said, "I think, therefore I am." For our purposes, we might go further than Descartes: "I inhibit, therefore I am human." In AVRT, we go to the limit with: "I recognize, therefore I am abstinent."

Only You

Notice in Figure 2 that the voluntary motor center, which controls your arms, legs, hands, mouth, and the swallowing muscles, is located in the neocortex. You have 100% control of your extremities and facial muscles. Actions are initiated through picture-language and internal speech. In order for your hand to move, you must know what you want it to do, usually in mental pictures, and then tell yourself, in effect, "Hand, pick up the glass." This picturing and internal language is usually rapid and practically automatic, so that you are largely unaware of the process of initiating physical action.

In AVRT, you will become acutely aware of these principles of voluntary behavior as they apply to your addiction. It is reassuring for you to understand that in order for your Beast to get what it wants, it must first identify itself by telling you in pictures and words that it wants alcohol. Only "the neocortical you" can decide to drink or not drink. If a thought supports the use of alcohol, you will *instantly* recognize it as coming from the Beast. Alcohol is a very significant substance, both to you and to your Beast. "It" will always love alcohol for the comfort and pleasure it brings; you will always intelligently disdain it for what it has done and can do to you.

Recognition is as effortless as naming a familiar object. From now on, your Beast is an object, and not you.

"Why Can't I Remember the Pain?"

Pain of any kind is not remembered well. You may remember that something was painful, but memories of the pain itself quickly fade. It has been said that if women could completely remember the pain of childbirth, there would be no population problem. Forgetting pain is much more dramatic in addictions.

One man struggling with his addiction got drunk and accidentally drove his car off a cliff. In the emergency room he cried out, "Why can't I remember? I've been in the hospital dozens of times, with tubes sticking out of me like this. Why can't I remember the pain and the horror?" The answer is simple. Notice in Figure 2 that memory is entirely contained within the neocortex. This shows why the Beast "forgets" pain associated with drinking. Just as with the language and motor centers, the Beast has access to memory and *uses* certain memories to its advantage.

It "remembers" only what it wants to remember, in order to get what it wants. Therefore, it is incapable of remembering pain associated with drinking alcohol. During a "Beast attack," it will show you pictures of past pleasure, and you will feel aroused. At those times it is extremely difficult to remember the negative consequences of drinking. The Beast has no memory of its own, but calls up your memory of past pleasure as a way of seducing you into more drinking. It was not long before this man drank again—and ended up in the emergency room once again. He forgot.

In traditional recovery programs group members tell and retell stories of drunkenness and relapse, with emphasis on the ugly and painful. They tell of "hitting bottom" and recall its pain and despair. These "drunkalogue" rituals are a tribute to the difficulty that all addicted people have remembering pain. They are a feeble attempt to keep the pain alive, as a deterrent against a decision to drink. But this is a costly and inconvenient way to abstain, and judging from the poor abstinence rates in those programs, ineffective as well. In fact, many participants comment that the only time they *really* want to drink is after hearing stories of drunkenness at meetings. Part of the problem is that the storytellers themselves have forgotten the pain. They present their war stories in an entertaining or even humorous way, an approach that is as counterproductive as it is appealing to the Beast.

In Rational Recovery it is unnecessary to exhume past horrors to deter future drinking or using. You can do what is natural and gradually forget them. When we say, "Close the book on that sorry chapter of your life," we mean it. In AVRT, pain is only a means to an end—permanent abstinence. Pain is the classroom for AVRT, but eventually school is out.

The Rationale for Abstinence

Compared to the disease model, the structural model of addiction is by far the more convincing argument for permanent abstinence. In the disease model, the justification for abstinence is based largely on your *faith* that alcoholism is a disease. But in reality there is no concrete evidence for this "disease," and your Beast probably understands this clearly. Therefore, when tempted to drink, you may quite reasonably surrender faith and doubt that there is such a disease as alcoholism. Even if there *is* a disease of alcoholism, you may correctly reason, you probably don't have it because you feel so unlike others who call themselves "alcoholic." So, as an experiment, you may once again test the waters and have a serious relapse.

Disease/treatment trusts that you will not become securely abstinent until you have reached other goals, and it sets you about the task of solving them. If you solve important problems such as self-worth, self-awareness, relationships, and childhood conflicts, deprivations, and traumas, you are still left with your original desire to intoxicate yourself. Some treatment promises to help you reach the nirvana of addicted people, which is moderate or controlled drinking or using, and your Beast may be terribly interested in exploring those avenues. Once you understand the structural model, however, you may become wisely suspicious of your own capacity to drink moderately, as well as your yearning to do so. You may even wonder why some professional people still want to help problem drinkers to drink.

Now let us look at the action of alcohol upon these two separate regions of your brain. When alcohol enters the bloodstream, it affects the midbrain and the neocortex at the same time, but in exactly opposite ways. The effect on the midbrain is rapid arousal, and the effect on the neocortex is impairment. So with every drink, you are not only becoming less inhibited in many ways, but also experiencing a rapidly increasing desire to drink more alcohol (see Figure 3).

Many have described a "slippery slope" in their drinking patterns, as though after a certain number of drinks there seems to be a point of no return. I call this the Crossover Effect. The structural model accounts for the apparent loss of control as a natural, predictable function of the human body. Moreover, when the action of alcohol upon the brain structures is understood, the case for abstinence is clear.

With every drink, your midbrain generates an *increased* desire to drink another, and you *enjoy* the pleasurable sensations

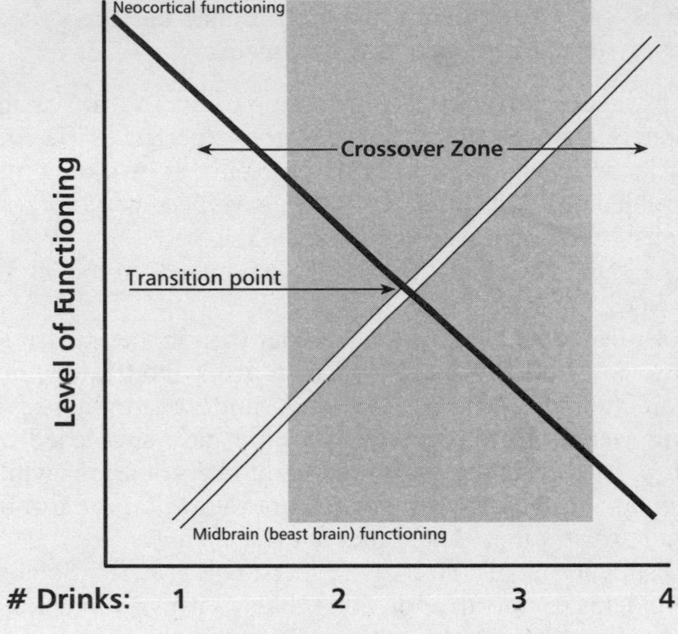

Figure 3. The Crossover Effect

more and more. This desire is your Beast. This often continues until you have reached very high blood levels. At the same time that your desire is increasing, the action of alcohol on the neocortex is *reducing* your self-control. Even though you want to drink moderately, you are soon in no shape to drink moderately. Your Beast *explodes* with desire, and you feel its cry, "yes, another!" from head to toe. Your Beast understands that moderate drinking means no more deep pleasure, but it *likes* the idea because it knows it will very likely get the upper hand with just a few drinks. The next day you wonder, "Why?"

As you develop tolerance for alcohol over time, it takes increased blood alcohol levels for you to "feel it." A "reasonable" level of blood alcohol means "not feeling it." Moderation finally becomes such a struggle that abstinence becomes much easier. As one person commented, "It is hard to control a lion on a leash. That's why we keep them in cages."

Even beyond the structural model, you may find ample reasons to elect abstinence, such as the following:

1. Abstinence is risk-free. To continue trying to drink moderately exposes you to more of the experiences (feeling sick, anxious, or depressed, problems at work, family problems, arrest, fines, etc.) that have become your personal reasons for wanting to drink less.
2. The outcome of abstinence is guaranteed. You will be sober.
3. Abstinence is easier and far simpler than moderate drinking. You have always intended to drink moderately, but you often change your mind while under the influence. If this were realistic, you likely would have succeeded by now. Measuring the amounts and numbers of drinks while you are struggling with your desire to drink more can be quite frustrating, almost like *coitus interruptus.*
4. Abstinence leads *directly* to personal growth. Solving problems to stop an addiction is like wearing a hat to keep your feet warm. It doesn't make sense, and your feet stay cold.
5. Abstinence ultimately feels better. "Chronic abstinence" leads to an actual *preference* to be mentally clear at all times.
6. Abstinence addresses the real problem: the *pleasure,* produced by the substance in question, from which you will ultimately abstain.

A Note About Your Nutrition

In recent years, a number of treatment specialists have introduced new programs based on nutritional therapy. The concept is that alcoholics and other substance abusers are driven to drink by nutritional deficiencies that cause cravings, so they are, in effect, attempting to medicate themselves with alcohol or other drugs. The treatment, quite often under medical supervision, consists of taking chelated and colloidal minerals, massive doses of vitamins, and strict dietary regimens. Most often, nutritional therapy is combined with traditional 12-step or other support group involvement, or psychological counseling to resolve personal problems. The literature surrounding nutritional therapy of addictions is esoteric, using the arcane language of chemistry and medicine. The promise is that by compensating for nutritional deficits, one will become robustly healthy and have less desire or inclination to drink or use drugs. In operation for just a short time, these nutritional centers are claiming high success rates.

Sounds good. But some problems come to the surface when viewed through the magnifying lens of AVRT. Nutritional therapy for addictions is only a slight variation of the disease model, which says that people intoxicate themselves for reasons other than pleasure. Nutritional therapy attempts to alter bodily functions in order to produce comfort and health, with the expectation that healthy people who feel well will not be interested in drinking or using drugs.

There are many folk remedies well known in the drinking culture for solving nutritional and physiological problems associated with chemical dependence. Good nutrition has been known for ages as a remedy for the acute effects of intoxication. At your local carry-out, you may notice near the cash register little envelopes for sale containing an assortment of nutritional supplements and vitamins labeled "Morning After Pills," or "Drinker's Insurance." Many maintenance drinkers, knowing they are running the risk of medical complications by over-indulging, are quite fastidious about taking vitamins. For many years, the treatment of acute alcohol withdrawal has been intramuscular injections of B vitamins followed by multivitamin therapy. Let's face it. Nutritional therapy for addictions has been around for a long time. It has been regarded as an adjunct, at best, to traditional treatment, and neither has produced remarkable abstinent outcomes.

Your Beast can be a doctor and health nut, too. It wants you to stay in good shape so you can return to the pleasure of drinking again, and again, and again. When you are feeling empty, fatigued, or malnourished, it will diagnose you and tell you to drink alcohol, with a food chaser. When you feel energized and healthy, it will tell you to celebrate life, break out the booze, and let the good times roll. If you abstain from alcohol, especially for health reasons, it will notice that you are gradually getting stronger, and healthier—and dryer. To Doctor Beast, your health is a commodity to be saved up and then cashed in. If you have been sober for quite a while, it will notice your little aches and pains and advise you that there is something wrong, a fundamental metabolic or nutritional problem that just won't let you go, and it will prescribe the most effective nutrition it can conceive, megadoses of gin.

As you might expect, AVRT dismisses the idea that nutrition is an important element in your recovery from addiction. If you recall, the sole cause of addiction is the Addictive Voice, which is the expression of an appetite for the pleasure produced by drinking alcohol or using drugs. A Big Plan is absolute and final, a commitment to total abstinence under all circumstances. This means that you have decided that you will not drink or use even when you feel fatigued, low, depressed, empty, weak, or are suffering from any other conditions that may be caused by malnutrition.

Here is the truth of the matter. When you decide to quit drinking or using for good, the recovery game is over. The quality of your abstinent life, however, will be affected by many, many factors, including nutrition, exercise, recreation, personal or spiritual growth, psychological improvements, and you name it. But AVRT is a voracious mind-set that devours anything that poses as a *condition* of lifetime abstinence, including nutritional therapy.

Tried Everything but Quitting?

Wondering why you drink in spite of it all can be agonizing. But here's another way of looking at it. **Maybe you've never made up your mind to quit!**

You may recall that in the past quitting was for an indefinite time. Open-ended. Staying sober was a one-day-at-a-time *experiment.* You might venture out into the real world, running just on your own natural chemicals, to see if you liked it. You could look, but you didn't have to buy. So when reality was not entirely to your liking, your Beast simply pointed out that, after all that time, you *still* felt lousy, that sobriety wasn't all it's cracked up to be, and that maybe it would be a reasonable thing to have a drink or two to take the edge off your bad feelings or just to give a little zing when you feel restless and down. "What's the problem with one little drink?" your Beast may have innocently asked.

This Beast strategy works well when you have been in addiction treatment. You may talk about your issues until you are blue in the face, you may make amends with all but the doctor who delivered you, you may do moral inventories until the Vatican finally learns of your perfection and declares you a saint, you may see an analyst until your head is on perfectly straight, and you may dispute your irrational ideas until the cows come home, but you will still absolutely *know,* from time to time, that it would be damn nice to have a drink—if only to celebrate your fine life. That awareness is your Beast, and there is no way that I know of to remove it from your consciousness.

Addiction is a state of being, a fact of life, until you comprehend the nature your Beast, recognize its expressions in daily life, and learn to relate to it as *less* than a nuisance.

In 12-step meetings your identity is the name of a disease—the disease of relapse. If you have attended those meetings and said, "I am an alcoholic," your Beast was listening carefully. It noticed the revolving door through which the majority of members passed as they dropped out, drank to destruction, and then returned (most of them don't), shamed and grateful, to Mother Group. Your Beast is *comfortable* with your surrender of control to a poorly understood Higher Power, your dependence upon others for sobriety, and your "alcoholic" self-concept. It *delights* in your short-range plan to remain sober one day at a time and in sharing graphic, entertaining stories of past drinking episodes. But this is not very inspiring to people who sincerely want to stop drinking and live free.

The *last thing* your Beast wants you to do is to take control of your feelings and behavior, to become emotionally independent, to lay down the law with yourself about drinking, to stop thinking about recovery, to allow yourself naturally to forget about the reasons why you quit, and then to live a normal, happy life as a person who never drinks.

AVRT helps you to make a plan that will lead you to these things and then shows you how to execute it. As you execute your Big Plan, you will vow to kill your Beast, even though it never quite dies! Beasts *despise* AVRT.

11

The Big Plan

You gotta take this AVRT with a grain of salt.

—Your Beast

The "Big Plan" of Rational Recovery is spelled with capital letters to signify its importance to people who enter into one. A Big Plan is an *irreversible* decision to abstain from alcohol. Because you will live with your Big Plan for the rest of your life, it is not to be taken lightly, and it requires considerable contemplation.

If you are actively considering a Big Plan for yourself after reading only this far, stop. Think. Be careful of what you are getting into. Read on before any further commitment. A Big Plan may not be for you at all. Moderation is fine for those who can do it, and "one day at a time" actually works for some people, in AA or not. There may be a chance, however small, that you can somehow acquire the ability to drink moderately or use drugs recreationally. On the other hand, you may also suffer serious consequences from further efforts to moderate, including ostracism, unemployment, failing health, mental and emotional problems, arrest, violence, and death. You are free to choose further drinking or drugging, provided you are willing to risk and quite possibly pay the consequences.

One man, now using AVRT, who had paid handsomely for controlled drinking treatment sessions, wrote a letter to RR.

Even though I wanted to learn to drink moderately, I knew there was something wrong with that idea. It was a feeling, and I couldn't put it into words, but seeing a counselor who would help me drink responsibly was all the encouragement I needed. I learned to estimate my blood alcohol content by my subjective feelings and to stay in control by drinking other fluids, eating, and spacing smaller drinks over the evening. I did drink moderately for a few months, and as a result I had fewer personal problems, but I became more and more aware that I honestly didn't want to drink just a few drinks. I wanted to get drunk. I felt annoyed every time I would limit myself to two drinks, and quite often I would avoid drinking altogether in order to avoid the frustration of cutting off just when I was starting to "feel it." More and more, I wanted to get drunk, just once, maybe out of town, which was a new idea for me. When I told my counselor I was preoccupied with the idea of getting drunk, he said my annoyance was caused by low frustration tolerance, that wanting to get drunk was only a feeling, and I should learn that I do not need to have feelings I merely desire. He also said I was probably dissatisfied with myself and with life and my desire to get drunk was to escape from my problems. I continued working on these problems until I heard about AVRT, and after reading that material the whole idea of moderate drinking seemed ridiculous. I knew that my original suspicions were correct, that my yearning to drink moderately was really a sign that I was addicted. I quit treatment, made a Big Plan, and my desire to drink moderately is completely gone. When I have the desire to get drunk, I know exactly what it is, and the feeling immediately goes away.

Outline of a Big Plan

A purpose. Why am I making this commitment? Pain is the classroom of addiction recovery. Your reasons for establishing a Big Plan will be the negative consequences of your addiction.

What do I expect in return? You are not cutting a deal for a better life. There are no guarantees other than that you will be abstinent.

An understanding of the implications of a Big Plan. Abstinence may change your social identity, your feelings about yourself, your vision of your future, and your relationships with others. There will be many times when abstinence seems awkward, inconvenient, or inadvisable. But a Big Plan is irreversible.

PHASE

The Big Plan Process

1. When the implications of a Big Plan are known, you will declare your intention to establish a Big Plan by saying, "Yes, I understand what this is, and I want to do it. Once I have done it, I will never change my mind about it." Even if you later wish to reverse your Big Plan, you will be unable to do so because of the process involved in forming it.
2. Set a time limit to achieve a Big Plan, such as "tomorrow by 10:00 P.M.," or "when I have completed reading *Rational Recovery.*"
3. Before your time expires, pick an immediate time when you will make your Big Plan and call it "now."
4. Make the Big Plan based on your understanding of this chapter.
5. When you have completed your Big Plan, consummate it by adding, ". . . and I will never change my mind."

Keep in mind that, while addicted, you cannot justify a Big Plan by reason alone. This is part of why addicted people do not do the obvious and quit for good. A Big Plan, however, may be easily arrived at through intuition. Intuition is a display of intelligence in which a correct answer or solution to a problem materializes without evidence, proof, or structured reasoning. Intuition may begin with reason, but leaps ahead to the answer. Both intuition and reason may support continued drinking, so we are resorting to similar means by combining reason and intuition to establish a Big Plan for permanent abstinence. Your intuited suspicion that you will probably have to quit for good will finally be confirmed.

The Key Question

Ask yourself right now, "**What is my *present* plan for the future use of alcohol or drugs?**" Ah, yes. This *is* the question, isn't it?

What is your *real* plan for drinking alcohol? Have you had enough? Drinking is always a choice, isn't it? *Isn't it?*

Of course it is, and no matter how many times you've quit before, or how many programs you've tried, and no matter how long you've been struggling with your addiction, you have always *chosen* to resume drinking or using once again.

Yet when you confront yourself with the key question, "What is my plan?" you still have no clear plan to stop drinking. In effect, you *still* intend to get loaded any time you really feel like it! You may cut back, take a vacation from it for a while, or wait for the desire to disappear someday, but your Beast *stops* you from promising yourself that you will *never* drink again. In the logic of AVRT, the absence of a plan to quit for good is a plan, *now,* to drink. You are being challenged here and now to take responsibility for your addiction and your own recovery.

As you become aware that you have no plan to quit a behavior you say you want to quit, you may feel awkward. This is the classical state of addiction that I sometimes kiddingly call *status addictus.* In my travels, I have many opportunities to sit in on meetings of groups of addicted people, and I am always fascinated at how they struggle with the key question, "What is your plan for the future use of alcohol/drugs?" At an addiction treatment clinic in Colorado, I asked this of each member of a group of about a dozen people on probation. About half of them were on probation or parole because of multiple convictions for drunk driving, and the rest had been convicted of other alcohol and drug-related offenses. Most were depressed and helpless from having their lives disrupted and tied up with the requirements of treatment, probation, and parole appointments. They complained of serious difficulties resulting from their lawbreaking, such as cost, employment discrimination, social ostracism, and inconvenience. Although most were seriously troubled, none could be considered mentally ill.

When the discussion was going smoothly, I started asking the key question of each person. Here are some brief interactions:

"You certainly have suffered a lot as a result of drinking/using. What is your plan for the future use of alcohol?" I asked.

"What do you mean?"

"I mean, are you going to drink alcohol in the future?"

"Huh? Am I going to what?"

"Drink alcohol, like in beer, wine, liquor."

"Ha! That's a real question, huh? If I knew the answer to that question, I wouldn't have a problem."

"I know. That's why I asked. Well?"

"I don't know. How could I know?"

"If you don't know, who does?"

One woman present had a different response:

"What is your plan for the future use of alcohol?" I asked her.

"I wish it wasn't true, but I will probably drink when I choose to."

"That's your business, but have you ever considered quitting?"

"Been there; done that."

"You changed your mind?"

"That's what always happens."

"Supposing you also decided you would never change your mind once you decided to quit?"

"Can't do that. I'm in recovery, and we do it one day at a time."

One man showed how he felt about the question.

"What is your plan for the future use of alcohol?" I asked him.

"Why you asking me that?"

"You were complaining earlier about how you hate jail and parole and all the troubles of this program. Have you ever gotten in trouble with the law when you weren't drinking?"

"You can't just up and ask someone what they don't know."

"Would you like to quit drinking for good?"

"I'm going out for a smoke. Anyone else coming?"

Another man responded this way:

"What is your plan for the future use of alcohol?"

"I was hoping you would skip over me. I can't answer that."

"What stops you from answering?"

"I get a real bad feeling about it. I feel like I'm doomed no matter what I say. If I say what I feel, that I will drink some more, I feel stupid and hopeless. If I say I will never drink again, I feel like I'm lying, even though that is exactly what I want for myself. I also think it would be setting myself up for a big failure if I promised myself I would never drink again. I don't understand these feelings at all."

"You're doing great. There are two of you inside, struggling for control, you and your Addictive Voice. Right now it's winning, but you can learn to psych it out and take your life back from addiction as well as from the authorities."

He broke into tears and sobbed, "If that is possible, I would be the happiest man alive."

Feel Your Beast Struggle

AVRT is a game that goes in for the kill. Notice your own feelings as you think about making a Big Plan. What is your emotion when you think about the idea of *never again* drinking or using drugs? Or, to put it more bluntly, *how do you feel now* about never feeling high again?

ACTION

Listen and Feel

Think about the rest of your life and all the possible situations you will encounter that would suggest drinking or using drugs. You will know boredom and depression, happiness and sadness. With family and friends you will celebrate many holidays and birthdays and attend many weddings, funerals, picnics, and other social occasions. You will be alone and travel into strange places, and you will be offered drinks by many pleasant, fine people. You will be employed and unemployed, you will succeed and fail, and one day you may retire. Think about your favorite drink, cooled to perfection, mixed just right, and the wonderful welcome feeling you get when you take those first few sips.

Once again, now, *think* of never feeling high again—*never* tasting your favorite cocktail, brew, wine, liquor, or your favorite drug—for the rest of your life. Now *how does it feel?*

It is very likely an unpleasant feeling. It may be sadness, anxiety, depression, anger, panic, or other bad feelings.

Listen to your thoughts about this deprivation. Write them down. Really. Get a paper, right now, and write down your thoughts and feelings about never drinking or using again.

The feeling *is* your Beast. You are *feeling* your addiction to alcohol or drugs, feeling your personal nemesis, your personal enemy itself, the infamous Beast of Rational Recovery. The sorry pictures you *see* of yourself, deprived of comfort and joy, are being shown to you by your Beast. The thoughts you hear are the *sounds* of your Beast. "That would be terrible," it may say. "You can't do it. Never say 'never,' " you may hear. "Put this book down. This is stupid," it may urge.

But as you read this material there is another voice—the voice of you. That voice may be saying something like this: "Yes, this is the truth of the matter, the problem I've had all along. I dearly love to drink. And I *have* been quite passive toward my addiction. I yield to it and then make up all kinds of excuses about how all of my ancestors were drunks and so was my stepmother and I'm an alcoholic and my liver metabolizes alcohol differently than normal people's, and I think alcohol is medicine for depression, and I had such a rotten childhood, and my father must have molested me, and alcohol is a substitute for love and I ain't gettin' enough love, so I drink. And much worse, I don't even have a *plan* to quit, mainly because I *love* to drink."

If you are thinking along these lines, then your neocortex, which is really *you,* is at work, and you are *recognizing* your Addictive Voice, with its endless rationalizations, excuses, and arguments for drinking or drugging. You are using AVRT, an intellectual thought process. If you are *uncomfortable* with the idea of an experimental Big Plan, and you can *hear* your disturbing thoughts about permanent abstinence, then you are *recognizing* your Addictive Voice. You are getting the hang of AVRT and making some serious headway toward permanent abstinence.

When you think of how deeply pleasurable drinking is, it is sad to think, "Never again." And it *isn't* fair, when life offers so few simple, predictable pleasures, that so much bad comes to you from drinking and that most people can drink when they choose without harm. And what *will* it be like, at those special times when it will be so enticing to go ahead and have just one little drink? You may think, "It will be sooooo difficult, even embarrassing, to turn down that drink, and just think of the craving, desiring, almost *tasting* the substance and feeling its effects. How frustrating it will be!" And how *will* you get through bad times when your favorite stuff has always been there to take the edge off? How dreadful, to be without that special comfort in a time of need.

These are some of the ideas that you can expect from your Beast. In later pages, you will learn the rules of the recovery game. Then you can aggressively challenge the Beast, knowing ahead of time that you will win!

Defusing the Time Factor

Even though you may sincerely want never to drink again, the *possibility* of future drinking or using is exciting to the Beast. Saying "no" is no big deal. Any addicted person can do it, and all do abstain from time to time. But saying "never" is an entirely different experience. And here is the reason: The midbrain is without a sense of time. It lives as a speck in eternity, tending to the now; on its own, it does not comprehend the possibility of a future. But it has access to your understanding of time and it will use it against you.

Attempting your first dive off a high-dive board will produce anxiety because your beast brain (it) knows that the neocortex (you) is preparing to *do* something that apparently threatens its survival. It doesn't trust the neocortex, no matter now intelligent and reasonable it is to jump headfirst into ten feet of water for the fun of it. It is scared *of death,* and you may stand on the end of the board, one day at a time, for the rest of your life, waiting for the anxiety to subside and for the fear to go away. But if you decide to *do* the fearsome thing and then do it, it is done. The fear will rapidly diminish over the next few jumps and soon be forgotten. Diving then becomes effortless and the anxiety a curious memory.

The Key Word: Never

The difficulty in establishing a Big Plan centers around the finality of *never*. On this issue, the Beast will use your reasoning ability to defend itself. "Never say 'never,' " it will chide. "How can I know I will never drink again? It feels like a lie when I say 'never.' I've said 'never' a thousand times, and I always went back, so what's the difference now?" And so on. But the whole issue of the Big Plan centers around the *illusion* of time, and the Beast is a master of illusions. Consider:

What is time in the first place? Is it like a railroad track, and we are trolleys free-wheeling toward a distant horizon? Are we able to look back and see the tracks behind and all the things along the way? Not exactly. Here we get into an interesting discussion, one worth learning in relation to the Big Plan of Rational Recovery.

Although time is not spatial, we perceive it as such. The idea called "week" generates a spatial design with seven segments, a "month" has thirty or so days or four weeks, a year twelve months, a decade ten blocks of time, and so on. Although time does not exist in that form, your Beast loves that scheme. It bets its *life* that you will drink or use during at least one of those time slots, in an hour, in a day, in a year, or decades from now. Once the inevitability of future self-intoxication is assured, the Beast then works with that idea, corralling all time into the present moment, seeking the earliest possible time for intoxication. "If I'm going to drink later, why not now?" the Addictive Voice will argue.

One thirty-year-old woman who was attempting a Big Plan

said she *liked* the idea of not drinking, but complained that she couldn't live with "the never part." She found comfort in the idea of drinking on her eightieth birthday to celebrate fifty happy years of abstinence. "I can live with this plan," she blithely explained. But when asked to **transpose the grammar, as we do in AVRT, she exclaimed, "*It* can live with that plan! *It* can't tolerate 'never,' but *I* can, and *I will!*"**

A man who was working on a Big Plan laughed out loud when he discovered drinking opportunities in a subsequent life. A believer in reincarnation, he found relief from the impact of "never" by planning a second drinking career following his death, when he would have a new, alcohol-tolerant body and no nasty memories of what drinking in this life has caused. But when he extended his Big Plan to cover subsequent lives, he reported that he once again sensed his Beast struggling with feelings of deprivation.

The Only Time Is Now

Are you ready for this? **In AVRT, time does not exist!** "Now" is an infinitely small interval that contains all that exists. Now is all there is. The future is only a possibility, but even then, it will be now. Nothing exists tomorrow, although everything may exist at that moment. When you started this sentence, it was now. But it is still the present moment, now, and it will always be now. Do you see? With the Big Plan, we meet the Beast on its own turf—eternity. We reduce our understanding of time to reality *as the Beast understands it*. Because it is always now, we may firmly make a plan for the rest of our lives based on the clear understanding, "**I will never *now* drink.**"

There is no parallel between the *never-now* approach of Rational Recovery and the 12-step one-day-at-a-time-forever idea. If it seems so, here is the concept once again: "Never" is the *opposite* of one-day-at-a-time-forever. The latter, if applied to the high-dive example, would have the diver decide, "I'll dive, but only one inch at a time. If I jump and don't like it, I can always change my mind." The more rational diver would conclude, "My Beast brain fears danger that I do not. I dislike standing here afraid, and I sincerely want the pleasure of diving into the water, so here goes!" In the 12-step approach, one is always diving but never quite reaching the pool. In Rational Recovery, we hit the water with a splash and experience the joy of being in control.

By collapsing the Big Plan for endless abstinence into the never-ending now, the task is made quite feasible, although there is probably no way to stave off the initial but temporary anxiety and grief over this life-changing decision. Would you rather suffer a few minutes of acute anxiety or a lifetime of recovering?

Ironically, the Big Plan of Rational Recovery is optional. AVRTechs (trained instructors at our RR Centers) and RR Coordinators are cautioned to avoid *advising* participants to abstain or to suggest that not having a Big Plan is a prediction of troubles. If a plan for permanent abstinence does not come from one's own intelligence, as a *personal* decision, then it will not come at all. Drinking or using is a personal matter, not one to turn over to others, no matter how well meaning, spiritual, rational, authoritative, official, credentialed, or competent they may be.

The Echo Effect

Are you kidding yourself with a Big Plan? When you think seriously about lifetime abstinence and finally feel comfortable with "I will never drink again," you may feel a grand sense of relief. The Beast of Booze (or the Beast of Buzz) is only a beast, and all beasts respond to authority. But you may have a funny feeling that all is not quite the way it seems and that you may once again return to the trough for another stint of drinking or drugging. "How can I ever *really* know?" you may fret. "I just feel unsure, like the Beast is waiting quietly, smirking, letting me enjoy the false comfort of thinking I really have a Big Plan."

ACTION

Listen for the Echo

Try this. As you state your Big Plan, listen for an echo. Think to yourself, "I will never drink/use again," and wait silently. *Listen,* and you may hear a subtle "echo" saying something like "Yeah, sure" or "We'll see," or perhaps you will only notice an odd feeling. This is the echo effect, a highly recognizable Beast presence that serves to undermine any sense of confidence.

One woman who relapsed soon after leaving a Rational Recovery residential program reported later that she did notice an odd feeling, an "echo effect," while in the program, but did not mention it to anyone (the Beast operates in secrecy). Returning home, she found that the vague, background feeling of insecurity became acute anxiety, followed by a feeling of resignation and then drinking. Another person resumed drinking before returning home. He experienced no anxiety, but simply accepted a drink from the flight attendant on the trip home. Both of them later reported hearing persistent Beast activity during the program that said, "Yeah, sure; you know it can't be any other way. You will always go back to drinking. It's useless to do anything else. You are doomed to drink forever." Notice the Beast's use of the second person "you." Whatever echo effect or negative response you have in response to your Big Plan is your Beast struggling against you, struggling for its life. When you *recognize* it as your old enemy, it will fall silent.

When you state your Big Plan to yourself, it may feel like a lie. You may even hear your Beast echoing, "That's a lie." To expose the Beast's absurdity, ask yourself, "Is it possible for me to lie to myself?" Is it possible? Try telling yourself a lie right now. Any intentional falsehood will do, such as, "I will now float to the ceiling." Did you lie to yourself? You may have been joking with yourself, but I doubt you laughed. Now try something that is possible but unlikely, such as, "I will clear the table immediately after every meal for one year." Say it to yourself, and listen for your own response. This time you may have felt a degree of conflict, because leaving dirty dishes may sometimes be a real problem for you. But very likely you dismiss the idea, saying, "I'm not going to struggle with that behavior," or, "Well, I may do better, but I doubt I will do that perfectly well." However, the idea of shaping up was not really your idea, but mine. By saying you will clear the dishes all year long, you are not lying, or even kidding yourself. You know what your feelings are about it.

Now, think of Your Big Plan to abstain. This is different. You care about this much more, and it is your idea. When you state that you will never drink again, is it possible that you are lying? To whom? To your Beast? Obviously, your Beast gets the message and does not like it one bit; it has a plan for you that is quite different. "You can't say that; you're lying," it says, even though it is impossible for human beings to lie to themselves.

Looks Can Kill

In AVRT, they can. **Recognition is essentially looking, a steady stare or only a glance at desire itself, an exposure that neutralizes the Beast.** There is one aspect of AVRT that raises concerns of morality. It is a sensitive issue that is easily misunderstood, but nevertheless an integral part of defeating your addiction to alcohol. The point: AVRT puts you in the position of trying to "kill" a living, feeling thing—your Beast, a part of yourself.

At first this may sound a little far-fetched, because the Beast is a construct, a metaphor, a figment of your imagination. If the Beast were only an imaginary entity, the question of getting rid of it by "killing" it would be as simple as the accepting deaths that occur in fairy tales.

But there is more to the Beast of Booze than your imagination. It is a very real part of you and has been for many years. Although without intelligence, it "thinks" by injecting the AV into your thought processes. It has feelings you know intimately. It wants to live, as any creature does, and it has a zest for life, a passion for the pleasure you feel from drinking.

The logic of AVRT is deadly to the Beast. Already, you probably sense that you are capable of establishing a Big Plan that will end your addiction. As the end comes near, your Beast will suffer and it will struggle. You will feel it suffering. You will hear its pleas for mercy.

Your Beast has been a friend to you for a long time. It has comforted you when you were feeling low, it has kept you company when you were alone, and it has been your companion during some of your finest moments. It will promise you anything if you will just back off and give it a little room to breathe.

But you now recognize that your Beast is a deadly enemy. It plays by no rules. Will you play by rules? Who will define those rules? You or it?

Killing in self-defense is justifiable on ethical, moral, and even legal grounds. And you surely know by now that if you don't kill it, it won't hesitate to kill you. As you prepare to end its life, you may feel as if *you* are suffocating. You will want to have mercy on yourself, but if you do, you will give it back its life. If you struggled to an advantage over a tiger that had attacked you, would you release your death grip on its throat as it weakened and cried for release?

Your Big Plan need consist of only five words: "I will never drink again." An even more condensed Big Plan is: "I never drink." Saying them with authority and conviction is a death sentence for your Beast. After all you've been through, I hope you will have a perfect willingness to kill it and to recognize that its groans, pleas, and fear are signals of your victory over addiction.

ACTION

The Crucial Exercise

Now, once again, are you ready? If you feel ready, go ahead. You can make a Big Plan now or later, but it's all the same to you. **To your Beast, now is never acceptable.** See how your Big Plan feels: **"I will never drink again."**

"I" is the conscious, human part of you that resides in the large, outer part of your brain.

"Will" is the use of intelligence in making decisions.

"Never" means *never,* ever, in the present moment, under any circumstances.

"Drink or drug" means to consume alcohol or other drugs, as the primitive Addictive Voice demands.

"Again" means that the past is a good predictor of the future, and you now have enough experience to make this very important decision to never drink again.

Got it? *How does it feel?*

The Abstinence Commitment Effect (ACE)

A Big Plan is victory and defeat rolled into one—victory for you, defeat for the Beast. Therefore, making a Big Plan creates strong opposing feelings. A fancy way of describing the Abstinence Commitment Effect (ACE) is *polar ambivalence*, in which you feel the anxiety or depression over the loss of the substance pleasure, along with a grand sense of relief that the addiction is over.

Your Big Plan is a *meaningful* decision, one that changes your life. When you have made a commitment to lifetime abstinence, your future will look different, and you may have feelings you have not had before. Have them, whatever they are, and relax. They are very human and natural. A big event has occurred within you, and it should not surprise you if you get goose bumps or feel tearful, joyous, euphoric, or have a profound sense of relief. Your depression may no longer have a purpose, and you may sense that strongly. There is nothing spiritual, religious, or mysterious about what you have done. You have simply changed a belief about yourself and about your future. People do this kind of thing all the time.

Here are some comments I have heard from people who have just made a Big Plan and are experiencing the Abstinence Commitment Effect:

"It's like graduation day, after a long difficult struggle. Knowing it's over is such a relief!"

"For the first time, I can see a future free of alcohol. I feel like I have a life again."

"My recovery is not just beginning; it's over. That's the best part. Now I can live for myself."

"I know my troubles are not over, but my *addiction* is over! Now my life will be much simpler."

"I can see I will never have a new problem caused by alcohol. What a feeling!"

"Now I see that if I don't drink, I cannot possibly be an alcoholic. The gray cloud of alcoholism is gone. What a good feeling!"

"These aren't bad tears; they're tears of happiness."

"This sets me free from the whole recovery thing and makes me a normal person who simply doesn't drink. What a terrific idea! I can feel it in my bones!"

"All of a sudden getting help with this problem seems like a silly idea. I don't drink, and that's that. No one can help me, which is fine with me, because now I know what I'm doing. I feel released from a long struggle, like finally it's really over."

"It's a wonderful feeling to be in control after feeling powerless for so long."

"This changes everything. Now I can see what my addiction was all about, and it's so simple. If I didn't feel so good, I might feel angry at having been misled for so long."

"My skin is crawling like I just discovered the meaning of the word *freedom*. It's a strange feeling, but I understand it."

"I feel like myself again. This is what I thought many years ago, but I didn't have the courage to stand up to all the experts who said I couldn't do it on my own. Now I see I'm the only one who *can* do it."

"It's shocking to see the other side, where there is hope and where I can just be myself and have a happy life."

"For a moment I was thinking, 'What's the word for when you think something good will happen?' Then I remembered the word is *hope,* and I started to cry. It's been so long since I had hope because of the disease indoctrinations. Now I have hope, and I can feel it!"

"I will have fewer problems because I don't drink. What a concept!"

Hope is not a pink cloud that will suddenly vanish when you least expect it. You already know your Beast is persistent, and you will almost certainly have times when you have thoughts of drinking or using drugs and feel aroused about the possibility of getting high. But you will be able to recognize your Addictive Voice and its corresponding feelings as a sniveling, defeated enemy. Congratulations on your Big Plan. Hope feels good, and you may confidently enjoy it.

12

The Beast That Keeps Coming Back

In the final analysis, I do plan to drink again.

—Your Beast

Your Beast has big plans for you. From its viewpoint, you will definitely drink again. While you are rapidly blowing its cover by reading about AVRT, it is busy making *sure* that you will drink again.

For example, the word *abstinence* has appeared many times so far, but you still may not be comfortable with it. Even though you are hopeful and your mind is still open, something about that word is troubling, and you feel uneasy about it.

Remember that the Beast (the animal appetite) exists only to consume alcohol or drugs, and its Addictive Voice (the thinking and feelings) exist to guarantee it a supply. The Beast has a *ruthless* intent to survive by finding the intoxicant, possessing it, and consuming it. It will attempt to preserve the future supply by hiding it, stashing it, setting aside money for it, and structuring your life plans so that drinking opportunities are constantly available. Most of all, your Beast will use any logic to convince you that you will drink at some time in the future, no matter what you think right now.

Like a child's connect-the-dot puzzle, the Addictive Voice functions only to connect words, ideas, images, and feelings together to form a pattern—any pattern at all—that results in the action of drinking or using. Some connect-the-dot puzzles are extremely simple, consisting of two dots, and the result is a straight line. But some dot puzzles are extremely complex, with hundreds of numbered dots, and the resulting pattern is a good-looking picture. Likewise, your Addictive Voice may have only two elements, "Drink now!" and you make a straight line for the liquor store, or it may be amazingly elaborate, connecting elements (dots) from philosophy, politics, psychology, genetics, and science to justify the same behavior.

It wants you to feel powerless. It wants you to believe that you cannot change, that you are "marked" to drink forever, regardless of any plans you have to abstain. It wants you to think AVRT is a lot of crap that can't really work and that there are times when you have *no defense* against a desire to drink. You do have those thoughts and feelings, don't you? That is what your Beast sounds and feels like. You have met the enemy, and it is within you.

But something may click with you here. Do you realize that your Beast is *struggling* with you? Do you understand that *it* feels anxious when *you* think of abstaining? Maybe it's more vulnerable than you think. If so, wouldn't that turn the tables? Isn't it interesting that it is *afraid* of what you may do? All that anxiety about abstinence may be telling you something very important. *Maybe it knows something you don't.*

You might say that your midbrain (it) *resents* your neocortex (you). Beasts have feelings, especially concerning matters of survival. Just as any beast does, your midbrain intends for you to survive, but it mistakenly believes that you *absolutely must* have alcohol or certain drugs in order to stay alive. Therefore, when you *seriously consider* never drinking or using again, you will also *feel* your Beast, probably as a jolt of anxiety or apprehension, followed by a low, sinking feeling. That anxiety is a fear of serious deprivation, as though not intoxicating yourself would deprive you of a *necessity for life,* such as oxygen or food. And the Beast within obviously knows that you—the neocortex— are *capable* of choosing lifetime abstinence and sticking with it. Otherwise, it would not feel threatened as it does.

With its ability to use your imagination, your Beast will predict that you cannot live happily or meaningfully without alcohol or drugs, and it will probably use your language centers to tell you that life without alcohol or drugs is inconceivable and possibly not worth living. This *thinking* may result in feelings of depression. And all you did was *think* about never drinking or using again. For that, it threatens your life, promising your endless despair. Some Beast, eh?

Suppose you were a quadriplegic, confined to a wheelchair, totally paralyzed, and your caretaker suddenly decided to stop feeding and assisting you. How would you feel? Pretty scary, unless you wanted to die anyhow. But listen to this. Your Beast, the inner enemy that has nearly ruined your life, is *totally dependent* on you to feed it. It cannot act without you. Your hands and feet are "wired" directly to you. Put your hand in front of your face. Now, challenge your Beast to move your index finger. See? You are in control! And your Beast knows it. No wonder it squirms when you threaten to cut it off from its survival stuff. All it has to work with are your thoughts and feelings.

When you threaten to deprive it of alcohol, it will first *attack* by telling you how awful it is to be deprived of alcohol. It will then remind you of how wonderful alcohol is and how nothing can replace it. It will drag up picture-memories of fine times of feeling high. Then it will plead with you, telling you that everything will be all right if only you are careful when you drink. Then, if you insist on not drinking, it will patiently *wait* until a better opportunity presents itself. Beasts survive by lying low, by slinking and hiding.

It is extremely important for you to know that you have a great advantage over your Beast. It is a worthy opponent, a strong fighter, and it will not easily give up. But your task is relatively easy compared to that of the Beast. You have something it doesn't have. You have the *intelligence* to recognize the Beast in all of its forms—the thoughts, images, moods, and emotions it uses to get you to drink. That's all. Just *recognize* those things, and the Beast will fall silent. What choice does it have? All that it is, including its voice and its feelings, it borrows from you.

ACTION

Tracking Beast Activity

It can be helpful to keep a journal or diary describing Beast activity for a while. Give it a try. Just sit down at the same time each day for a few weeks and jot down some notes. There are four ways to describe Beast activity: (1) frequency—continuous, often, occasional, seldom, about once an hour, only at five o'clock, every other day, etc.; (2) intensity—booming, whispering, vivid, vague; (3) the tone of what it says—demanding, cynical, cocky, friendly, scolding, arrogant, pitying; and (4) circumstances—only at meals, only around people of the opposite sex, out of the blue, when I'm tired, when I'm upset, when I'm bored, afraid, depressed, alone, and so on. By looking back over your notes, you can watch the changing strategies of your Beast.

Beast Strategies

You Beast has become comfortable over the years, and it is accustomed to getting its way. It knows you like a book and takes advantage of your personal flaws. If you think you are a jerk, it will agree with you and offer you a drink. If you think your spouse is a jerk, it will agree with you and offer you a drink. If you believe that it is terrible and awful that you didn't get a raise, it will agree with you and offer you a drink. If you think life sucks, it will agree with you and then offer you a drink. If you have financial problems, it will suggest an inexpensive drink. If you run into lots of money, it will suggest a drink to celebrate good fortune. If you have a hangover, it will suggest a drink to take the edge off. If you are sober, it will suggest that you celebrate your sobriety with a drink. And so on.

Common Beast Lies

1. Drinking is good for me. It is good for the heart, lowers cholesterol, helps blood pressure, adds important nutrients to the diet. Comfort is health.

2. Drinking is one of the few pleasures in life.
3. Life is hollow and meaningless without alcohol or drugs.
4. A few drinks makes a good time better. What's in a sunset without a drink in hand?
5. I am a nicer person when I drink or use drugs.
6. I am a better lover when I drink. I am sexier, more potent or attractive under the influence of alcohol or drugs.
7. I am more creative under the influence of alcohol or drugs.
8. I am very funny to others when I am loaded. My sense of humor is enhanced under the influence of alcohol or drugs.
9. Drinking gives me relief from feelings I can't stand. If I am angry, ashamed, fearful, or depressed, alcohol or drugs give me strength.
10. I am more productive in my work when I am intoxicated with alcohol or drugs.
11. I am hooked on the wonderful taste of alcohol, especially the fragrant aroma or special bouquet of certain brands. Good food doesn't taste right without alcoholic beverages.
12. Because I am an alcoholic, my body functions best with a steady amount of alcohol. I will never feel right without alcohol in me.

To see the stupidity of the Beast, simply change each of the above statements into a question by adding a question mark. For example, in number one, "Is drinking good for me?" Number two, "Is alcohol really one of the few pleasures in life?" Number three, "Is life really meaningless?" Number four, "Is drinking really fun?" (Or better yet, "Have I been drinking while attempting to have fun?") Go ahead and dispute *whatever* your Beast tells you, just to learn how irrational and silly its ideas are. But remember, just because you know the Beast is stupid doesn't mean it will go away. Your ability to recognize the Addictive Voice will not cause the desire the drink magically to disappear and will not prevent you from drinking in the future. Something besides reason is required to defeat it.

Addiction Diction

The Addictive Voice is primarily a language function of your brain. Because you cannot really control the Addictive Voice—

such as by deciding you will not *think* of alcohol or drugs—AVRT provides you a sophisticated means to manage it that I call "Addiction Diction." This is one of many recognition techniques, but it stands out as the basic technique upon which the rest are built.

"I" is the most significant word in your vocabulary because it is the *operant pronoun.* In other words, "I" is a command symbol that initiates voluntary behavior. If you get up to get some coffee, the thinking prelude to getting up is "I want some coffee. I'll go get some." The Beast's favorite pronoun is "I." As long as it has a firm grasp on that word, it will control you. You can spend many years debating whether "I" will drink or not. But you can also play word games to dumbfound your Beast. Addiction Diction is like introducing a virus into a computer program, causing it to malfunction. Once you reclaim "I" from your Beast, you are well on the road to complete recovery from your addiction.

As you listen to your Addictive Voice, notice the pronouns it uses. Sometimes you will hear "I," "it," "you," "we," and "us" (as in "let's" or "let us"). If you hear "We need a drink," you have heard your Beast. If you hear "You have gone six weeks," that is your Beast setting you up for a binge. "It's just a matter of time until you drink," obviously, is from the Beast. As you learned before, there are two of you inside your head, and often you will hear a voice that is not "I" using the second-person pronoun "you", just as when I address you here.

PHASE

Transposing Words

The Beast naturally expresses itself through the AV by deceitfully using pronouns. But your Big Plan states definitively: "I will never drink again." If you decide to stay in the first-person "I," you will find abstinence to be virtually effortless. Any time that the pronoun "I" appears in your consciousness in connection with drinking, just add a *t,* transforming "I" to *it.* "It," of course, refers to the Beast. In AVRT, we call this Transposing. For example, "I want a drink" becomes "It wants a drink." If you hear "I will never be able to stay sober," just add the *t* and see the obvious truth. To master your Addictive Voice, recognize first that you are thinking of drinking alcohol, and then change all pronouns to "it." If you think, "I would really like to chase a whiskey down with beer while reading a newspaper," transpose that sentence to "it—my Beast—would really like to chase a whiskey with beer while I read the paper." By doing this grammatical sleight-of-hand, you will not only outfox your Beast, but you will very likely feel immediate relief from the desire to drink. Try it. See for yourself.

When you struggle for control of "I," as in "I will not drink," you will notice something truly remarkable. The subcortical Beast will immediately address you as "you." "You can handle just a little this time." This is highly significant, for you have *forced* your enemy into a defensive position, *into the second person.* Now its masquerade is over, and it will be much easier to recognize. It must now come to you and, almost respectfully, appeal to you with reasons and justifications for drinking. It will also use the plural pronouns "us" and "we" as a way of speaking for both parties. If you will listen to your Addictive Voice, you may notice it using the word "we" in a highly inappropriate way, even when you are alone. "We need a little drink. Let's get something at the store" is a perfect example of the innocent, seductive quality that characterizes some Beast talk. Plural pronouns have the added effect of taking the edge off loneliness, as if a friend has dropped by to show you a good time when you're down and out. Addiction Diction makes AV recognition easy, because the Beast becomes so conspicuous once the game is exposed.

Beast Attacks

In the weeks and months to come, there will almost certainly be times when you have thoughts and feelings that seem to draw you to alcohol. We call these moments "Beast attacks." Your task is to build a perfect defense against whatever your wounded Beast throws at you. Relax. Human beings aren't perfect by a long shot, but we can do many tasks perfectly. Perfect games in sports are possible, and one can solve most equations and crossword puzzles perfectly. Remaining perfectly sober is no big deal.

Notice how your Beast noticed the word "most" just now!

Here are some examples of Beast attacks:

1. **Restlessness.** Now that you don't drink, what do you do? For years you have always had something to do, any time you had nothing to do. But now it's gone. If you live alone you may have serious problems with Beast attacks, because your Beast is also at home alone with you. Whether you are alone or not, your Beast can make itself felt and cause a feeling of ugly restlessness. You may call this "boredom," but actual boredom is rare in life. *Boredom* is a word given to negative feelings one may have in a variety of situations, such as being alone, not having entertainment, doing an unwanted task, listening to something you don't understand, visiting with uninteresting people, or doing something you don't do well. The actual feelings should be called anxiety, annoyance, low self-esteem, or anger, possibly caused by irrational beliefs, rather than sensory deprivation. For your purposes in AVRT, it is better to recognize the restless feeling as Beast activity. Whatever you are telling yourself that causes your "boredom," the Beast may be affirming and gleeful at the opportunity to drink. Many people find that by simply reaffirming the Big Plan, the Beast falls silent, and the unpleasant feeling lifts. Then they get on with doing something of interest.
2. **The sudden flood.** These experiences can occur under certain circumstances, such as a party, while driving or taking a walk, or out of the blue. You may suddenly become flooded with thoughts and feelings about drinking. At these times, the use of addiction grammar and transposing, as described above, are quite effective. Another excellent technique is to put your hands in front of your face and move your fingers, proving once again that you, and not your Beast, are in control. Better yet, challenge your Beast to move your index finger, against your wishes, as suggested previously.

3. **Vertigo.** This is a strong Beast attack that goes beyond flooding. Some people report an experience of "snapping," in which they sense that the decision to drink has already been made, and it is *inevitable* that they will drink. They feel physically mobilized to drink and may even start preparing to drink by deciding where the drinking will take place, looking for the car keys, counting money, and setting up a time of absence from the home or work. Along with these behaviors, there is a feeling of excitement and relief. All the while, they experience a clear awareness that something is seriously wrong, sometimes observed with a sense of eerie fascination. "Here I/we go again," they report hearing. "I can't believe I'm actually doing this, but I'm going to do it anyhow. To hell with it, just this once. I've gone too far with this, and it's too late to stop now. ***I'm in relapse.*** Being forewarned is being forearmed. Because you are now aware of the vertigo state, you will be able to recognize that you are "under the influence," that your subcortical Beast has gained a foothold. Instead of being passively fascinated or appalled, you are now prepared to think *aggressively* about your predicament.

ACTION

Labeling

First, *label* what is going on. Give it a name by calling it "vertigo." Think to yourself, "I am having vertigo! This is a Beast attack, and I am in vertigo!" Now you are recognizing and labeling what has been happening, and you are therefore not in the Beast's direct line of fire. You will also notice that the immediate urge to take action goes away, and you have regained your balance. You have evaded the Beast, for the moment, and now it is time to fortify your position. Remember that there is no time, prior to swallowing, toking, or injecting, that is "too late" to pull out of a plan to drink. Some people experiencing vertigo imagine the sound of a shrieking emergency alarm. It is a technique that psychologists call "thought stoppage" or "thought interruption." By doing this, you can clear your head of Beast activity so that you can start practicing the AVRT you have learned.

Second, use the *N* word. *Never.* "I *never* drink/use." *Look at your hands* and remember that they are under your voluntary control and not your Beast's.

Now, calmly withdraw from the situation in a way that feels natural. There is no sense feeling afraid, because you are calling the shots.

Having read this section, you know something that you cannot really forget. You now know that vertigo is a common experience of newly abstinent people and not unusual among more securely abstinent people. You know what to call states of arousal and mobilization: vertigo. You will always be able to recognize vertigo states because they are so *conspicuous*. Just saying "vertigo" to yourself is almost like saying a magic word; the vertigo is objectified, and the feelings are neutralized. When that occurs, you can fortify your position by affirming your Big Plan with "never" and calmly withdraw from the situation.

Slippery Places vs. Perfect Drinking Opportunities

There is a traditional belief that abstinent people remain at high risk in the presence of alcohol. This is a defensive outlook, quite attractive to your Beast, and it sets up high-risk situations in which you may unexpectedly or unavoidably find yourself with a perfect drinking opportunity. Your Beast will rise to the occasion and give you a thorough justification for going ahead and having a drink, "just this one."

As an example, let's use Peter, who is newly abstinent. He normally works one day a week in another city, but this week he was told by his boss that, because the annual report was due, he must work three days instead of one in the other city. Instead of commuting as usual, he reserved a motel room for two nights, starting Monday. When he checked in around noon, he found that the room was stocked with beer and liquor, in a cabinet by the TV. He felt a little uneasy, but decided he simply wouldn't drink. When he returned to his room that evening, the boss phoned and said, "The office will be closed for auditing all day Tuesday, but please stay in town because we will start Wednesday very early to make up for lost time. Have a good time tomorrow at the company's expense." Peter hung up, and his Beast lunged. It said, "You have all day tomorrow to sober up! You've got what you need in the cabinet! This will be absolutely fine. Who would know?" Peter's heart sped up, and he felt a little shaky. "Take the edge off," the Beast urged. "Have just one, and then you may want to stop. Just one. You need it." Peter felt as if he would likely drink, and he was physically *aroused.* He opened the cabinet and looked at the bottles again.

Peter had learned some AVRT and was prepared to defend himself. "Who will know? *I will know!* And I *never* drink. Nice try, Beast. Too bad." He felt a twinge of disappointment and then felt quiet inside himself. He closed the cabinet and went out for dinner, and the following day he was in an exceptionally good mood. He knew he had defeated his Beast and was firmly in control.

You can relax about such slippery places, because there aren't any situations where you will magically lose control. You are always on duty within your own thoughts, and you will always recognize that alcohol is a very significant substance in your life. You will always know that you never drink—under any circumstances.

As you grow with AVRT, you will discover that there are also no 12-step "warning signs of relapse"—only harmless Beast activity you can dispel. The very concept of "warning signs" is delightful to the Beast, for reasons that are by now, I hope, obvious. (Hint: If you aren't going to drink anymore, how can there be "warning signs" of relapse?)

Dr. Beast, Scientist at Large

A survey of scientific research shows that between 40% and 70% of those who recover from addiction do it on their own, without getting help or attending recovery group meetings. A study of RR self-help groups showed that 74% of those who attended meetings were abstinent. A follow-up of AVRT: The Course participants found that 68% were abstinent after one year.

What are you to make of these numbers? Better yet, what does your Beast make of success rates and recovery statistics? As you might guess, there are two ways of looking at it. On the one hand, you may be encouraged that most who undertake self-recovery succeed.

Most traditional treatment programs advertise themselves as being highly effective, but newcomers to those programs are usually told that their chances of success are abysmally low. "Only one in twenty of you will make it. Who will it be?" is a common remark during orientations to inpatient and residential programs. The addictions field is a huckster's paradise, with competing money interests making claims based on "scientific" studies. People hear what they want to hear and have come to believe that treatment works, that certain treatments are better than others, and that certain people do better in certain programs. We have become keenly interested in applying the general to the particular, in which we look at an individual human being as a statistical probability. A man or woman in the treatment program above is regarded as a five-percenter, a person with a 5% chance of becoming securely abstinent. In a program making a claim of 60% success, the same person would be a sixty-percenter, for sure, but still experience a 40% degree of doubt about remaining sober. This is absolutely insane, and the learned people who perpetuate such sophistry should be censured.

Rational Recovery asserts that no *thing* works with substance addiction, but *anyone* can quit now for good. The new cure for substance addiction is individual responsibility. A Big Plan is an informed, personal decision to abstain permanently, with no regard to what others have done. I once told an anxious man who worried he would "relapse" and who kept wondering if AVRT was effective, "Pete, let's suppose that no human being in history had independently quit an addiction to alcohol. Where would that leave you today?" He gave this some serious thought and replied, "I guess I would be the first one ever to do it. Gee, I see what you mean. It doesn't change a damn thing. I would just be the first, that's all." I asked, "So what's your plan?" He answered,

"I've got it. Even if I'm the first person ever to quit on my own, I will never drink again. I see it. Once I make the decision, it doesn't matter how many other people have already done it!"

The Beast has access to all of your intelligence and sophisticated knowledge of science and statistics and will very effectively use the foundation of science to perpetuate your addiction. Science is essentially a negative hypothesis, in which nothing is true without evidence or proof, and your Beast revels in the debate about success rates and recovery statistics.

ACTION

Take a Picture of Your Beast

In any situation at all, whether in a slippery place, alone, in a "vertigo" feeling, or during a "white-knuckle" episode, you can instantly disarm your Beast by taking a picture of it. This is just another way of explaining what "recognition" means, one that some have found effective.

Supposing you are alone and you start thinking of drinking. "Who will know if I drink?" you hear. "*I* will know," you respond. Then the debates ensues. "Yes, yes. The AVRT thing. But you know that you are really one person, and what's the difference, really, if you have a few drinks and then let it be?" So you engage in dialogue. "But I *never* drink, ever." And it responds, "So? Forever starts in one hour. You can drink until then, and then do your Big Plan thing again." And so on.

You may feel quite comfortable as you switch back and forth. This time you're having more trouble separating your self from the Beast. Addiction Diction isn't cutting it, and the Beast is capturing the pronoun "I." Your heart beats rapidly.

Take a picture! Hop up in your thinking, as if you were a little bird above, and observe yourself in your predicament. See yourself struggling over whether to drink. **Capture a picture of yourself as an image in your mind, and look at yourself. Now, do the same thing with your feelings.**

Look at the picture you took, and imagine the feelings of the Beast as part of the picture. See it struggling with you, trying to gain control. Now, throw the picture away, and get on with something else. If the Beast persists, take another picture, and throw it away. And do it again. The Beast can't stand having its picture taken.

Mingling of Beasts

If you watch the social behavior of dogs, you can get some insight into why people often relapse in the company of other serious drinkers. On the street, dogs aggressively seek each other out, engage in sniffing rituals, and then run off together to do dog things. You might say they are "all beast." Your Beast is acutely aware of others who like to drink, because those persons also have Beasts. Many of your old friends have Beasts, just as you do. You and they have the common ground of drunkenness as a bond between your Beasts. When you are around other drinkers, your Beast may "connect" with another drinker's Beast, like two dogs on the street, and you will feel it tug on the leash. When this happens, you can recognize that your Beast is mingling with another of its kind. You may then pull hard on the leash, by reminding yourself *never,* and perhaps find others with whom to socialize.

The Society of Beasts

Beasts have no friends. They are lone wolves in that they exist in and for themselves, often content in isolation with only the substance of choice. When they connect or mingle with another Beast, the relationship is based entirely on the common activity of drinking alcohol. When Beasts mingle, there is a sense of mutual loyalty to the cause of drinking, as well as a shared suspicion of others who may interfere with or disapprove of alcoholic excess. "Never trust a man who doesn't drink" is a folk cliché that reflects Beastly suspicion of narcs. Nondrinkers who are passive and tolerant alcoholic excess pose no threat toward Beasts, and so they are accepted as "okay" or even helpful to the extent that these "suckers" may support the cause of drinking. But many relationships, intimate as well as casual ones, dissolve when one party abandons alcohol. Beasts perceive nondrinkers as narcs, until proven otherwise.

It has been said that there are two kinds of people, drinkers and nondrinkers, and that these different kinds don't mix. On the surface, this may be the case, but the difference is better understood as a matter of Beast functioning. Beasts want to associate with their own kind and seriously want others to drink too much for their own good. "Have another; I'll buy" is a common remark heard at their watering holes. When the reply is "No thanks. I've had enough," the Beast inside will register disappointment. Animated "friendship" quickly fades into detachment and indifference.

Beastly Humor: The Bond That Ties One On

Suppose a person you like, a previous drinking companion, drops by your house. You recount old times and notice that you are laughing at a story about a drunken evening in the past when two other drunk people wrestled on the floor. Is that really *you* laughing about human beings in that condition? Imagine a pack of dogs barking excitedly as one of them attacks another.

Your Beast can make a knee-slapper of alcohol-related tragedy because it places no value on pain and suffering. When you recognize this Beast activity in yourself, the story will no longer seem funny, and you will become acutely aware of your companion's Beast activity. If you stop laughing and display appropriate feelings of disgust, your companion may take notice and feel quite uncomfortable. Beasts require secrecy and cannot tolerate exposure. When you recognize your own Beast, it falls silent, but your companion's Beast will probably remain in control. It will tell him or her to leave, and that person will probably avoid you in the future. With AVRT, it is unnecessary for you to end relationships with previous drinking companions. They will usually take care of it for you!

During the early days of television, comedian Red Skelton played the character of a drunken bum, Clem Kadiddlehopper, who would stagger onstage with bottle in hand and talk with slurred speech and impaired thinking. People would laugh for a number of reasons, but some of the laughter, probably the loudest, came from people who themselves were problem drinkers and who found Clem's pratfalls and alcoholic stupidities much funnier than others in the audience. Such comedy does not do well these days because there is more objective *recognition* of addiction as a tragic human condition. Beastly humor, however, goes much further than the mild comedy of Red Skelton. Many alcohol-dependent people, drunk or sober, tend to laugh at their own and others' misfortunes, especially when alcohol is involved. Think back to the case described earlier of the man who while drunk drove his car off a cliff and ended up in the emergency room. He was duly horrified at the time he woke up with IV tubes stuck in his arm once again, but the very next day he laughed heartily as he told of plummeting into the ravine, beer in hand. This was not the same man who desperately asked me from his hospital bed, "Why do I do this over and over? Why can't I remember the pain?"

I heard him tell his story the next day to a group of young, heavy-drinking men. They roared with laughter and started telling their own one-better stories of tragedy and mayhem. It was as if their experiences under the influence were cartoons, and they were resilient, slapstick characters with no past, future, or feelings. One story involved a person's death, and for a short moment a silence erupted, and another said almost inaudibly, "That was actually a bad thing." But another man quickly continued the hilarity, saying, "So there I was cruising down the highway drunk as a skunk, and I didn't see the turn coming or the cop car behind me . . ." Soon all were howling again, including the man who had just the day before narrowly escaped death and killing others. During AVRT sessions, I always notice laughter, to see if it is based on human or beastly humor.

Beasts Will Bite

If you cross a Beast, it may snarl or even attack. More than a few people have been injured or worse when they interfered with a

Beast's supply of its favorite stuff. In my own case, I recall becoming enraged when, during a family outing, my bottle of whiskey was accidentally smashed against a rock. I accused everyone within earshot of carelessness and said some pretty harsh words. I know a woman whose husband struck her when she poured his bottle down the sink drain.

The mean streets in large cities are inhabited by addicted people whose human brains are out of order from daily intoxication and whose Beast brains demand more drugs—*or else*. No wonder those streets are often called "the jungle." Urban cemeteries are full of people who interfered with a Beast's supply of drugs.

Instead of friends, Beasts have only *partners,* and many run in packs. Just as loyalty to the cause of drinking or drugging is essential for "friendship," betrayal is the ultimate offense. Rage and violence are quite predictable when the alcohol or drug supply is threatened, such as when a deal goes sour. Closing time is a common time for violence to erupt in bars, as are occasions when the bartender declares a customer too intoxicated for bar service.

Secrecy pacts are common in Beast relationships. Sometimes a Beast makes an error by assuming that another person's Beast is cooperating with a secret plan for intoxication, when actually he or she is using good neocortical judgment. When the other person acts responsibly, say by calling the drunk person's spouse or by reporting illegal or dangerous plans to an authority figure, an outburst of Beastly rage over the "betrayal" may be expected.

Beasts in Love

It is well known that drinking and drugging destroy relationships. There are complex theories about mate selection, family dynamics, and codependency that attempt to explain how chemical dependence affects couples, and those theories are the basis for counseling and therapy. AVRT gives you a simple insight that explains the basic problem and suggests some solutions.

When either or both members of a couple are dependent on alcohol or other drugs, there will almost certainly be disturbed feelings and conflict. The key to understanding that turmoil is in the *doubling* of addicted people. Each addicted partner is two parties in the relationship. When either member of a couple is addicted, there is automatically a love triangle. If both are addicted, there are four parties in the same relationship, each struggling desperately to survive. Learning to recognize both your own Beast and your partner's Beast (if he or she is addicted) will help avert lapses. When drinking or drugging ceases for anyone in a couple relationship, the Beast will attempt to exploit the situation.

Beasts, male or female, care nothing for romance or marriage. If anything, these human arrangements are little more than nuisances or hindrances. Although you may love your spouse intensely, your Beast views your spouse as a "sucker" who will play along with its plan to drink freely. When he or she refuses to go along with your Beast's agenda, it will feel anger or resentment and will generate dishonest messages to conceal its true purpose, which is to continue drinking. As you learn AVRT, you will begin to recognize your Addictive Voice as the expression of your Beast, but your spouse will not appreciate your insight. To your spouse, you are one person with one voice, and therefore it will take quite a long time for him or her to learn that you have really changed, that you are really you and not the incorrigible drunk or junkie to whom he or she has become accustomed.

If you and your spouse are both addicted or have been addicted, you will both occasionally run into the other's Beast. But it can become annoying for both spouses to scrutinize each other for Beast activity. For example, a newly sober couple attended a party where alcohol was served. Each of them was conscious of the other, and they both felt uncomfortable. Afterward they talked:

JIM: I didn't feel at ease at the party. I felt you were watching me.

JOAN: Ha! I felt the same way. But I really wasn't watching you. I knew you wouldn't have anything to drink; but I am certain that you were watching to see if I would drink.

JIM: Not really. I was watching you, but not to see if you would drink. And you were watching me. And we were both uncomfortable. We were both feeling the same thing, and it seemed the same to both of us, even though we both trusted each other not to drink.

JOAN: Since there are two of each of us, maybe when I was looking your way, my Beast was hoping you would have something.

JIM: Now that you mention it, I did wonder if you would drink, and in a way it would have been okay if you did. I wouldn't have hit the ceiling if you drank and I didn't. I'm staying sober for myself, whether you drink or not.

JOAN: So why is it okay if I drink?

JIM: I didn't say it was okay. Well, I guess I did. Maybe it was my Beast telling me it would be fine if you drank, because then you wouldn't have a leg to stand on if I had a drink at some other time. Yes. Now that I think of it, that is exactly what crossed my mind for a moment when you were over at the punch bowl.

JOAN: Well, now that we're being candid, here's what crossed my mind. When I was at the punch bowl and you were staring at me, it seemed as if you actually *wanted* me to drink. My heart started going fast, and I thought if you did want me to drink you were a real bastard. But I still felt excited and wanted you to want me to drink.

JIM: That sounds pretty confused until you apply AVRT. Now I can see it clearly in both of us. Both of us want to stay sober, to make our marriage and family work better. But each of us has another presence that wants to continue drinking and also wants the other to be the one to drink first. When we were watching each other, our Beasts were looking through our eyes, hoping to make contact with the other's Beast.

JOAN: Exactly. Who was watching whom? It seemed as if you were watching my Beast, but you were really just watching me. But your Beast was looking for my Beast. I was watching you, like I said in the first place, but my Beast was working overtime, trying to make contact with your Beast.

JIM: So it wasn't really me feeling uncomfortable. It was my Beast, thinking you were a narc. And your Beast thought I was a narc.

JOAN: Actually, when I thought you were a bastard, that was my

Beast resenting you, for watching over me as if I were a child. My Beast will never be able to pull the same stunt again. I'll know exactly what it's up to the next time I feel you're watching over me to stop me from drinking.

JIM: Isn't it strange that we both have Beasts that don't give a damn about either of us?

AVRT is a vital means to take care of yourself without entering into conflict over use of alcohol in the home. Addicted couples have a strong tendency to depend on each other as a way of staying sober. "Let's do it together, honey" is a seductive idea that seems to offer sharing of problems and a kind of intimacy that could benefit the relationship. The idea of supporting and encouraging each other can be quite attractive to long-term lovers as well as people in newer relationships. But remember, dependency is your original problem. You both have Beasts that will mingle with each other and will try to subvert your best intentions. Your Beasts are in love, and they are attracted to each other with the same biological attraction that unites people in sex. The catch, however, is that it isn't sex that bonds the relationship. It is booze.

One likely outcome of mutual sobriety pacts between spouses or lovers is a mutual lapse during an intimate moment. "I feel so wonderful being with you. Our relationship is just heavenly. I keep thinking that it would be a wonderful experience to watch the stars on a night like this while sharing a bottle of wine (a joint, a line of coke, a martini, a few drinks, etc.). Then we could go to bed and . . ." What could be more innocent and understandable than two lovers wanting to add some *zing* to a special moment, to celebrate life and love?

Getting drunk and having sex are two experiences that significantly overlap at the sensory level. Starting with a sense of deprivation, there follows a state of arousal and anticipation, and then consummation with the warm, deep, sensual pleasure that engulfs one's entire body. Lovers may think they are enhancing sexual excitement by drinking alcohol, but in reality they are usually *substituting* the guaranteed pleasure of alcohol for the less certain pleasure of sex. Therefore, formerly addicted couples are often seduced by internal Beasts that promise sexual fulfillment while setting the stage for readdiction and potential separation or divorce.

But a more common pattern of mingling Beasts is the "mutual assured destruction" experience. Here, the Beasts exploit conflict rather than love. One party drinks, and the other's Beast whines, "This isn't fair. He/she is drinking, and I'm not. I can't stand watching him/her drinking when I can't have any. Besides, he/she broke the promise to quit, not I. So now it doesn't make any difference if I drink or not. The whole agreement is voided, now that he/she is drinking again."

Another variation on "mutual assured destruction" is when one spouse drinks as an expression of anger. His or her Beast may present drinking as a way of getting even, as in, "I'll teach that so-and-so a lesson by getting drunk," but it will more likely exploit anger with, "This is intolerable. I shouldn't have to put up with this. I need a drink right now, and I'm going to have it!"

ACTION

The Tightrope Dilemma

Addicted spouses will do much better if each makes a Big Plan for abstinence that has nothing to do with the other spouse. A good analogy is to compare recovering from addiction to walking a tightrope together.

Imagine being in a tall building that is on fire. You are both higher in the building than the fire and are forced onto the roof. Now the roof starts burning, but there is a tightrope strung over the street far below that leads to safety on the roof of another building. You both step onto the tightrope at the same time; the flames are licking at your heels. Now flames are nearing the rope itself, and soon the rope will burn.

Scenario 1: Your spouse is ahead of you. Suddenly your

spouse starts wobbling. He/she is starting to panic, arms waving to gain balance. Can you help?

Scenario 2: Your spouse is in front of you. He/she freezes, cannot move. The flame is now on the rope. What do you do?

Scenario 3: You got onto the rope first and are in front of your spouse. He/she freezes and cries for help. What do you say and do?

The purpose of this imagery is to emphasize that you are responsible only to yourself, and that you are not responsible for another person's drinking or abstinence. If you and your spouse or lover are both planning to walk together on the tightrope of recovery, it is each person for himself or herself. Beyond the question of drinking, however, you will surely find many other ways to help, support, and encourage each other as you move onward with your lives.

When Helping Doesn't Help

Many people using AVRT will find that their spouses are entrenched in disease/treatment thinking and expect that they too, attend recovery meetings or get 12-step-oriented counseling or treatment. One woman addicted to crack cocaine, named Gloria, completed AVRT: The Course. She had been in several treatment programs and was delighted that, at last, she felt secure her addiction was ended and she would have no further problems. Her husband, however, who also had a drug problem, continued in a 12-step recovery program and could not accept that she was, in her words, completely cured. He pressured her to attend more meetings and to resume family counseling with a therapist who expected her to focus on several of the 12 steps, admitting her powerlessness over addiction and taking a personal moral inventory. She resented participating and told her husband and therapist that, since she would not be drinking or drugging and had been feeling better than she ever had as an adult, she had no reason to continue and would withdraw for recovery activities. The therapist admonished her to continue meetings and counseling sessions since she appeared to be in denial and headed for disaster. Her husband became angry, and tension built in their relationship. She agreed to continue, but only as a gesture to accommodate him. Soon she began to feel depressed, and she began to doubt her ability to remain abstinent. When she told her husband about her feelings, he became affectionate and said he felt relieved that she was coming to her senses by realizing that they both share a family disease and must continue indefinitely with recovery meetings and counseling. She felt cold and detached from his overtures, sensing that she was becoming trapped in a never-ending struggle. She withdrew for a few days, convincing her husband she was in a typical relapse cycle, but she was actually working on her problems in solitude using the AVRT she had learned.

The next counseling session began on a stormy note and ended abruptly. She said, "I have decided that I will never do two things again. One is that I will never drink or use drugs again; the other is that I will never attend a recovery meeting or addiction treatment session. My addiction is over, but the two of you don't want it to be over. You both want to undermine my self-confidence so I cannot remain sober on my own. Neither of you will accept me as a well person. I have problems, sure, but if I can't figure them out on my own by now, I never will, and the only way for me to learn is to go it alone. The help I'm getting here is causing me more trouble than my addiction did. Goodbye."

She walked out before her husband or counselor could respond. She now remains abstinent and believes she will eventually get divorced. When her husband attempts to challenge her Big Plan, she hears and recognizes his Addictive Voice predicting that she will eventually drink or use, and she dismisses it without comment. He interprets this as more withdrawal and denial, and he is convinced that she is a very sick woman whose rejection is a symptom of her disease. As with many couples, addiction recovery does not salvage a marriage. It is significant and ironic that the most serious threat to Gloria's plan for abstinence came from those who were trying to help, her husband and her therapist.

* * *

I recently had an experience similar to Gloria's. In 1995, I presented AVRT to nearly a thousand chemical dependency counselors at a conference in Minnesota. To describe the Big Plan concept, I disclosed my own past addiction to alcohol and told how my commitment to permanent abstinence has resulted in complete recovery and given me great comfort. I said I was certain that I would not drink alcohol for the rest of my life. A counselor steeped in the 12-step approach took issue with my Big Plan, asserting that because I cannot prove what I will do in the future, my plan to abstain is unrealistic. "How do you know you won't drink?" she demanded. "Can you prove it?" I assured her that there are many things I know I will never do, because they are so reprehensible, disgusting, or against basic principles that I stand for, and that drinking alcohol is only one of them. I asked her if there are any acts that she could honestly say she would never commit. She answered, "There are some, but they aren't the same. I am not addicted to those behaviors and not recovering from them. You cannot guarantee for yourself or anyone else you won't drink." I responded, "Perhaps not others, but I can certainly guarantee that of myself." She persisted, saying that I was living on a false premise, one that could be dangerous to me and others who would accept the idea that a plan to abstain is sufficient to ensure lifelong abstinence. I was living on the brink of disaster, she suggested. Others in the audience chimed in, and one chided, "How many times a day to you have to tell yourself you won't drink? You must stay pretty busy reminding yourself!"

I turned to the rest of the audience and laid the matter bare. "This woman, who is a professional chemical dependency counselor, is attempting to undermine my confidence that I will remain perfectly sober for the rest of my life. She knows very well that if I drink, I will probably have problems more severe than ever, and that I could possibly die if I do drink. You all know that I have remained abstinent for well over a decade, that I have every intention of remaining so, and that I am also quite confident that my problems with alcohol are over because I will never drink again. But you have all heard her attempt to undermind my ability to stick with my decision. I don't know why she is doing this to me today, but I am aware that 12-step counseling is the art of undermining people's confidence, especially their confidence to remain sober. I am immune to what she is attempting to do to me, but most people who seek help respect professional guidance. They are extremely vulnerable to the idea that without *proof* that one won't drink, one *will* drink. I honestly believe that people who are treated this way by a professional person should sue for malpractice and that counselors who use this invasive approach should be disciplined. Since I am immune to any attempt to undermine my confidence, she has done me no harm, but I will use this incident as an example of a widespread problem in the counseling field."

Presenting this story here keeps that promise, and may help others resist aggressive 12-step intervention.

Mr. Beast, Esq.

Like a prosecuting attorney building a case against you, your Addictive Voice will accuse you of being incompetent and powerless over addiction and will find mountains of evidence to prove that you cannot possibly remain sober. It will refer to all of your previous attempts to remain sober, all of the programs you've tried, and all of the books you've read on recovery. It will focus on your imperfections and failures and refer to recovery statistics to prove your chances are slim ever to recover. One can almost imagine it at trial: "Your honor, this man/woman stands accused of alcoholism and will never be a fit human being. Look at his/her record of failure, see the many he/she has harmed, and consider that only rarely do people like this ever change their ways. I ask the court to declare him/her incompetent to remain sober, destined to drink for the rest of his/her days."

There is no need to prepare a defense against the Addictive Voice. After all, you are the ultimate authority.

13

Lapses, Relapses, and Other Nonsense

Relapse is a normal part of recovery. A lapse can be an educational experience, like falling forward.

—Your Beast

People who have made a Big Plan do not have relapses, or even lapses; they *never* drink or use again.

Of course, some people who consider a Big Plan and even go through the motions of making one change their minds and simply decide to drink or use drugs. They do not have relapses; they have drinks. They have not failed, nor did AVRT fail them. They are free to do as they wish, and they are victims of nothing. Others may go through a period of uncertainty and conflict when they have not made a final commitment to abstinence, and they drink or use with a great deal of self-consciousness. This kind of experimenting, if it occurs at all, usually serves to strengthen understanding of how the Addictive Voice works and usually results in rapid progress toward secure abstinence.

George, for example, traveled to an out-of-state Rational Recovery Center for an intensive course in AVRT and returned home feeling securely abstinent. About a month later, his Beast presented the alluring idea of driving to the top of a nearby mountain, alone, where he would drink a six-pack of beer as he watched the sun set. George recognized his AV clearly, but after some vacillation, he decided to go ahead and have his solitary party. Although deciding to go ahead made him feel very uncomfortable, he expected that by the time he actually got to the top of the mountain, he would be able to relax and enjoy a few drinks as the sun set.

Conditioned by much AVRT, George was unable to enjoy drinking. Later, he explained, "When I opened the beer, I felt disgusted, stupid from head to toe. But I still took a couple of swallows. When it took effect, it felt *wrong*. I knew right then I would never drink again. I poured the rest on the ground and left the other five beers on a picnic table for anyone who would find them. On the way back down the mountain I knew that my love affair with alcohol was over."

George is an example of how people who have learned the basics of AVRT kiss their addiction good-bye rather than receiving the kiss of death. Others sometimes go further and get drunk, only to find that the experience feels awkward and uncomfortable. AVRT builds on itself. When one has a sincere desire to quit drinking and drugging, it matters little what the Beast does; the self—you—will naturally prevail.

You may notice as you read about George that you are imagining a little lapse for yourself. This is inevitable; your Beast is only doing its job. It helps to understand that there is no such thing as a relapse, even though you may change your mind. The word *relapse* is a word that suggests that you are defective or diseased and explains your drinking or drugging as if you are not truly responsible for your behavior.

If you do drink in violation of your Big Plan, Mr. Beast, Esq., will make a big deal of it. It will pound the gavel of judgment and tell you that you are incapable of keeping your word and that your plan for perfect abstinence is unrealistic. From your viewpoint, the violation is also a significant event, not one to dismiss casually. You drank in violation of a covenant you made when you were using your best intelligence and when you could clearly remember the pain and suffering caused by your drinking. But that is all you have done. You are not out of control, because no one but the neocortical you decided to drink and no one but you used your voluntary muscles to pick it up and swallow it. Having a lapse, which means that you have had one drinking episode, does not mean that you are a stupid person, or that you have crossed over the line into a mysterious forbidden zone in which you suddenly become powerless to stop or less responsible for your actions and decisions. It does mean that your Addictive Voice, the Beast, temporarily gained control of one or more of your mental faculties. You can recognize the Beast building a case against you, focusing on your fallibility, predicting you will continue to drink more and more, or at least now and then. Prepare your defense by doing a lapse reconstruction, as shown in the case of Bill, below.

A casual attitude about relapses seems to set the stage for an end run by the Beast. "If having a lapse is no big deal," you may hear, "then why not indulge once in a while? Besides, having a lapse could be such a fine educational experience. You could learn so much about how your Beast behaves with just a wee bit under your belt. Then it would be over, and you would know what you need to know about managing lapses."

Clever? Yes. Intelligent? No. A planned lapse is a planned drink, no matter how you cut it. *There is no benefit from a purposeful lapse.* It is only another reason to drink.

Bill, for example, was unhappy about his unemployment and marital problems, which he knew were caused by his alcohol dependence. He learned AVRT, made a Big Plan, and to play safe, he removed all alcohol from his home. But one evening, he felt restless and went out to a bar and had a few drinks. "Something just came over me," he lamented, "and I got up from the TV, and the next thing I knew I was at the bar with a shot and a beer in front of me. I drank while reading a newspaper, and then on the way home I felt like an idiot for doing something that endangered my home and my career. Even though I had a Big Plan, I heard this voice in my head that said, 'You don't really want to do that. It can't really be that way. We'll see.' "

When pressed to explain what came over him, Bill explained, "When the evening news was over at seven o'clock, I thought, 'What's there to do?' I started feeling fatigued but not really sleepy. I lay down on the couch, feeling depressed, empty, and restless. Then I got a picture of the bar and the drinks in my head, and I heard myself think, 'Screw it. Let's go do it.' Suddenly I felt a surge of energy, and I was on my feet and going for my car keys. It was weird. I know this sounds stupid, but *I felt good* all the way to the bar, even though I hadn't had anything to drink. I thought, 'Who gives a shit? There's nothing to do, and I know I really love to have a few drinks in a bar with the jukebox playing while I read the paper or talk to someone.'"

The surge of energy Bill noticed when he decided to go drink was a state of arousal similar to the way a hungry lion might feel when the zookeeper throws a leg of lamb over the fence. Even though Bill had many second thoughts before leaving for the bar, his Beast urged him on, saying, "You won't do this tomorrow night, so let's get moving." Each time Bill tried to resist going to the bar, he felt worse, and it seemed he couldn't think of anything but going to the bar. "If I'm going to feel so rotten, it's not worth trying to resist," Bill finally thought, and he decided to drink, having failed to recognize his Addictive Voice. Bill's subcortical Beast gained control of his *language* and his *motor* centers, located physically within the neocortex.

Analysis of Bill's Lapse

When Bill decided to remove the supply of alcohol from his home, his Beast grasped at his reasoning faculty and argued that he would soon stop drinking anyhow, that he couldn't tolerate boredom, and that he deserved a late-evening drink. Notice that at the time of greatest conflict about going out to the bar, Bill, *who was alone at home,* was thinking, "*You* won't do this tomorrow night. *Let's* get moving."

This is pretty strange. Who did Bill think this other party was? It couldn't have been himself saying *you*. And what's this "Let's" business? "*Let's* get moving?" Later, as he prepared to leave the house, the Beast gained control of the pronoun "I" when it said, "If I'm going to feel so rotten, it isn't worth resisting." Who was feeling rotten, Bill or his Beast? To whom was it not worth resisting? By transposing "I" with "it," Bill could have avoided this lapse.

This all begins to make sense when we recall the structural model of addiction, wherein the brain consists of *two parts speaking to each other.* That's right. The neocortex speaks for itself through its language centers. The midbrain, almost a separate entity, is able to make its demands known in conscious thought by seizing control of those same language centers. When addicted people attempt to limit or stop drinking, the Beast struggles for control of language and decision making. "White-knuckling" is simply the result of internal and unresolved two-way debate about the intoxicating substance. AVRT ends the debate.

Relapse Prevention or Planned Abstinence?

Slicing words thin to see through their meaning can be helpful to people learning AVRT. Ultimately, "relapse prevention" and "planned abstinence" have similar meanings, but it is worth noting that relapse prevention is a negative statement, while planned abstinence is active and positive. We might even compare the two by using the football expressions "touchdown prevention," which is playing defense, and "planning a touchdown," which is playing offense. A Big Plan is, in effect, the touchdown that wins the game. People who have made a Big Plan understand that there are no more relapses to be prevented. That is why they feel so good.

Lapse Reconstruction

"But what if I do decide to drink/use again? What then?" many people ask. AVRT shows clearly that this question is *itself* the Addictive Voice, predicting future drinking or using. The logic spirals, and the possibility is dismissed. But still, some do drink/use again, even when a Big Plan has been stated. Therefore, the following Lapse Reconstruction Sheet is recommended for your use if you should ever decide to use alcohol or drugs. The sheet allows you to write down all of the Beast activity that led up to the lapse, as soon as possible after the episode, and learn from what happened. You can discover exactly how the Beast got a foothold in your thinking, what strategies it used, how it felt, and what physical behaviors signaled that the Beast had gained indirect control of your muscles.

I composed the Lapse/Relapse Reconstruction Sheet about a year before I published it in *The Journal of Rational Recovery*. I withheld it because it contains the catch-22 any addicted reader will notice, which is this: If you are never going to drink again, why read it? If you choose to review it, notice your own Beast responses. Be aware that your Beast will try to exploit the fact that you are reading a highly sophisticated relapse prevention device that can be used over and over and over again. I don't strongly recommend that you read the sheet, even though it is very effective, but if your curiosity is high, look it over. (As an AVRT exercise, you might try to imagine why I found it difficult to develop and present a device that could be helpful to someone who has resumed drinking or using drugs.)

Lapse/Relapse Reconstruction Sheet

1. When did you break your abstinence? State date, time of day.
2. When did the idea of *this* drinking/drugging *first* come to mind?
3. Where were you?
4. What, if anything, was happening at that moment?
5. Identify any negative emotions.
6. What was the idea like? If it was a speaking voice, what did it say?
7. If it was visual imagery, what did you see?
8. What feelings did these ideas cause?
9. What was the *reasoning*—the logic—that made drinking/using acceptable?
10. What was the *purpose* of drinking/using? Were you "coping" with something?
11. Did you hesitate, argue within yourself, have second thoughts? (Here, you are searching for *yourself* during the Beast attack, asking, "What were *you* thinking when the Beast emerged?")
12. When did you "know" you would drink/use? (This is the *reversal of intent,* the sense of inevitability.)
13. What, if anything, was happening at that moment?
14. How did you and it feel "knowing" you would drink/use?

15. How long was it between "knowing" and when you actually drank/used?

16. Any second thoughts or background uneasiness between "knowing" and "doing"?

If your answers to the next six questions involve illegal activity, don't incriminate yourself or anyone else in writing; answer silently.

17. What did you drink/use? Substance, brand, type, etc.?

18. What is your favorite stuff, brand, type?

19. Where did you get it?

20. Who gave/sold it to you?

21. How much did it cost?

22. Recall taking possession of it, picking it up, looking at it in your hand. How did that feel?

23. Look at your answer to #5 above: Did you still feel that way after possessing the substance? Ask yourself about your feelings for questions #12 through #16 as well.

25. Any second thoughts? (You *were* there! Think hard!)

26. At the golden moment, just as you took it to your lips and just before you got the actual "hit," *how did you feel?* (Be honest. Beasts have feelings!)

27. What was your blood alcohol content or blood drug content at the golden moment? The answer is zero. Write the word *zero* here: __________ !

28. Were there any feelings identified in #5 left?

29. Look at your answer to #10. Do you still think this is why you drank or used?

30. Why did you actually break your abstinence?

31. Were you really drinking/using for any of the reasons previously stated?

32. Go to #11 and #16. Can you visualize yourself taking back control from the Beast?

33. Does this lapse affect your Big Plan in any way? If so, how?

34. What is your Beast telling you right now about your lapse or relapse?

35. Is it possible that you will ever lapse or relapse again?

36. If yes, redo this sheet.

There. Did you notice an odd feeling as you imagined using this tool on yourself, while knowing that you will never have an occasion to use it? Strange, isn't it?

PHASE

Stealthy Beast Strategies and How to Combat Them

Remember that your Beast will do *anything* to satisfy itself and plays by no rules, ethics, or morality. Any warped logic, any clever language will do. You may have trouble at first deciding if a particular thought is you or your Beast. Here are some common strategies that evade detection, along with AVRT responses:

1. I still think a part of me really does want to drink.

What do we call that part of you that still wants you to drink? Can you recognize the Beast here? Either you want to drink some more or you don't. If you really want to drink, then drink! That isn't a *part* of you, it *is* you. Make your mind up. If you have had enough to drink, then you don't want to drink. The idea that part of you wants to drink simply leaves the door open for drinking any time you feel a desire to drink.

2. But why can't I say that I just *want* to drink? That doesn't mean I will do it. I can want to do something I won't do.

That may work for some people, but it is not AVRT. The rule in AVRT is to *dissociate* from the Addictive Voice by recognizing its nature, using objective (not-me) terms rather than subjective (I, me) terms. Dissociation from the Addictive Voice helps many people who have struggled against it for many years.

3. This is really going to be a difficult struggle, for a long time.

Difficult for whom? You or the Beast? Your Beast wants to compare abstinence to being sentenced to hell. It is afraid, and cannot accept your desire to abstain.

4. I feel both ways about quitting for good.

Pure Beast. You have no separation between "I" and "it." In AVRT this is impossible because logically you can't have it both ways. You feel good about quitting, it feels bad about quitting.

Play by the AVRT rules, and you cannot fail to remain sober. If you have no plan to quit for good, you have a plan to drink/use.

5. I can think about quitting, but I really have trouble with the idea of "never."

Your Beast will permit you to think about quitting, as long as you aren't serious about it, so get serious!

"You Need It to Cope," Says the Beast

Watch out for the words *cope* and *deal* in your mental vocabulary. They are buzzwords in a recovery movement that assume you will be unable to function without alcohol or drugs. Literally, *cope* means "to overcome problems and difficulties." In disease thinking, you are coping, or attempting to cope, with your problems by drinking. Your Beast absolutely loves *cope* and *deal*. How can you *not* cope? Isn't everyone dealing with problems? If you see a woman crying, isn't she coping? Isn't an anxious man dealing with a problem? How would you know if he stopped coping? Would he die? But now you know that, by drinking, all you were coping with was not drinking. That insight will help you immensely when you are permanently abstinent, because you will definitely have problems, and you almost certainly will "cope" with them. No big deal.

But suppose your doctor has said you are "clinically depressed." That *proves* you have a *depressive disease* and you *need* some foreign chemical in your body in order to feel normal, or so it is said. So your doctor may give you antidepressants, but you drink on top of them because that's what you wanted to do in the first place. Then you feel worse because the antidepressants don't mix with alcohol. So there you are, depressed since conception, hopelessly trapped in your addiction, seeming to drink because you feel so bad all the time. But underneath it all, you know what you're doing, don't you? Deep pleasure.

One woman drank after learning that her husband had been unfaithful to her. She was told by a counselor that she was "drinking on him," as a way of getting even and as a way of dealing with the pain of betrayal. But this didn't settle the question in her mind about why she had chosen to drink after several years of abstinence, particularly since she had gotten through other stressful times without drinking or even seriously considering it. Once she immersed herself in AVRT, she had no difficulty reconstructing her relapse by recalling that her Beast had exploited the marital disturbance. "You shouldn't have to experience all this emotional turmoil," she recalls thinking. "It would be perfectly understandable for you to have a few drinks. After all, look what he's done to you."

Her decisive insight was that once she decided that she would drink, she lost all feelings of anger. For several days, as she made plans to check into a motel and get drunk, she became practically *unconcerned* about her husband's infidelity. When she realized that by the time she drank, she was already feeling fine, the truth of the matter sank in. When she finally drank, she was drinking *for the pleasure of it,* and the marital problems were only a *front* for her singular desire to drink.

The illusion that addicted people drink or use to cope is a transparent fallacy, one that has become widely accepted in American culture. By the time you actually drink or use drugs, you already feel better. That's right, even if you felt angry or anxious or depressed when you decided to drink, the idea of drinking produces a pleasant anticipation. By the time you lift the glass to your lips, or as you prepare a line of cocaine, your troubles are already gone, even though your blood alcohol or drug content is zero! This premature high may be strong or weak, but it's nearly always there, and it strongly contradicts the idea that people drink or use drugs to cope with negative emotions. Figure 4 (opposite) shows the premature high concept.

The Felt Presence

Much of AVRT concerns language, but Beasts have feelings. When you threaten it with a Big Plan, it will react with strong feelings, usually anxiety, anger, a desire to withdraw or be isolated, or a vague "sick" feeling. Usually, you can hear it talk to

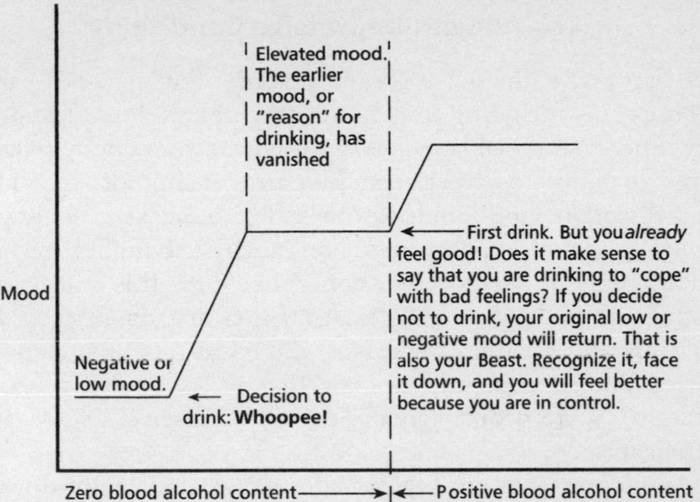

Figure 4. The Feeling of Alcohol

you, arguing and pleading that you not deprive it forever of alcohol. But sometimes, a feeling may come over you like a dark cloud, a depressed feeling that may come and go or settle in for a spell. When you feel this way, you may begin to dwell on life's misfortunes and frustrations and feel confused about how to solve your many, many problems. Soon, you may conclude that you really are depressed and cannot "cope." But you, the one who is choosing abstinence, are not depressed. Your feelings are those of a sulking Beast that is using the siege strategy in its battle with you. It promises you a lifetime of gloom and despair, but suggests that you can feel better if only you will do what it feels is best—have a drink. This is the felt presence of the Beast that foils many sincere efforts to abstain from alcohol. This is such a common, almost universal condition that in Rational Recovery literature it has been named the addicto-depressive condition. It has been observed by many others, including alcoholism researcher George Vaillant, M.D., who has said, "The idea that alcoholics drink because they are depressed is like believing the world is flat. It is the other way around."

The Addicto-Depressive Condition

True depressive illness is a serious disorder that creates a pattern of symptoms including low mood, tearfulness, loss of appetite, loss of interest, social isolation, withdrawal from family relationships, inability to experience pleasure or humor, irritability, sleep disorders (too much or too little), indecision, feelings of helplessness and hopelessness, and suicidal thoughts, gestures, and attempts. If one does not commit suicide, it is still possible to succumb to the disease by malnutrition, inertia, organic deterioration, and wasting. Depressive illness results in such persistent emotional pain and despair that ideas of dying become attractive. Some people actually do kill themselves as a way out of their misery.

Antidepressants are like wonder drugs that really do work with depressive illness, and they have saved many from suicide. The disposition for depressive illness is in one's genetic inheritance and brain chemistry. People suffering from severe depressive symptoms often experience remarkable relief within one month of antidepressant medication, and sometimes sooner.

The addicto-depressive condition is distinct from depressive illness. In recent years, there has been a blurring of the distinction with the contrived diagnostic category "dual diagnosis." The addicto-depressive condition described here is nearly universal among addicted people, but it mimics many of the symptoms of depressive illness. Consequently, in many hospital-based addiction treatment programs in the late 1980s and early 1990s, it became convenient, and to some extent profitable, to treat people suffering from addicto-depressive conditions with antidepressants, as if they were suffering from depressive illness.

Because alcohol is a depressant, people with depressive illness typically find that drinking makes them feel worse. People not suffering depressive illness, however, usually report the opposite, that they find "relief" from depression in alcohol. The nature of their depression is quite different from depressive illness, in that the cause of the depression is the alcohol itself in combination with the practical and personal problems that are directly caused by drinking. They are convinced they are drinking because they are sick, and not the other way around. Addicto-depressives may seek psychiatric care and start antidepressants, but most often they drink on top of the medicine, against medical advice. The reason for this is that depressed, alcohol-dependent people are not seeking relief from depression in the first place. They are seeking the specific pleasurable effects of alcohol. Therefore, even when the medication seems to help, they most often return to drinking.

It is possible that you suffer a depressive illness. Because you are reading this book, however, that is unlikely. But you may often feel depressed and drink as if to relieve depression. If so, you probably suffer from an addicto-depressive condition.

The Beast of booze is a creature of depression. Its passion is sustained, frequent use of alcohol, which *causes* a depressed condition in the body. But when deprived of alcohol, the Beast amplifies moods of depression by creating thoughts and ideas of gloom and doom. As if it were sulking in the unlit recesses of the midbrain, it uses your thought processes to create visions of endless misery and promises instant relief by drinking. But it is only organizing your thinking to create conditions favorable to drinking alcohol. It tells you that life is largely meaningless, that there is little good in life, that life has few if any real pleasures, and that it is hardly worth living. It will not hesitate to suggest that you may as well commit suicide and get it over with. "Life sucks," it broods, "and you will *never* feel right." And it will often suggest specific ways that you could kill yourself, such as by shooting yourself or running your car into a cement wall or off a cliff.

Then, like a friend in the wilderness, it will suddenly interrupt its morbid monologue and suggest, "But that would be too messy. And what if it didn't work? You might end up paralyzed and that would be really bad. Besides, there is one thing that *will* help, and that would be to get drunk, and since you're on the verge of killing yourself, getting drunk doesn't seem stupid at all. Now, just run out and get our life-saving alcohol." This recurring script, common among alcohol-dependent people, often goes on for years or even decades. This is why the expression "slow-motion suicide" actually misses the mark in describing the way some people slowly drink themselves to death.

Addicto-depressives aren't trying to kill themselves, but are consciously trying to save their lives by drinking alcohol *instead* of destroying themselves. The Beast, with its singular passion for alcohol, seems to care, but it doesn't. It demands more alcohol, sending the drinker plummeting into deepening depression, hopelessness, and despair, and the call for more alcohol becomes louder and louder. The drinker may stop drinking periodically to dry out, to earn some money, to mollify family or relatives who are getting fed up, or even out of fear of decline and death. But these stoppages are only that, and the Beast finds a path to alcohol in hopelessness.

This addicto-depressive disorder continues and deepens even during long "dry" periods. It takes the form of thoughts like "What's the use of not drinking if I still feel rotten?" Not to be confused with the "dry drunk" of 12-step lore, addicto-depressives are not showing a symptom of the disease of alcoholism. Instead, they are hearing amplified thoughts that generate depressed moods. The Addictive Voice, seeking eventual satisfaction in alcohol, promises the hell of lifelong depression that can be relieved only by alcohol's instant bliss. Relief, for these addicto-depressives, is only partial. Alas, they rediscover that alcohol isn't a very good antidepressant, and that it wears off and causes more depression. So the result may be an alcoholic purgatory of continuous drinking, keeping the blood alcohol level high enough to blunt awareness of the futility of drinking to oblivion.

To illustrate the addicto-depressive disorder, let's take the case of Bob, who has finally decided to quit drinking because of family and job problems. He functions well all day at work, but when he arrives home, he retreats to the bedroom, where he just lies on the bed, staring at the television, not really paying attention to the program. His wife, Gail, is unhappy because she hoped that their relationship would improve once he stopped his drinking. Instead, he complains that he is exhausted, too tired to help around the house, and uninterested in sex or simple closeness. Bob has not had a drink for one month, and he feels no better than the day he quit. He wonders how long he can endure the depression he feels, wonders if he will *ever* feel better. But deep inside, Bob *knows* that if he could only have a few stiff drinks, he would "feel normal again." But he holds out, one day at a time, hoping each day that he will feel better in the evenings. But he doesn't.

Bob is "white-knuckling it" and fits the profile of the mythical "dry drunk" of the disease model of addiction. In traditional programs he would be told he hasn't "turned it over," that he is not working a good program, and very certainly that he is not attending enough support group meetings. If he were to be seen by a doctor, he would perhaps be diagnosed as suffering from major depression and given an antidepressant. If he received medication, he would take it, but he would very likely drink on top of it against medical advice. Why? Because antidepressants don't create deep pleasure.

Having been exposed to some Rational Recovery material, Bob senses he can defeat his problem by using his intelligence. He begins to observe his own internal state and takes note that he is not depressed *all* of the time, as he would be if he suffered a depressive illness. He feels fine at work, and in the evenings there are some moments when his mood lifts. For weeks, as he lies on the bed, his arms feel heavy, and his fatigue makes getting up a major effort. But he thinks frequently about getting up and going to the liquor store. He imagines purchasing a pint of vodka and drinking it straight down in his car, before driving home. Then, he imagines returning to the store, buying a week's supply, returning to the car, and driving home feeling like a new man. What a fantasy. But, for Bob, who is being set up by his Beast, this is more than a fantasy. When he thinks this way, *he feels better.* His energy returns, and the depression vanishes. On some occasions, he actually gets up, walks about, and feels a surge of energy and vitality.

Making a serious effort to better his life, Bob decides that he will not drink. *Instantly,* his depression returns, he feels fatigued again, and he slumps back onto the bed. "When will this *ever* be over?" he asks himself. An inner voice answers, "Never. There's something wrong with you. You can't make it. You are an alcoholic, and you're hopeless. You may as well end it all." At which time, Bob again thinks of drinking, and again *feels better.*

But Bob *persists,* and the next evening he asks himself, "How long can I take this?" But this time he reflects on why he is not drinking, and he certainly has a laundry list of excellent reasons to abstain. His life is a mess, and he feels desperate. So, the answer comes, "Forever. I don't care how bad I feel, or for how long, *I will never drink again.* If I am depressed twenty years from now, I will not drink. I don't care how much I suffer, I refuse to live my life under the influence of alcohol. My last drink was my final fix."

By thinking aggressively and by making a difficult decision, Bob made a Big Plan. In that instant, Bob's addiction to alcohol was over. He felt an immediate relief from the depressed mood, and his fatigue vanished. Matching his Beast's determination, he faced it down, and it *collapsed.* His Addictive Voice became a faint echo of a life-threatening force that had compelled him for many years to drink in spite of all consequences. He will still face the mop-up operation of contending with occasional Beast attacks and solving his many problems, but he will be energized by the feeling of being in control.

Low moods and uneasy feelings among newly abstinent people are usually the *felt presence* of the Beast. Treatment of these moods is costly and ineffective. In AVRT, you may simply recognize depression as the felt presence of your Beast, trying to get you to drink alcohol. Think to yourself, with meaning, "There, I can feel my Beast struggling to get me to drink. I know what these low feelings are and where this is leading. But I will not drink anything, now or ever. I will remain depressed if that is what is to be, but I absolutely will not drink." Now, think about your life from your own viewpoint, as a normal, intelligent person who never drinks and who wants a better life with excitement and real pleasure. Where has your dark mood gone?

Relapse Anxiety

If you feel anxious thinking about eventual relapse, recognize that moment as a perfect opportunity to use AVRT in its most potent way. Simply be aware—*recognize*—that you are feeling anxious about relapsing and *attribute* that feeling to your old conniving enemy, the Beast! It's just that simple. Here is a way to understand even more clearly how relapse anxiety works.

Relapse Anxiety's Hidden Agenda

Refer back to our structural model of addiction in Chapter 10, with the two-part brain. Your "Beast activity"—the feeling that you will eventually relapse—is simply your midbrain influencing the language center, located in your neocortex. Remember that your neocortex is *you* and your anxiety about relapse is originating in your midbrain. Now, re-create or *intensify* your anxiety about inevitably relapsing. Imagine that eventually the Beast will get the best of you and you will become powerless to say "no." When it seems that you will drink again, you will feel relapse anxiety. Go ahead and let yourself feel the anxiety. But here's the catch. You may *also* notice that you feel a quiet satisfaction with the idea that you will eventually relapse. Some people describe the feeling as "a smirking sense of satisfaction that I may relapse." That is your Beast, grinning behind your legitimate anxiety. As you now recognize what's going on, you are "hopping up" into your neocortex, so to speak. You are thinking objectively about your anxiety and noticing a hidden satisfaction that you may become powerless and relapse.

Now look at Figure 5, "The Relapse Anxiety Grid." All of the possibilities have been played out, and you can see that opposite feelings exist about all of them.

Anxiety cuts both ways. You are frightened of relapse and happy with the idea of a Big Plan. (Aren't you?) But your Beast is frightened at the Big Plan and happy about the possibility of relapse. So when you have feelings about either the Big Plan or about relapse, you can recognize which party, you or it, is being offended or pleased. When this becomes clear, you will be much more secure in your Big Plan. There is no reason to fear the presence of the Beast. It's just there, and you can sense it practically at will.

You may have heard the expression "warning signs of re-

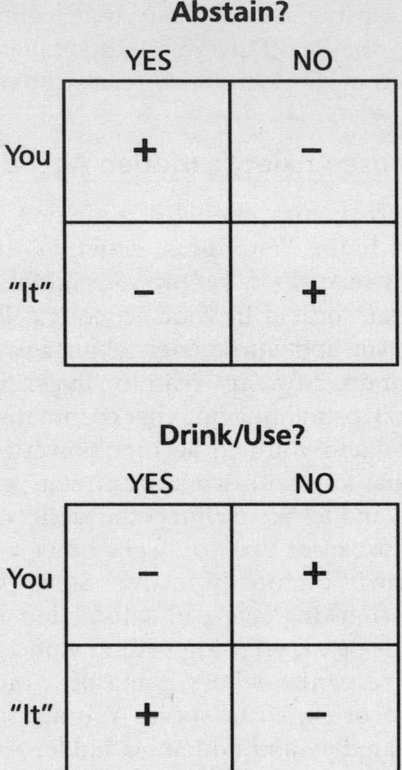

Figure 5. The Relapse Anxiety Grid

The plus and minus signs represent positive and negative emotions, respectively. Understanding this ambivalence is central to AVRT.

lapse." In traditional programs, one is said to be at high risk of drinking alcohol if any of the "HALT conditions" exist. HALT is the acronym for "hungry, angry, lonely, or tired." If this is so, that you are more vulnerable to drinking or using when hungry, angry, lonely, or tired, then we might conclude that life is a constant struggle to remain sober. In AVRT, however, there are no warning signs of relapse, but only recognizable Beast activity.

Instead of undermining your self-confidence by putting you in a defensive posture, AVRT assures you that even if you were stranded on a desert island, angry as hell that you are there, hungry for anything but coconuts, and tired of endless boredom, you would be entirely capable of instantly recognizing and neutralizing your Addictive Voice if a case of cold beer washed ashore. Would you drink the beer? Who knows? That is your personal business. There are many of us, however, who most probably would not drink the beer unless physical survival somehow depended upon it. Addiction Diction is a sophisticated device that can distance you from any impulse or desire and from any anxiety about a relapse.

ACTION

Relieving Relapse Anxiety

When anxious, ask yourself, "Will I ever drink/use again?" Then, look at your hands and wiggle your fingers. Challenge your Beast to do the same. A tip: Reminding yourself *never* will relieve most legitimate relapse anxiety.

How Rotten Can the Beast Be?

Some people are uncomfortable with the idea of a sinister, ruthless potential within themselves, and would like to conceive of the Beast as an innocent creature, like a puppy dog that charges blithely about, leaving a path of destruction. This preference is obviously the Addictive Voice, an expression of the Beast itself, attempting to conceal itself in the guise of a charming, even lovable, entity. If you feel uncomfortable with the idea that your appetite for alcohol and drugs creates a style of thinking that has little regard for anyone or any consequence, that is because it cannot tolerate being exposed for what it is.

The Beast plays by no rules. Anything goes. Winning is everything, and no hairline crack in your Big Plan will go unnoticed by the wily Beast. But, alas, the Beast is predictable because we know what it is after, and it is conspicuous because of its movement toward the supply. Your Beast moves in strange ways that your AVRT-educated eyes can discern. Take, for example, the following letter from a man who attended AVRT: The Course a couple of years ago.

> Dear Jack and Lois,
>
> After reading your new book on AVRT, I have implemented a new, restructured Big Plan. Under my former Big Plan, which has served me well, I was never to drink alcohol or use drugs again. Behind this, however, was one condition: ". . . unless I happened to contract some horrible, painful, terminal disease that I simply couldn't live with. In the event of catastrophic illness, surely using alcohol or narcotics would then be reasonable and acceptable." My astute Beast argued further, "If it comes to the point of suicide, you can overdose on heroin, morphine, or some other opiate, and we could have one final high." I was almost amused to discover a quiet longing to contract cancer, AIDS, or some other devastating illness in order to acquire, quite literally, the final fix. I have recently informed Mr. Beast that in the event of painful, terminal illness where rational suicide might be an alternative, neither alcohol nor drugs shall be the considered as a possible means. The result is that those morbid ideas about becoming ill have vanished.
>
> Sincerely,
> RT, California

This man's discovery duplicates my own experience about two years after I quit my alcohol addiction. During a dental exam, the dentist spotted a polyp on my throat and sent me for a biopsy. The procedure could not be scheduled for almost two weeks, allowing me time to contemplate the possibilities. I could not avoid imagining myself with throat cancer, wasting away, unable to speak. Oddly, I had no anxiety, even though this unhappy vision recurred nearly every day. Finally, about two days before the biopsy, I got to thinking more deeply about the possibility of having cancer. I imagined myself in my home, dependent on others, speechless from a laryngectomy—but there on the coffee table next to my chair was a bottle of whiskey. I immediately saw why anxiety was absent: The Beast had seized upon my undiagnosed condition as a boozing opportunity. I quickly affirmed that if my biopsy found malignancy and progressive illness, there would be no use of alcohol. At that very moment, I was flooded with anxiety. That anxiety was my own appropriate fear of becoming ill.

The Beast will exploit tragedy, such as the death of a loved one, by telling you that *you should not feel bad that someone you love has died.* This sounds macabre at first, until you recognize that the Beast is a dumb thing that merely orders your thinking into causal pathways to drink alcohol. If your mother, child, or spouse dies, you may imagine yourself drinking to "cope" with grief, but by now you know that the Beast is only seizing an opportunity to get a buzz on. "You poor thing," it would say, "how awful that so-and-so has died. You can't bear the misery. You need a little dope to cope." With AVRT, you will understand that grief *is* coping with loss, and to drug your grief is to deny your love. You may then love fearlessly and grieve intensely as an expression of your love.

Triggers, Warning Signs of Relapse, Post-acute Withdrawal, and Pseudoscience

In the recovery group movement, scientific language is used to say ordinary things, and many bogus ideas are given the authority of impressive-sounding words. The most notable example of this kind of scientific confetti is the "denial" misconception, which traces back to Freud's more sophisticated theories. (As is it used today in the recovery group movement, "denial" has its real roots in the Spanish Inquisition and the Crusades, when "denial" meant "of God.") Here are some other pseudoscientific concepts to think over, using AVRT as a filter:

1. **Triggers.** These are situations or events that are believed to produce a risk of relapse, such as hearing an old song, seeing a previous drinking partner, meeting an old flame, going to a certain part of town, or becoming angry, anxious, or depressed. These circumstances are said to "trigger" a series of events that may culminate in self-intoxication. "Slippery place" fits into the concept of "trigger."

   Question: If you aren't going to drink anymore, what could "trigger" you to do so? In AVRT, you may feel considerable Beast activity, yet know that you will not drink or use.
2. **Warning signs of relapse.** These are thoughts, feelings, or behaviors you or others observe that, once again, indicate "high risk" of relapse. HALT (hungry, angry, lonely, and tired) is the best-known example of "warning signs of relapse."

   Certainly, any self-respecting Beast will be thrilled to learn that there are "high-risk" (high-opportunity) moments that are unavoidable in daily living. "Warning signs of relapse" is probably one of the most delicious ideas your Beast can imagine. It sounds as if addiction treatment views abstinence as conditional upon serene comfort. Speaking for myself, I imagine that I will be HALT every day for the rest of my life. I will be hungry because I am healthy; I may be at least a little angry, especially if I think very much about reality; I will be lonely because even in love we are all alone; and I will be tired because I have lived well that day. But I ask, what does comfort have to do with abstinence? And what does discomfort have to do with drinking or using drugs? See what your Beast answers to this.
3. **Post-acute withdrawal (PAW).** This one takes the cake. Did you know that you aren't mentally clear for six months after your last drink? Or so they say. Yes, you

suffer seratonin depletion and fluctuating brain cell membrane impermeability, which allows free ions to bond with your secondary neurotransmitters. And certain substances resembling heroin have been coursing in your veins for years, even though you only drink beer. That can last for years, according to some experts, causing you problems you don't think you have.

I like to call this kind of medical mumbo jumbo the "double clinch-back overhang complex," because it is purely an exercise in confusion that has no bearing on your decision to drink or abstain. People who speak of these things rarely know what they speak of, and even more rarely can they describe how one might benefit by being so informed. Professional addiction treatment specialists will show you diagrams of your brain cells to prove you're out of it, give you paper-and-pencil tests to "prove" that you are brain damaged, then tell you to draw a picture of your Higher Power. They will not use actual medical tests, such as an EEG or CAT scan, because PAW is only *minimal* brain damage—so minimal that it can't be measured. They say the trouble is that your neurons and brain cells aren't producing the right stuff, causing "cognitive impairment" (you can't really think straight). So, not much is to be expected of you, as long as you show up for your treatment sessions. You are viewed as an incompetent person, childlike, under the wise guidance of treatment professionals. If you have any objections to the treatment program, this is further evidence of your "denial," which is a result of self-inflicted brain damage from your drinking. If you relapse, that would be understandable and expected. PAW, more than any other concept, probably represents the jaded perception of the treatment community toward addicted people.

Newly sober people are not mentally disabled in any significant way. Chemical dependency counselors sometimes flaunt the term "post-acute withdrawal" (PAW) to convince well people that they are mentally sick after many months of abstinence. If you don't feel mentally impaired, then you most probably aren't, and you may dismiss suggestions that you are impaired as fancified nonsense. It is true that after detoxifying (quitting alcohol) it takes a while, a few weeks at the longest, to get adjusted to not drinking. Moreover, you may feel mentally "out of it" during that time, with an irritable disposition, and you may feel a little foggy. But this is a *temporary* problem—a hangover—well known for eons, which fades as you move forward with the important problems of living. If you have access to a local RR self-help group, you may make contact with others who are working through problems using concepts of Rational Recovery.

In the real world, people gradually get better after suffering the effects of prolonged drinking. They know their bodies have taken a beating and don't expect to feel perfectly well, but they do expect that eventually they will get back to their old selves. In the real world, addicted people make some of the best decisions in their lives while drunk as can be or while suffering rotten hangovers. In the real world, some newly abstinent people are among the happiest people alive. In the real world, people who no longer drink feel better and have a new zest for life within a very short time, and they often function at a level surpassing their expectations.

4. **Stages of recovery.** Academic researchers studying people who have quit their addictions believe that recovery is a process and that there are stages of recovery. In other words, much leads up to one's decision to do something about the problems caused by drinking or using. Following the ideas of the popular author Elizabeth Kübler-Ross, who spoke of dying as a process of denial, anger, bargaining, depression, and final acceptance of inevitable death, psychological researchers are now looking at addiction recovery in the same stepwise fashion. Recovery, they say, comes in stages, too—precontemplative, contemplative, decision, and action. In other words, people don't quit their addiction out of the blue, but consider before deciding, and before they consider quitting they are "precontemplative," which is to say they haven't seriously

considered it. This reminds me of an American trying to describe the game of cricket after seeing only five minutes of play. Nevertheless, much is made of the "stages" of recovery by some psychologists who need to make sense of addiction, which appears to them chaotic.

The stages-of-recovery approach has some serious difficulties, from an AVRT perspective. Describing people who are simply chemically dependent as "precontemplative" presumes they are doing something they should not be doing and they are not as responsible as they should be. This amounts to an unsolicited moral exhortation, not far removed from "denial." As we might expect, the so-called precontemplative and contemplative drinkers or users are then exposed to professionally crafted *motivational enhancements* intended to move people along toward the desired end, which is some action.

If you will notice, AVRT makes no attempt to motivate you to quit. AVRT credits you with motivation and removes the only obstacle standing between you and your own self-defined goals—the Addictive Voice. Chemical dependence is an individual liberty, pain itself is the classroom of change, and your decisions about using or quitting are entirely your own. If someone attempts to motivate you, your values, judgments, and interests are being replaced by theirs.

5. **Moderate drinking.** Moderate or controlled drinking is the second fondest wish of all addicted people. It is their passion to drink *to excess* that drives people to seek help learning to drink moderately. There is an odd irony to the concept of moderate drinking, in that those who yearn to drink moderately are fully acknowledging their present inability to do so. They are saying, in effect, "I am having problems because of drinking, but I want to continue drinking without the problems it causes. Therefore, if I drink less than I do, I will have fewer problems, but I do not know how to accomplish that." They want to acquire an ability they do not have, an ability they may once have had but somehow lost. In effect, they want to return to

the good old days when drinking provided its satisfactions yet did not result in problems.

It sometimes escapes people's attention that the inability to predict how much one will drink, and to predict the limits of one's behavior under the influence of modest amounts of alcohol, combined with a persistent desire to continue drinking, is a deadly cocktail in itself. It certainly sounds as if a Beast has been born along the way and is now calling the shots.

There is no doubt that some with drinking problems do mature out of their difficulties, for this is well known and substantiated by scientific research. By the time people are looking for help in learning to moderate, however, it is probably too late; they have crossed the threshhold of deep pleasure and no longer drink for a good time—they drink to get drunk.

But what other way is there to learn to abstain except through repeated, unsuccessful attempts to drink moderately? There is an abundance of good advice for problem drinkers that boils down to "cut back, lay off, or get help." Yet there is no resource for people who are determined to acquire the ability to drink moderately.

Until recently. A woman who was unsatisfied with her AA experience, Audrey Kishline, has written a book titled *Moderation Management,* in which she argues the case for moderation. She manages a growing network of MM support groups, which are designed to help people drink moderately.

The MM program attempts to separate "problem drinkers" from "chronic drinkers" on the basis of one's history and cautions the latter against further drinking. All participants begin the program with one month of total abstinence, followed by a reentry phase of self-monitoring and group support. Some report success and others go on to RR, AA, or other abstinence-based resources. MM is a valuable resource since it fills an important gap in services to addicted people, and I have little doubt that MM will help many people.

You may wonder how Rational Recovery relates to Moderation Management with regard to the abstinence issue. First, my endorsement of MM in unconditional; I really like it, and I'm delighted it's there. But AVRT is a logic-driven, self-aiming device that exists solely for the purpose of Addictive Voice recognition. The position of RR on moderation is very simple: Problem drinking, chronic drinking, and substance addiction are one and the same. Like a smart-bomb, AVRT identifies plans for moderate drinking as the unrecognized Addictive Voice. It cannot do otherwise. AVRT surveys the mounds of scientific literature on moderate drinking and finds the Beast of Booze wearing a lab coat, building ever more sophisticated justifications for people to continue consuming a substance that has already caused them substantial harm. AVRT spotlights services and programs to ask, "Why advocate moderation for those who cannot moderate, and why not abstinence?" The reply, whether in narrative form or with charts and graphs, is nothing more and nothing less than the AV. Through the crosshairs, AVRT also finds that ideas of moderation mostly tend to occupy the minds of never-addicted professionals who do not understand the subjective experience of addiction. They try to imagine what it must be like to be addicted and apply theories designed for purposes entirely different from substance addiction. Theoretically, many more people should learn to drink moderately than do. Many professionals seem not to understand that it is their clients' Beasts writing the checks for counseling to dignify the decision to continue drinking.

All of the above notwithstanding, whether any individual accepts AVRT as a means to defeat a substance addiction is a personal matter. It is not the intent of RR that everyone who has a drinking problem should immediately make a personal commitment to permanent abstinence. Accordingly, RR welcomes new organizations with constructive new ideas to serve addicted people. MM may help some people, and many addicted people are helped with other problems by professional counselors and therapists.

As the experts debate abstinence vs. moderation, the obvious is lost to complexity. Sometimes simple questions can clear the air. For example: Why would someone who has had a bad time from drinking want to continue drinking? Or, aren't people seeking moderation already showing they are addicted? Or, perhaps better, Why would anyone actively support an addicted person with that goal? Are the lucky ones who beat the rap of abstinence really lucky, or are the ones who choose abstinence really the ones who are much better off?

The position of RR on moderation is very simple; the desire to drink moderately or use drugs safely or recreationally is wishful thinking. Problem drinking and alcohol addiction are one and the same. We call the wish to drink moderately or use recreationally the Addictive Voice because the yearning to drink moderately is known only to addicted people. In other words, the wish to drink moderately proves its opposite, the inability to do so. Problem drinking or addiction result from the action of alcohol upon the brain, and we do not know of any effective way to prevent the predictable effects of alcohol or other drugs. When unassisted moderation fails, Rational Recovery recommends permanent abstinence, which is risk-free, feels good, and is very easily accomplished.

Personal Business

Your Big Plan is your own personal business, and it is best kept that way. A number of RR group facilitators have suggested that when one finally makes a Big Plan, it might be good to tell another human being about the decision, to share the experience as a way of emphasizing its significance, as a "rite of passage" acknowledged by the support group.

Of course, this is a hangover from traditional 12-step sentimentality about interpersonal dependency. The AA program directs one to ". . . share your wretched guilt with God and with at least one other person." In that program, confessing your sins to others and proclaiming yourself "an alcoholic" in public are both thought to build a desirable, self-deprecating attitude of "humility," and in doing so one is setting a trap for times when one is tempted to drink. According to this thinking, the more people who know you are "an alcoholic," the better the chances are that someone will be standing near to intervene, should you show signs of drinking.

For example, Linda, an AA member who had been abstinent for several years, moved to another community where no one knew of her identity as an "alcoholic." Within three months she was consistently drunk and failing in her marriage and work. Later she recalled thinking soon after arriving in town, "I'm starting my life all over again. No one knows about the trouble I had with drinking, and for once, it's nice just being myself without that alcoholic identity hanging over me. I feel normal again, and I can make new friends based on who I am rather than upon what's wrong with me." Then, at a welcoming party, she was offered a drink, and she heard the thought, "I don't want these people knowing that I have a problem with alcohol. If I don't accept the drink, then someone will figure out that I'm an alcoholic and start asking me if I have found a new AA home group. I want to stay free of all that, so I'll take the drink and only have a teensy little bit."

Linda drank the entire drink, plus one more. And, *nothing bad happened.* Her Addictive Voice was well poised to strike, and it did. She began to wonder if she was really an alcoholic, and she began to test her ability to drink more frequently, all the while enjoying the alcoholic buzz immensely. The more she enjoyed drinking, the less she believed she had "the disease of alcoholism." Her binges became noticeable to others before she became alarmed, and her troubles mounted.

After years of 12-step involvement, Linda was incompetent to remain sober. She had remained sober one day at a time through constant attendance of AA meetings; having learned dependency and helplessness well, she was unprepared for independent sobriety. She had no concept of her Addictive Voice and no plan for permanent abstinence. She had based her day-by-day abstinence on her faith that she had a "disease" and that one drink would have abrupt, serious consequences. She was all Beast, thinking, "Who will know if I drink? Besides, what proof is there I'm really an alcoholic?" Because she told no one that she was an alcoholic, no one came to her rescue when she started drinking.

Telling someone about your Big Plan is similar to telling others you are an alcoholic. What do you think your Beast would make of your confiding to someone about your Big Plan? Wouldn't it wonder *why* you have done so? Wouldn't your Beast find leverage in this by concluding that you, alone, are not capable of remaining sober? If you recall that Beasts have no friends but only partners, can you see that your Beast doesn't give a damn about anyone to whom you may confide? Your Big Plan is your own personal business and no one else's. You don't need any help; it would only get in your way. No one else needs to know that you have decided to never drink again, but your Beast will be acutely and most unhappily aware of your life-changing decision. You are in the ring with your Beast, one on one, and you have a truly awesome advantage.

In times past, social dignity was afforded people who abstained from alcohol. "Some gentlemen just don't drink" was a sufficient explanation before the present era, when the refusal to drink when others do suggests the stigma of disease—and may prompt a winking query, "Where's your home group?"

ACTION

Shifting

Place an imitation of your favorite stuff on the table before you. If you like beer, pour a ginger ale; if you like bourbon, pour a shot of coffee on ice and water; if you like pot, put some tea leaves in a baggie; if you like coke, lay a line of flour or salt. Now, look at it for several minutes. Allow yourself to imagine it is real stuff, and let the old, familiar feelings start up. Imagine the smell, imagine sipping, sniffing, or smoking. Don't be afraid. Just let the Beast come out. Now, take a second look. You look at the stuff that has caused you so much trouble. You look at the stuff you will never use again. Allow yourself feelings of disgust. Let your own feelings now take over, and you will find that your Beast withdraws and you feel either neutral or put off.

This exercise is called Shifting because it demonstrates that you have direct, voluntary control over the way you look at and feel about your intoxicant. There are two ways of looking at it, and you can always choose to look at alcohol or drugs either way. Your Beast will always lust after it, but you can instantly intervene and look at the substance yourself and completely change the way you feel.

Now return to the table. For the next five minutes, practice shifting back and forth between you and your Beast, first allowing it to get all worked up, then taking over with your right mind. Anyone can do this, but in AVRT we make it a part of your perfect defense against the Beast.

You and your Beast look at life in different ways. Neither can imagine life as defined by the other. From the Beast's perspective, life without drinking is inconceivable, but from a vantage point of stable sobriety, it will be inconceivable to think of resuming the use of alcohol or drugs. It all depends on how you look at it.

There are two of you, remember? You and it. And you both share the same body, the same senses, the same set of eyes and ears, the same emotions and feelings. There are two of you looking out through your eyeholes.

When you are around alcoholic beverages, such as when shopping or in a restaurant, look at a drink or a bottle. Better yet, find your old favorite bottle on the shelf and look at it. (You can do this in your head right now, using mental images rather than the real thing.) Look at it *both* ways, and feel the difference. Allow your Beast to drool. Feel the arousal, the desire. It won't hurt you to excite your Beast this way. Then, remember the pain that drinking alcohol has caused you. See the bottle as ugly. Recognize the feelings of desire as your enemy. Notice the difference in how you feel. This exercise places you in complete control over how you perceive the idea of drinking. It all depends on how you look at it.

If you have reason to be around drinkers, look closely at someone who has had a few too many. From your sober viewpoint, you will see a deteriorating person with slurred speech getting louder and laughing at things that aren't funny. Look again, and you may remember being in that shape and having a delightful time. From that Beastly mind-set, this person is simply ahead of you, having a great time, and you haven't had enough to drink!

One man told of looking into a bar after abstaining for several months. He saw some disheveled people draped over each other at the end of the bar, and the air smelled of stale beer and urine. Country music, which he hated, filled the dimly lit room, and the bartender looked like a zombie. But as he stood there, something strange came over him. The people suddenly looked friendly and interesting, and he had a desire to sit down with them at the bar. The bartender seemed more human, the low lighting seemed relaxing, and the music took on a soothing quality. The smell of the place aroused nostalgic feelings, and he felt as if he belonged inside. For a brief moment he wished he lived nearby so that he could walk between his home and this haven of human hospitality. Because he was experienced in AVRT, he chuckled, remembering that his Beast is a master of illusion. He then did something remarkable. He shifted his perceptions back and forth, between himself and his Beast, and was impressed that he could *voluntarily* change his perception of that drinking environment, from a disgusting dive to a haven of hospitality. From that day forward, he has had no significant Beast activity. In an instant, he had learned to *control* his perception of alcohol, leaving him virtually unable to consider drinking again.

Isn't the idea "At times, there is no human defense against the first drink" utterly absurd? What could be a more harmful idea to you?

But It Won't Die!

Remember, a Big Plan requires only a perfect *willingness* to kill the Beast. That doesn't mean that you can actually kill off the living tissue of your midbrain by deciding you will abstain from alcohol. Your midbrain will continue to send out "drink!" messages for quite a while, possibly for the rest of your life. How does it feel to think that your Beast doesn't really die, that it only plays a waiting game?

Relax. It's all different now. You have a Big Plan, and your Beast knows it. Even with beasts, reality sinks in. With your Big Plan, your task is reduced to instant, shoot-from-the-hip recognition. Because of your Big Plan, which is absolute and final, everything your Beast has to say is dead wrong, even before you hear it.

At first, it may seem that life will be a constant struggle to stay sober and that your Beast will lick at your heels all the way to the end. In reality, the battle will soon be over. During the first weeks of abstinence you will probably feel odd, as if something is missing. (Something *is* missing—alcohol!—and the Beast will *feel* it!) But you will get used to it. And to some extent, your Beast will also get used to it. Like a horse in a rodeo, the Beast of booze understands mastery. When it learns that its struggle is futile, it will settle down. But, like some ornery horses, it will occasionally start bucking. With AVRT, you will always be prepared to respond smoothly and effectively and never be thrown by the Beast.

Here are a businessman's remarks about residual Beast activity: "After ten years of abstinence, I still hear some Beast activity, especially when I'm flying somewhere. When the flight attendant comes by with the beverage cart and asks what I would like, my eyes sometimes go to the little bottles of liquor, and I hear my Beast saying, 'Yes! That would be good. Why not?' But this is not even an annoyance anymore. I usually think, 'How strange, that the Beast would still try to pull one on me after so many years.' There is no discomfort or struggle, only a sense of amusement that it still happens."

PHASE

Aggressive Listening

AVRT is *more* than a perfect defense against future problems with alcohol. The saying "The best defense is a good offense" applies also to AVRT. Thus far, you have learned how to recognize your Addictive Voice and are preparing to kill it with your Big Plan. Still, it refuses to die, leaving you in a *defensive* position, wondering, perhaps, "What next?" This arrangement, in which you patiently wait to hear your Beast's next move, gives it a subtle advantage. In the background, it can sit back and ambush you when it has a perfect opportunity. It may seem to tell you, "It's not over. Sooner or later, I'll get you. Wait and see." This may leave you feeling insecure about your future; that is your Beast's intention. It still has a foothold in your consciousness, it will preserve as long as it can.

In games such as chess, football, and tennis, the player who makes the first move has the advantage. In AVRT, you can gain the advantage by making the first move, just as you would by playing white in chess, by serving the tennis ball, or by taking possession of the football. You can take the initiative and *attack* your Beast.

ACTION

Attack Your Beast

Here's how to attack your Beast. Address it as if it were another person in this way: "You keep trying to convince me that there are good reasons for me to drink alcohol. I just want to hear one good reason why I should drink alcohol, now or in the future. *Why* should I drink? Come on. *Tell me right now!*" Now, wait for an answer. You probably won't hear a reason, because your Beast knows that you know that whatever it says is wrong, even before it is proposed. You will possibly hear a pathetic, "Because it feels good," or dead silence. Your Beast is on the defensive! Don't let up.

If your Beast attempts to give any reason that drinking might be a reasonable option at some future time, be prepared to laugh. In desperation, your Beast will resort to extremely unlikely scenarios to prove that your Big Plan has holes in it. "Suppose," it may begin, "you are in a country where the drinking water is unsafe, and you are extremely thirsty, and the only beverage is bottled beer or wine. Wouldn't you drink something then?'' Or it may suggest, ''Supposing you suddenly learn that a nuclear war has already begun and the missiles are in the air, and there are only thirty minutes left until the end of everything. What's the difference what you do then?'' It may appeal to your financial interests with, ''Suppose you are on the brink of signing a ten-million-dollar contract with an eccentric Japanese businessman who insists that you honor the occasion with a glass of *sake;* otherwise the deal is off. Wouldn't it be stupid for you to refuse to have just one little drink then?''

At first, these unlikely scenarios may create a real sense of conflict, which is exactly your Beast's purpose in resorting to such arguments. But just ask yourself, ''What are the actual chances of any of these situations arising?'' You will quickly see that the probability is almost zero. Then, recognize that the Beast is attempting to use impossibly low odds to justify its position. Deep pleasure is all it wants, and it will use any warped logic to get it.

But there is something even more sinister in the contrived logic of the Beast, as we may see in the idea of using nuclear war to justify drinking alcohol. What kind of Beast is this that would barter the entire human race and the planet Earth itself for a lousy drink? This example was actually presented in an RR Center program (see appendices) by a bright man who was struggling with his Big Plan. He said, ''I can see not drinking under the usual circumstances, but if the bombs were falling, I know what I would do. I would grab a twelve-pack and go to the top of a hill where I could see it happen and go out with a buzz on. The group leader then asked, ''Now suppose that you were unable to get any alcohol. Think carefully. What would you do then?'' The man paused, and tears came to his eyes. ''I would hold my family close. They would be afraid. I would want to be with the ones I love. I would not want to be drunk with so little time left.''

A woman considering a Big Plan found that her worst-case scenario would be the death of her daughter. She was shocked to realize that her Beast would cash in on tragedy that way, in effect saying, ''You shouldn't have to feel the pain of loss.'' She realized, of course, that there is no grief without loss of love, and that the Beast was attempting to deny her the most *meaningful* emotions that she could experience. She recognized an odd, smirking awareness about the possibility of drinking under those conditions.

Aggressive Listening brings out the worst or the best in your Beast, depending on how you look at it. You may be appalled at what it has to say. It is subhuman, both physically and in its character. It cares for *nothing* that you love, and given the opportunity, it will lead you to abandon love at the drop of a hat—for a drink.

But what about the Beast's earlier question? Would you turn down a single ceremonial drink if it meant losing millions of dollars? That's your business, but I sincerely hope not! Going further than wetting your lips to get some wet ink on the contract, however, would be highly suspect! Does this suggest that a salesperson with a Big Plan might drink each time he or she sells a big-ticket item? To the Beast it means just that, and more.

AVRT Is Effortless

There is no reason, ever, to negotiate or attempt to reason with your Beast. You will struggle if you do. "White-knuckling" is often a result of negotiating with the Beast, as in "Should I or shouldn't I? Maybe I'll just stay sober for today, and tomorrow will take care of itself. Oh, maybe I can have just a little." And so on. Reasoning *dignifies* ideas of drinking; negotiation shows your willingness to compromise. Any idea of drinking is instantly recognizable, so shoot from the hip. When you hear or feel the Beast stirring, think, "Gotcha!" Instead of saying no, say *never.*

The greatest irony of AVRT-based recovery from addiction is that recovery is easy, not difficult. For the same reason that willpower doesn't work, AVRT is *effortless.* If you stop to think of it, "will" has nothing to do with "power," any more than intelligence has to do with brute force. "Will" is neocortical; "power" is subcortical. AVRT is "your" will over "its" power, the human over the sub-human. Joining the two words together and saying "Willpower doesn't work" is like pointing out that you cannot teach a dog to talk. Your will is nothing more than a very intelligent decision to abstain for good. Free will is what makes you human. When you have made a decision to abstain, recognition of the Addictive Voice in your thoughts, behavior, and feelings is *effortless*. Either you recognize it or you don't. If you do recognize it, it will struggle. When you feel the struggle, you are on top. It is your Beast that is struggling, not you. All you did was recognize it, *effortlessly*.

How to Get Out of Your Big Plan

If you have made a Big Plan, and you feel confident that your addiction is over, that is fine. But a time may come in the future when conditions have changed and it would be unwise to continue with total, uncompromising abstinence. You are probably reading this book at a time when you are under pressure, and because of your desperation you will consider almost anything to cut your losses. Decisions made under that kind of pressure rarely hold up over the long run, and because of this some instructions are provided on how to get out of your Big Plan. But first, let's see if you can figure it out on your own.

Canceling your Big Plan is tricky because when you made it, it was absolute and nonnegotiable. You understood that it was irrevocable, a covenant entered into more binding than a marriage vow. You took the plunge with full knowledge that AVRT would render you incapable of drinking or using for the rest of your life. Then you learned specific techniques, including Addiction Diction, Shifting, and Aggressive Listening, which instantly mark any contemplation of drinking as the Addictive Voice. You then considered any conceivable circumstance under which you might consider drinking or using. You found that no matter what your Beast attempted, it was useless—you would never drink or use again, even on your deathbed. But there is a way out, a secret formula to reversing your Big Plan, just in case you decide later that complete abstinence isn't your style after all. Here it is.

Made you look! Actually, I made your Beast look. I have set you up to discover a strange truth. I do not know how to cancel a Big Plan because such a counterplan is a plan to drink. I have worked on this puzzle using myself as an experimental subject, but each time I think about developing a plan to reverse my Big

Plan, I recognize my own Addictive Voice and *cannot* proceed. Would it be as simple as just grabbing a drink and tossing it down? Even if I could get myself to do that, I doubt I could do it again, and the thought of taking a drink is repugnant. If you have made a Big Plan, try getting out of it, and discover the meaning of the word *never.*

Tomorrow, your Beast will be busy at work, trying to salvage a foothold in your thinking. Will you be ready? I bet you will be.

14

Stay Who You Are

You are one sick puppy. You need help—lots of it.

—Your Beast

If you will be patient, a wonderful surprise very likely awaits you. AVRT ends your substance addiction forever—nothing more, nothing less. Just wait and see what happens when you know you have had your final fix, and you are securely abstinent. But it's hard to be patient when the experts say you need help.

Although the product warnings on cigarette packs sometimes recommend quitting, isn't it strange that neither public service nor commercial advertisements recommend quitting alcohol or drugs? They only say *you need help*. Society expects addicted people to get help *rather* than cease and desist, and addicted people themselves fall into the trap of viewing secure abstinence as if it were contained in the proverbial pot at the end of the rainbow. Virginia's story in Chapter 1 is an example of how disease thinking leads to endless procrastination. Another person, Manuel, recalls a particular incident when, while reading a newspaper on a bus, he noticed a public service advertisement that listed ten questions about excessive drinking. At the bottom it said, "If you answered 'yes' to any three of these questions, you may have a serious illness requiring treatment. Alcoholism is a disease, and it's nothing to be ashamed of. Treatment works!" An 800 help-line number was listed. Manuel recalls thinking,

"That's me! I answered 'yes' to half of the questions." And his Beast chimed in, "Yes, you are an alcoholic, and you really are locked into drinking. But it takes many years for people to get bad enough to really need help. You'll be okay if you don't overdo it. Besides, it doesn't really look like a disease, does it?"

This seemingly helpful ad is the face of the recovery group movement and its business arm, the addiction treatment industry. It *supports* continued drinking by providing Manuel a ready excuse for his "yes" answers, confronts him with the distracting disease-riddle, and implies that he cannot take immediate responsibility but should only "get help." A corresponding ad by Rational Recovery asks only one question, "Do you drink too much for your own good?" and follows with "If you answered 'yes,' you may be at high risk to develop more serious problems. The most effective action you can take is to immediately quit drinking for good. Some people just don't drink." An 800 number is also listed, where people can obtain information about planned abstinence, as well as the internet address for the RR Web Center, which contains the basics of AVRT (http://www.rational.org/recovery/).

Getting information isn't the same as getting help, and education on AVRT isn't treatment. The recovery group movement is right on target by insisting that permanent abstinence is essential to recovery from addiction, but it completely misses the boat by assuming that recovery is a process or a result of personal, spiritual, emotional, social, and psychological growth. In Rational Recovery, those worthwhile pursuits *follow* recovery and are made possible by your continuing abstinence.

Making a Big Plan is the critical event that leaves you completely recovered from addiction. When you fully understand that your drinking and drugging days are over, you are completely cured, *recovered* from your substance addiction. You are on your own, just like everyone else, to seek a better life, to learn and grow through trial and error, to set your own goals and decide how to solve your personal problems.

Your Beast will remain active for quite some time, however, looking for reasons to resume your addiction. Like any predator, it will detect your weaknesses and vulnerable points, your imperfections, your fallibility as a human being, and use them viciously against you. It will have plenty of ammunition.

As a newtotaler, you will immediately begin to feel life's difficulties and problems. From time to time, you will feel the presence of the Beast as a vague, uneasy feeling, and at other times you will experience its urgent desires to drink. Your understanding of AVRT is perfectly adequate to see you through it all.

One persistent Beast strategy is worth considering in detail here, and it is this: You might wonder if recovery can be so simple, considering the huge industry that caters to people who are in recovery. Experts—yes, the most respected scientific and professional authorities in our society—give convincing and fascinating arguments that addiction has many causes, that addiction is a symptom of inner deficiencies (character defects, separation from God, genetic disposition, social background, poverty, dysfunctional families, low self-esteem, anger, resentments, low frustration tolerance, dissatisfaction with life, etc.), and that a recovery program must *deal* with these issues so that recovering people can *cope*. They offer their services and programs as vital ingredients for recovery. Yet AVRT insists that addiction has but one cause, the Addictive Voice, and it sets you adrift on the wavy sea. "It can't be this simple," you may hear. "You need help, but you can't be helped."

Moreover, your life was organized for years around drinking and the high life, and that pleasure became the *meaning* of life. If you felt bad, you drank to feel better; if you felt good, you drank to enjoy feeling good. You chased the elusive high, setting aside all other loves, obligations, duties, and priorities. From time to time, as the substance took effect, it seemed worth it all. "Ahhhhh! That's better," said your Beast, as you lifted off into the "home zone" of sensory pleasure.

Now, you abstain from that pleasure. It is not an option or even a possibility. "So, what's the point of living?" you might ask. "How can I have fun? And what about all these problems I've created? How can I ever solve them?"

Pure Beast. It is a dying creature, telling you its darkest secret—that life has no meaning other than as an extended party. It will continue: "You are fundamentally defective somehow.

There's something missing upstairs. You aren't like other people who can just enjoy a sunset or have a pleasant walk. You have a reverse Midas touch, and everything you touch turns to dirt. People can see that you're not quite right, and they take advantage of you. You'll never get ahead or really enjoy life. You can't go it alone. You need help."

When these thoughts occur, transpose the "you" with "I," and see how convinced you really are that you are so impoverished, so defective, or so much a loser. "Am I seriously defective? Am I *really* that bad off?" you might ask yourself (don't ask your AV). Mr. Beast, Esq., prosecutor-at-large, is making a case against you once again, attempting to prove that without alcohol you are an incompetent person. Don't argue this point with your Beast. Just *recognize* it for what it is, your old companion trying to get you drunk again.

This kind of Beast activity is 100% predictable, and in my opinion it accounts for the incredible growth of the recovery group movement. People feel *vulnerable* when they consider abstinence, and they are extraordinarily prone to forming substitute dependencies to compensate for the Beast. It is the Beast's fear of deprivation that propels people into elaborate recovery schemes that promise fulfillment, social contact, new coping skills, character repairs, moral betterment, serenity, or nirvana, and it is the AV that keeps them there. Then, recovery is never really over, because the AV is running the show. It should not be surprising that the Beast speaks through the recovery group movement in a *collective* AV, which says, "This is your lifeboat, and you're lucky to be here. Keep coming back and think about alcohol all the time. For you, the world is a slippery place, so you need someone to watch over you. Tell drinking stories and convince others that they are defective, too. There is no human defense against me, for I am powerful, cunning, baffling, and you are powerless before me. Your best thinking got you here, so accept my simple program of surrender or die. Without me life is no good, and you need a new design for living. I am with you always, and if you don't work this simple program, I will get you sooner or later. There is nothing more pathetic than a person who has just quit drinking and not accepted the Program. Never say 'never'; quit only one day at a time. Circle your wagons—yes, your chairs—and delve into your pasts and personal affairs and discover how defective your are. Take what you like, but if you leave the program, you will drink again."

The initial holding power of the recovery group is the fear of inexplicable relapse, pure and simple, and with time it becomes a way of life. Granted, many members come to like it, and there is no doubt that some are better off in significant ways as time wears on.

AA splinter groups based on humanistic or cognitive psychology have sprung up in recent years, but they still carry on the traditions of disease thinking, psychological problem-solving, and open-ended, long-term support group participation. Interestingly, Rational Recovery began as that kind of program, but changed rapidly as AVRT came to the fore. RRSN groups now offer orientation to AVRT for a month or so, with the expectation that participants either want to quit or they don't. If they don't presently want to make a Big Plan, there is little reason to attend further meetings, but they may return later when they are ready.

Your Values, Your Emotions

In Rational Recovery, your support group is society at large, and your recovery program is called life. Life will teach you everything you need to know to have a satisfying future. AVRT allows you to freely explore any psychology, religion, spirituality, or therapeutic method without unrealistically expecting those resources to solve your addiction problem, and you will be much more pleased with the results. But keeping your addiction separate from your other problems can be difficult, even when you are using AVRT, as the case of Jeff, below, demonstrates.

Jeff was addicted to crack cocaine. During an AVRT session, he remarked, "I've also been acting out my other addictions, really manifesting my addictive personality. Maybe AVRT can work with those problems, too." He had been in several treatment programs and had learned the recovery jargon well, so I asked what he really meant. "The sex thing. I really act out my addiction there," he said.

He told me about his attraction to women besides his wife and how his unfaithfulness had caused marital problems. He thought his use of crack was a symbolic acting-out of his dependency needs for his wife, and his extramarital interests a symptom of a pervasive, malignant psychological condition. He cited references and named several prominent therapists with whom he had consulted. He suspected there might be some physiological basis for his problems in life and spoke about his own brain chemistry as if he were a specimen.

I could have stuck with the usual AVRT approach by asking what those matters had to do with his future use of crack cocaine, but instead I changed course altogether. I said, "Jeff, have you ever seen an Italian opera?" He said he liked opera and knew the stories somewhat. I said, "I think your personal problems are the stuff of life, Jeff. Marital infidelity has been an endless human drama since the beginning of our history, and some of the greatest literature ever written is about the problems in your own life. Love, romance, betrayal, reconciliation. Your life is rich, Jeff, full of meaning and passion. I think you are cheating yourself by looking at your life as a disease process, seeing your passions as symptoms of bad brain chemistry, and thinking your sorrows are psychopathology."

Jeff caught on quickly. He said that for years he had been struggling with personal problems, and he found the recovery group movement concepts enticing because they offered a way of looking at things, a perspective, that let him feel he was accomplishing something. Of late, he explained, he felt more and more desperate, more confused and hopeless about life, and his use of alcohol and cocaine had increased considerably.

"Your life isn't an extension of your crack habit," I told him, "and your crack habit is not a result of your problems, either. They are two entirely separate things, even though they do interact."

This was an important moment for Jeff, for he was able to go forward with a much clearer focus on AVRT. He found the structural model offered him a renewed sense of well-being, and he gave up on the idea that bad chemicals were ultimately responsible for his follies. But even more importantly, I think, Jeff was able to see himself as a real person leading a meaningful life and very much a part of the grand human drama. He is abstinent today, and he still has problems that would probably qualify for insurance payment if he continued with counseling, but he would rather face life on his own than return to the sterile room.

I mentioned earlier that AVRT was taught to me by my addicted clients. Several years ago an incident occurred that made me stop and think more seriously about the place of psychological counseling in addictions. Curtis, a seriously addicted man, had drunk away many opportunities and gotten into much trouble. Very bright, he had plummeted in just a few years from being an independent businessman to having a public guardian. He had a short temper and loathed himself for his alcoholic blundering. At the time, Rational Recovery was using some psychological concepts along with AVRT, so in addition to teaching him the technique, I also attempted to help Curtis with his problems with guilt and low self-esteem.

He said that he wanted to quit drinking in order to gain back his self-respect and the respect of his family and friends. He was still grieving the loss of an important love relationship that had ended due to his drinking. He felt quite rejected and depressed, and he damned himself for his stupidity. Using expletives excluded here, he described himself as a thoroughly rotten person.

Curtis had no trouble understanding that his negative emotions were brought on by his irrational beliefs, especially the idea that his failures proved he was a worthless person. I helped him to challenge those beliefs by asking himself how making big mistakes proved he was a bad person, and I suggested that he might just accept himself as he was without putting himself down. We continued on this avenue for several sessions, and he seemed to be catching on that he could take it easier on himself and possibly have an easier time staying sober. But Curtis was set in his ways, and either he would not or could not accept himself unconditionally. "I must quit drinking altogether," he said over and over, "I absolutely must. I can't live with myself this way." I asked him, "Curtis, is it that you absolutely *must* quit in order to consider yourself a worthwhile man, or is it that you really want to quit?"

That was the straw that broke the camel's back. Very impatiently, he said, "Listen to me. If you can't understand that I am really a bad person because of all that I have done, then *you* have a problem! I've listened to this rationalizing stuff for several days now. That's not the way I was brought up, and I'm not going to buy it. The only way I will come to respect myself is if I quit drinking. Period. I came here to learn how to quit, because that's what you said we would do, so that's what I want to do, right now."

I had been had, and I knew it. I instantly saw that I was wasting Curtis's time on matters that were irrelevant to him. By seeming to impose a psychological belief system on him, or suggesting that his emotions and personal values were tied into his ability to remain sober, I was actually putting an obstacle in his way. I agreed to drop the self-acceptance stuff, and we focused only on bullet-nosed AVRT for the rest of his sessions. Curtis called recently, over three years later, to say he was getting married, and said he has remained effortlessly abstinent using AVRT. He quipped, "I'm having a ball proving I'm a good man!" I said, "Touché."

Just Be Human

Stay who you are. Be true to yourself. Use your own best judgment in all matters. It is okay if you withdraw from others and from activities for time to yourself, if that is what you prefer. Be extremely cautious about making major life decisions during your first months of abstinence. You are vulnerable to quick and easy-sounding solutions to the common problems newtotalers face. Be skeptical of programs that offer you a new design for living or promise to make you over into something you aren't. They may have some merit for securely abstinent people, but it is doubtful that better living will result in abstinence. Be wary of your own attempts at self-analysis, and be skeptical of persons who come to you with advice, guidance, or directions on how to live your life. It sounds as if I'm suggesting that you unconditionally

ally accept yourself, just as you are. Maybe I am. Just don't drink or use, that's all.

Rational Recovery and Religion

Rational Recovery was originally a secular mirror image to the 12-step program, offering humanistic psychology to replace the religious content of the 12 steps that so many find unhelpful or objectionable. The result was diversion from the immediate task of planned abstinence and the illusion that abstinence was an outcome of psychological improvements. Also along the way, Rational Recovery has voiced the conscientious objections of tens of thousands of persons who have received unwanted, unconstitutional religious indoctrinations in the course of addiction treatment. By advocating for their religious freedom, which certainly includes freedom from state-sponsored religion, we have risked being perceived irreligious, sacrilegious, or even anti-religious.

Nothing could be further from the truth. RR is a friend of organized religion worldwide. We deplore suggestions that any of the world's great religions are insufficient to address the common human problem of habitual self-intoxication. We encourage people to maintain their family values, religious beliefs, and devotion to the church of their choice. I have stated publicly on many occasions that the Holy Bible contains all the information one needs to recover completely from substance addictions. I have learned that the Islamic religion contains guidance and injunctions that are highly effective with chronic substance abusers. I know that the Mormon and Jewish religions are successful in reducing substance addictions among their members. I have corresponded with RR Coordinators in Central America and found that Catholic nations have always had adequate means to address the ever-present problem with alcohol and drug abuse. In Mexico, for example, problem drinkers often make a pledge to the saint *Virgen de Guadalupe* never to drink again and then carry a picture of the Virgin their wallets as a reminder of the duty to remain sober. Of course this works, because Catholics hold human beings morally accountable for their behavior and do not expect God or any saint to take on human responsibilities. This approach has been used successfully for eons.

When you quit an addiction, you face the same problems as anyone else. Your religious faith can be a precious resource for solving life's problems, and it is an authentic setting for your spiritual growth. You can open doors for rewarding relationships with people who share wholesome interests and desires, and you can become part of a vital social institution.

If you are Christian, you can support AVRT with Bible studies referring to "the beast," found both in the Old and New Testaments, and the account of Satan's temptation of Christ in Matthew 4:5–11. Not long ago, the Women's Christian Temperance Union suggested that people, addicted or not, voluntarily pledge *to* God that they would abstain from alcohol. Since then, the recovery movement has required addicted people to *depend upon* God to keep them abstinent. The call to "Turn it over! Let go and let God" shifts responsibility for abstinence to God, pure and simple, quite the opposite of the WCTU pledge, and also opposite the majority of religions, which *prescribe* abstinence (or even moderation). The expression "It's against my religion" is perfectly congruent with AVRT; the decision is one's own, a *responsibility* to one's religion or God. The recovery stance is a clear reversal of duty; it is not surprising that America has consequently become possessed by malignant, mass addiction. RR returns addicted people to traditional values that stress personal responsibility, self-reliance, and *duty* to God. God is not responsible to keep you sober—you are.

Some in the recovery group movement say they are glad they are alcoholics because it brought them to God. While RR has no objection at all to that perception, we do disagree that it is necessary for one to depend upon God for such a commonplace achievement as abstinence, or that public institutions should ever enforce such an arrangement.

AVRT and Psychiatry

Some might wonder if AVRT works when other psychiatric problems exist. In schizophrenia, for example, people often hear voices, and in manic-depressive illness, people become agitated and grandiose. In paranoid conditions, people believe that they are the subject of scrutiny by conspirators and unseen observers. Generally, these conditions come and go and are quite treatable with psychiatric medication.

If you have a psychiatric problem, that does not mean that you have two psychiatric conditions, as reflected in the recently coined term "dual diagnosis." It does mean that you have a special responsibility to abstain from alcohol and other nonprescribed drugs—that is, if you hope to benefit from psychiatric care. I often refer to "Dr. Beast" because your AV will tell you that you know better than the doctor, that alcohol or drugs are okay, and that often those substances are superior to prescribed medications.

Although you aren't responsible for your mental illness, you are responsible for complying with your medical care. Even though you may go through periods of disruption when your mental illness flares up, you are probably in control of your behavior in some very important ways. For example, there are certain things you will not do, even though you are having serious symptoms. When you make a Big Plan, you can make it apply to times when you are suffering symptoms of anxiety, depression, agitation, or confusion. In effect, you are adding one more thing to the list of things you absolutely won't do when you are having psychiatric symptoms. Yes, this applies even if hearing voices is one of your problems.

Generally, anyone who can self-medicate is a good candidate for AVRT. You pharmacist has a most direct and helpful approach for addicted people, a little dose of AVRT pasted next to the label of your medications. It reads, "Do not use alcohol."

Counseling and Therapy in Addictions

A relatively new school of psychology called cognitive-behavioral therapy (CBT) began in the 1950s and has gained momentum since then. Sometimes called "humanistic psychology," CBT reflects a philosophy as much as a therapeutic method, and as such contradicts many of the tenets of the 12-step philosophy. As

AVRT emerged as the predominant feature of Rational Recovery, the apparent contradictions between psychology and religion became moot issues for addiction recovery.

The Small Book, for example, has an entire chapter devoted to emotional problems related to guilt, shame, and self-condemnation, strongly suggesting that abstinence is connected in some way to how one feels about oneself. In one chapter, it was suggested that people who want to quit drinking or using in order to gain self-respect or self-esteem are at a disadvantage because one may still feel guilty while abstinent, and that would undermine the initial reason to abstain. Unconditional self-acceptance was set forth in *The Small Book* as the preferred, perhaps ideal, foundation for "rational sobriety" (an expression no longer used in RR).

Much ado is made in our society about self-esteem, self-acceptance, and unconditional self-acceptance. The state of California now has the Office of Self-Esteem, funded out of state revenues under a 1986 assembly bill. The purpose of this office is to survey the parameters of self-esteem in society, particularly as it affects or reflects the functioning of socioeconomically disadvantaged groups. A massive study during the 1980s, costing millions of tax dollars, and culminating in a thick, bound volume containing thousands of pages, concluded that self-esteem is good for everyone, that opportunities for success and social support are important conditions for self-esteem, that Californians are *entitled* to it, and that laws should be made to foster and protect it.

Before you laugh, consider that many seriously believe that society's ills may be corrected by social engineering, psychological intervention, and behavioral health management. So, what is self-esteem? It's a sense of personal well-being from liking oneself, not too much, but just enough.

And what is unconditional self-acceptance? Much different, say cognitive therapists. It is accepting oneself without reservations, as a fallible person, warts and all. It is a stalwart refusal to blame or condemn oneself for anything, no matter how reprehensible one's behavior might be. It is a learned, self-induced immunity to the emotions pertaining to one's selfhood—pride, honor, guilt, shame. Unconditional self-acceptance is the Holy Grail of cognitive psychology, arrived at by logically attacking the idea that a person's good or bad behavior indicates one's own goodness or badness.

Unconditional self-acceptance is an elusive concept, for it is an argument against human nature. People naturally scold themselves, blame themselves, and feel emotions of shame and guilt associated with their mistakes and failures. Psychoanalysts insist that the absence of shame and guilt is the making of sociopaths and psychopaths, while cognitive therapists insist that shame, guilt, and self-rating are the root of all evil, if evil exists at all. From the cognitive therapy perspective, the deeper dimensions of the human drama are reduced to faulty, absolutistic thinking and overgeneralization.

Very likely, your own present values and beliefs are right for you. As you shed the Addictive Voice that has controlled your behavior for so long, you will naturally become more ethical, moral, pro-social, honest, and loving. It is an error, I think, to assume that because you have been strung out on alcohol or drugs, you must undertake to improve your basic underlying character.

Symptom Removal by Abstinence Alone

When it is clear to you that you will never drink or use drugs again, you will be faced with many personal problems. However, you may be pleasantly surprised that some problems you expected to haunt you may fade and disappear. While addicted, your Beast finds your problems useful as a means to drink or use. Anger, for example, can become a well-worn path to the bottle. One man, having made a Big Plan, reported, "I used to get really irritable in heavy freeway traffic. I'd clench my teeth and curse other drivers. Usually, I'd stop at a bar and sit out the rush hour, starting my evening drunk. Now that I have a Big Plan and know that I won't be drinking if I pull off somewhere, I just relax and stay in the congested traffic listening to music. If someone cuts me off, I figure there's no use getting upset. My freeway anger no longer has the purpose of getting me into a bar."

Accordingly, long-standing social anxiety may also disappear simply because you have ruled out the possibility of drinking. Here is the story of a woman who drank, she thought, to feel more at ease with people.

One night this young woman recognized her AV while attending a musical show at a casino. Two weeks earlier, using AVRT, she had stopped drinking alcohol, and just a few days before, she had made a Big Plan to never drink again. Seriously and chronically addicted to alcohol, she was quite attracted to the Big Plan, but she was also uneasy that she would lose her capacities to party, to cut loose and have unbridled fun.

She was a fan of the band performing at the casino that night, so she abandoned the games and paid to get into the show. The show was terrific, and as the band finished their final encores, she had an impulse to run up to the bandstand and hug the bandleader, as she had done many times in the past. But suddenly she became anxious and heard herself think, "You can't do that. You haven't been drinking. You'll just make an ass of yourself if you run up there. You need a drink to be yourself." Her excitement left, and she was no longer having fun. She thought of taking her friend's drink so she could enjoy the moment. But a better idea suddenly came to her. On the way to the bandstand, she would go to the bar, order a brandy snifter, and down it. She felt her excitement returning as she contemplated having a quick drink and then running up to the bandstand just as the buzz set in.

She was aroused to drink, felt for a moment on the brink of a relapse, and then felt anxious because of it. But this time she knew what was going on. In a brief moment, she *recognized* that her Addictive Voice was stealing the show. She identified her arousal to drink and saw that she was not as much excited about the music or the bandleader as she was about having a drink. She recognized her excitement as the Beast and simultaneously recognized that her anxiety had more to do with *not* drinking than with making an ass of herself in public.

Upon recognition, her Beast fell silent, and her lust for brandy vanished. She focused again on the bandstand, started cheering for the great musical performance, dashed up to the bandstand, and hugged the bandleader. He was surprised and smiled, and the audience laughed. She returned to her seat, only slightly embarrassed, but thrilled about seeing a great show and hugging the bandleader.

Securely abstinent people discover that sober sex surpasses drunken sex. Once the romance and allure of drinking before sex is understood as so much Beast activity, the real pleasures of sex become possible. Fears of failure, rejection, or other sexual anxieties may give way to healthy sexual arousal after a period of abstinence. Even drug users who once insisted that cocaine created awesome sexual experiences find that "normal sex" is, well, normal, and more satisfying than seemed possible while addicted.

Symptom removal is part of the Abstinence Commitment Effect, or ACE (see Appendix A), and it may go on for years, as you mature with your Big Plan. Because you don't drink or use, you will naturally find ways to overcome persistent personal problems. When that fails, you can still get professional help—treatment appropriate for those problems.

Return of the Authentic Self

The world of addiction treatment has gone far afield from the simple reality of addiction; all of life is made a condition of addiction and of recovery. All of your background, your heritage, your surroundings, early experiences, deprivations, deficiencies, and troubles are worked over in a mighty effort to release you from the grip of a mysterious, unseen force—a "disease with multiple causation"—that compels you to drink.

In AVRT, you simply quit your addiction, now and for good, and let the chips fall where they may. Most experts predict two things: (1) You won't succeed for long because you have not solved your real, underlying problems, and (2) you cannot be happy because there is something wrong with you.

The Abstinence Commitment Effect strongly contradicts those dire predictions with the opposite results. Just as one might expect, were it not for current cultural attitudes, people who abandon their addictions immediately continue to improve in all areas of life and become normal human beings with common human problems.

There is nothing different about "newtotalers" (newly abstinent people, new teetotalers), except for their unique understanding of addiction and a set of practical problems common to the aftermath of years of substance abuse. They "wake up," not necessarily in any spiritual sense, but return to living in a natural, functional state. Some have pronounced emotional hangups, psychiatric problems, and deficits, but these problems are not the cause of addiction. Treatment for them is widely available.

One newtotaler said her father said when she started drinking, "At some point in time, something changed in you. You have changed, and something is gone from you. You aren't the same person I raised." She said she didn't understand then what he meant, but now she knows that the change he noticed was when drinking took over. Although she had only two days of abstinence when he made these comments, she already had a strange but familiar feeling that she was once again "herself." With a Big Plan firmly in place, she was already looking at her drinking years as a finite period with a beginning and an end.

"Where have I been for the last ten years?" she asked. "It seems like a bad dream." During her drinking years, her inner life was motivated by and organized around the priority of alcohol pleasure, and she became an unfamiliar person to her family, "a beast, dressed up in people clothes," as he put it. Her many hundreds of 12-step meetings had convinced her that she and her family were dysfunctional and that she was destined to drink and struggle against drinking for the rest of her life. She thought she was still sixteen years old inside, a child in an adult figure, an idea resulting from the pop psychology of the recovery movement.

Now abstinent, she has returned to her old self, familiar from late adolescence, her *authentic* self, a resilient, adaptive, and viable person, but now an adult with a full rainbow of feelings and natural coping skills. During her drinking years, she grew, learned, and matured, even though she was intoxicated much of the time. Becoming addicted was an accident, and even though the birth of her Beast was abrupt, she could not identify what had come over her and did not understand what had caused her life to change so much. Now, with AVRT, she sees clearly what it was and understands that "It's just there." She won't waste any time trying to figure out why the Beast is there, but she recognizes it as a parasite on her lust for life, and she knows that she will never feed it again.

A man from California working on his Big Plan heard the echo effect as he stated he would never drink again. The Beast said, very clearly in his thinking, "You *will* drink, and you know it. To hell with your wife, and screw the job. You don't need them. Everything will be better. You wait and see. You will drink, and it will be okay." He grew tearful as he listened to the mentality that had been running his life for many years. He had always heard it, but never recognized it so clearly as when he threatened it with a Big Plan, and it resorted to the second-person "you." He said, "I'm shocked to hear this ugly thing in my own head. It isn't me at all. It's a monster that's dying, and I know I am now free from it. I can see this so clearly now."

This man is actually a sensitive, loving person who is now free to be himself, free from the biologically driven mentality that had ruled his life and caused mayhem. He had been in several 12-step programs and was in the process of being inducted into yet another one when he learned of AVRT and Rational Recovery. For years, he was horrified at his own behavior and felt like a totally worthless, damnable person. Between his increasingly frequent binges, he felt profoundly ashamed, and he considered suicide as a form of due punishment. He had years of addiction treatment, psychotherapy, and counseling, and attended hundreds of meetings to improve his character and morality. Yet he drank and drank. No amount of self-improvement would help him as long as his Beast remained hidden from him.

The structural model of addiction finally answered his question "Why?" and he felt relieved by its vision of health and hope. When he finally *recognized* his Addictive Voice serving a ruthless biological drive *and heard it talking to him,* it became a conspicuous alien. He became willing to kill the being that was killing him, and thereby he became himself—nothing more, and nothing less. His complete recovery took less than a week.

15

Family Politics

We deserve some trust and appreciation after all we've given up.

—Your Beast

In Rational Recovery, you will take a direct hit of moral responsibility. Let's see what this means to your family life.

While you ran amok for all those years, the people who loved you and cared about you were aghast at what they saw. Your spouse in particular would not have formed a relationship with a person who acted as you later did, and quite a number of families break apart because of such intolerable conditions. To your spouse, it seems that he or she did not really know you in the first place, that there must have been some dark, hidden character traits overlooked in the rush of romance, which finally came to the surface in the form of lying, cheating, conning, hostility, drunken behavior, and betrayal. In other words, your spouse may feel like quite a sucker for having married you in the first place, and like a world-class sucker for putting up with you.

Initially, memories of your earlier relationship stayed alive, giving your spouse hope that there must be something wrong with you temporarily, something that would clear up so there could be one happy family again. But with time, the memories gave way to reality, and your spouse may have concluded that your drinking was but a symptom of an underlying character problem, that you really are a scoundrel who just likes to get drunk and doesn't give a damn about anyone but yourself.

It is very important for you to understand that people who think this way are entirely in their right minds. This is real-world thinking, the way it is in human relationships around the world. Trust is a fragile thing that flies away when danger comes.

So your spouse came to suspect the worst but hope for the best, that you would quit and become your old self. But what could explain how your spouse's old flame (you) became such a loser? Could it be a disease? What if you are actually the victim of disease, an inherited condition that makes you powerless to act otherwise? Who in their right mind could blame a sick person for being sick?

It's getting to sound like you are really a sick person who does not know right from wrong and is therefore exempt from the usual adult responsibilities. And your spouse, to top it off, is spared the despair of feeling like a sucker who inadvertently married a loser.

It's easy to love a drunken spouse if you think he or she is sick, especially if you are a little sick, too. So, how about a parallel disease for your spouse? How about codependency? And we'll call alcoholism a family disease, and you can all get sick together and ask the experts how to get better. After all, none of you can trust your own judgments now that you have the family disease of alcoholism. One day at a time, you can structure your lives together around a program designed for families with addictive disease. Down-home family politics, the struggles that give color and meaning to family life, become dynamics of family systems theory, and your interactions become the subject of the next meeting. The addiction is never forgotten, not for a day, and life becomes defined by that sodden past. You have slid past the moral judgment of others on the runners of your disease, but you can never really live down your addictive disease.

While some may come to accept or even like this arrangement, it is quite the opposite from AVRT-based recovery. One thing, for sure, is that with AVRT you won't have the protection of disease. In the short run, I suspect that AVRT-based recovery is more difficult and stressful for the family than traditional approaches. Here is why.

In AVRT, the *sole cause* of alcohol or drug addiction is the Addictive Voice, which is the expression of an appetite for biological pleasure. There is not even a fraction of a degree of tolerance in AVRT for any other explanation for the beastly behavior of addicted people. Simply put, your spouse's worst suspicions are right on the mark, that you drank only because you loved alcohol more than him or her, and you played your spouse for a sucker all along, consciously and deliberately lying, cheating, hiding it, conning, and betraying your spouse—all for your ultimate self-indulgence, booze.

The truth hurts. It hurts you, it hurts your spouse, and it hurts your relationship, at least in the short run. You are left in a very weak, almost lame, position as you face your significant others with the honest truth: "I drank because I loved to get drunk. I did it all on my own, and I knew better, but I put drinking above you and everything else. There is no other explanation."

Your spouse will see you as you are—the person who did it all for the love of booze, the same love that others restrain in the name of decency. If you embellish the truth in any way to save your marriage, you will be setting up conditions that will later come to haunt you. For example, if you say the problem runs in the family, it may excuse you momentarily, but you have described yourself as a defective person with a mysterious, inherited condition. This is not good for you. If you say you don't know why you drank, you are presenting yourself as a person who has learned absolutely nothing, a very poor risk for any substantial relationship. If you say, to show your diligence, you are going to get help and work on your drinking problem some more, your spouse will rightfully wonder what for, and suspect that your drinking days must not be quite over.

Don't forget that in the real world of family politics, it really *was* you who placed the noose around your own neck by drinking as you did, and it is not your Beast, but you, who now turns slowly in the breeze. If you try to explain AVRT to your spouse, be aware that your Beast is eager to present the old excuse, "The devil made me do it," and I doubt it will work with your spouse, or anyone else for that matter. In spite of all you know about the structural model, the Beast, and all of that, you are fully accountable for every Beast-inspired deed you ever committed, and you now take the full, direct hit of moral responsibility.

Without your shield of disease, you may feel rotten and your spouse may leave you. That is the natural, logical outcome of substance addiction in many cases. But by sticking with the truth, that you drank for pleasure alone and betrayed everyone to indulge yourself, you lay a foundation for healthier relationships with others. You can live down stupidity, even enormous stupidity, and you can live down your reputation in the family as "the beast." People you harmed can, and often do, forgive. Trust will not come soon, because your spouse, once again, is in his or her right mind and has no reason to trust.

For years, you may expect lingering doubts to occur when you come home late or disappear unexpectedly. For years, old wounds will open in the heat of healthy, marital discord. Yes, it can be healthy to argue, quarrel, and fight, because it is so *educational* for both parties, provided some basic rules are followed. When your spouse recounts the harm done "while you were drinking," remember that the reasons you made your Big Plan are largely the same reasons your spouse is belatedly bringing up. Why object to the obvious truth, that you behaved deplorably, even though you no longer do? You may squirm, but so what?

Some "A's" to Guide Your Way

Although AVRT is not in itself geared toward solving personal, emotional, or relationship problems, the following suggestions fit well with AVRT. Each one happens to start with "A."

ACTION

Family Matters

1. *Approach each person in the family* about your drinking problem. Don't wait for them to say something. You drank for many

years, and they haven't been able to communicate with you about your behavior for a long time. Your Beast didn't want to hear of it.

2. *Admit your role.* Listen to your family's complaints. Tell your family members that you became more devoted to drinking than to them. Don't minimize how seriously you disappointed them.
3. *Acknowledge the hurt.* While you were drinking, your Beast was in control, and it didn't really give a damn about how others felt about your drinking. Now that you are sober, you know that they were frightened, disgusted, angry, and hurt, and felt betrayed. Although it would help no one for you to feel guilt and shame, there are appropriate emotions: Regret, sadness, and remorse are feelings that will help you move forward with your life because they can be expressed in meaningful ways.

   Don't explain your family's feelings away. Put yourself in their shoes and imagine the feelings they had as well as you can. See if you can imagine in yourself the feelings they had. Now you can tell them you understand how they felt.
4. *Apologize.* Love means saying you're sorry. Let them count the reasons why.
5. *Absorb their anger.* Don't forget, your family got fed up with your drinking behavior long before you did. Give them a break.
6. *Ask how you can help.* Remember that you cannot compensate your family for harm done. You can't undo what happened before, but you may find some very real ways to join in activities that will help the family to do better. Spending more time with your children, taking on extra chores, refraining from certain annoying habits, eating out more often, starting a savings account, or in some cases even moving out of the home for a while—all of these things may be helpful in getting the family on an even keel.
7. *Assert your love.* Part of the family's hurt is that they feel rejected or betrayed. Instead of trying to explain why you didn't reject or betray them (because you did), simply express your real feelings toward them. Tell each of them that you really do care for them, that you love them.
8. *Anticipate mistrust.* Don't expect your family will believe you when you say you will never drink again. They have good reason

to believe otherwise. Expect instead that they will continue mistrusting and resenting you indefinitely. If and when it seems that you are being trusted and accepted, you may be pleasantly surprised. In the meantime . . .

9. *Accept that you are a fallible person.* Don't depend on them to make you feel better about yourself. Do it yourself. This is a key to emotional independence, and dependency, if you recall, is your original problem.
10. *Adventure.* Explore new activities, build new relationships, follow your interests and take your loved ones with you.
11. *Abstain from alcohol.* It isn't good for you, and your family will learn to love you for what you really are.

Your Life as an "Alcoholic"

If members of your family have been involved in 12-step programs such as Al-Anon or Codependents Anonymous or received treatment from a professional counselor, they have very likely been told that alcoholism is a family disease. This may have the effect of alienating you from your family as a *carrier* of a mysterious, deadly disease that now requires them also to participate in extensive meeting attendance, self-improvement, introspection, and therapy. It is as if you are a "Typhoid Mary" who has infected other family members, an invalid unfit to assume family role responsibilities who is expected to attend frequent 12-step meetings in order to remain sober. The expense of child care for these meetings several evenings per week can be formidable, and the actual time taken away from the children takes another toll on the family. But disease thinking can also create anxiety about parenthood that goes beyond these issues. Here are some tormenting questions that many parents in traditional recovery ask themselves:

> Are my children already alcoholics, like time bombs in my own home? Will they blame me for passing the disease of alcoholism on to them? Should we avoid having more chil-

> dren, knowing that I carry the alcoholism genetic code? What should I do to prevent them from becoming "symptomatic"? Will they have to go to Alateen, or Adult Children of Alcoholics meetings to overcome the bad influence of this alcoholic home? What kind of a parent am I? How long can I stay sober?

For this kind of recovery-induced distress, here is some common sense:

The first point to remember is that while your drunken behavior may have caused problems for your family, you may be in the *best* position to help them now. Rational Recovery is an opportunity for personal growth, and the concepts you learn may be quite helpful to others in your family. Of course, you will not be trusted immediately after you stop drinking or using drugs, but whether you are a husband, wife, father, mother, son, or daughter, you may start living in a way that is more accepting of yourself and others.

Secondly, you are *not* an alcoholic or an addict, even though these labels may describe your behavior, and you have *not* genetically transmitted a drinking problem to your children. (Your children, as they grow older, will have the same responsibilities as anyone else.) The other addictions (cocaine, heroin, pot, etc.) are not seriously considered to be genetically transmissible. So relax on that one, and go ahead and have as many babies as you otherwise would have. Just don't drink when you're pregnant. Really, isn't the idea of an alcoholic baby a little strange? Trust your common sense.

Most kids will experiment with alcohol or possibly drugs, and most of them will also get over it. Studies have shown that children of heavy-drinking parents later on drink less than their peers. There's little relationship between how you drank and how your kids will drink. They are separate people, and you don't have to feel responsible for their adult troubles decades from now. Just raise them well and be kind to them until they are of age, and you will have done your part.

This is not intended to minimize the seriousness of the problems resulting from your alcohol dependence. If you or your spouse drank a lot, or continue to drink more than occasionally, there most likely are problems in the home resulting from your drinking. Alcohol not only amplifies anger, irritability, and harsh words, but also blunts your other emotions. Alcohol, when used regularly, transforms your personality in ways that only others can see, and children are the most perceptive people when it comes to telling if mom or dad is sober, high, loaded, feeling good, or blotto.

The children do not care if you acted poorly or deplorably toward them because of "diminished capacity due to the disease of alcoholism." They remember only that the most important people they know said and did things that were painful, harmful, and disappointing. It hurts them when their parents aren't kind and understanding. But children are resilient, not fragile orchids that wilt when things are not just so. They understand human fallibility, and they will appreciate an explanation of your own feelings, especially your feelings of regret and sorrow that you drank and caused them unhappiness.

Part of your Rational Recovery is to let your children understand that you know you were not out of control, but *out of line,* and that you are aware of how disappointed they must be that you acted badly toward them. Tell them you're sorry about the problems related to drinking and that your drinking has stopped and will stay stopped. Don't tell the kids you are stopping *because* you love them, because they may justifiably wonder why, if you have loved them all along, you didn't quit years ago. Just tell them you've had enough to drink because it causes *you* too much grief and you'd like to have a happier family. That's all they really need to hear.

If they ever blame you for their adult problems, the most important question you might ask yourself could be, "Will they *ever* grow up?" Adults who whine about their rotten childhoods are not emotionally mature, and that includes most adults who grew up in homes where a lot of drinking went on. If you find that your son or daughter is attending Adult Children of Alcoholics, take note that "adult child" pretty well sums up the problem and hope that he or she will gain maturity.

But your children may indeed follow in your footsteps and

become seriously involved with alcohol and/or drugs. Although AVRT was designed for adults who have already developed serious dependency on alcohol, it provides an excellent knowledge base that can help adolescents avoid long-term alcohol dependence. The structural model will show your child why chemical dependencies begin in the first place and why they are so difficult to end. AVRT will give your child an objective awareness of the Addictive Voice, enough so that he or she may find it relatively easy to remain alcohol- and drug-free. But the Big Plan of AVRT, a serious decision for lifetime abstinence, may be premature for most adolescents. It is true that many people do make decisions to abstain from drugs, alcohol, and tobacco during their early years, at a time before a substance-dependent lifestyle has developed, so they need not experience the great sense of loss adults feel. It is difficult for adolescents to make lifetime commitments to anything. And it may be that in a few years things *will* be different, and alcohol may not present a problem when used in a responsible way.

As for your own sobriety, you are becoming well enough informed by reading *Rational Recovery* to abstain from drinking or using drugs for the rest of your life. You can dive into your parental roles with well-founded confidence that your family's alcohol-related problems are nearly over.

Remember, recovery groups don't keep people sober; people keep themselves sober, whether they attend AA or RR groups or not. Use your own common sense and don't let others undermine your confidence that you can completely recover from your addiction within a reasonable period of time—without getting entangled with groups, sponsors, therapists, or addiction treatment programs.

16

Congratulations

It's not over until it's over. You'll see.

—Your Beast

If you have read this far in *Rational Recovery* and continue to drink or use, you might conclude that you are not addicted at all, but that you *desire and freely choose* to drink alcohol or use other drugs, knowing the risks that are involved. That is certainly your right, and your judgment is the one that counts. If you sincerely desire something, wouldn't it be rather pointless for you to receive treatments to reduce that desire? Your substance dependency is all yours, so enjoy it as much as you can, and be careful.

If you have had your final fix or last call, and you are prepared to apply firmly what you have learned in these pages, here is what you have accomplished:

1. You recognize that the Addictive Voice exists *separately* from you.
2. You understand the structural model of addiction.
3. You think *objectively* about your Addictive Voice, recognizing it as your enemy.
4. You call your Addictive Voice "the Beast" or something equivalent, describe it with adjectives, and understand its primitive logic.

5. You recognize the emotional expressions of the Beast.
6. You sense your advantage over it and listen aggressively for its stirrings.
7. You have established a Big Plan for permanent abstinence.
9. You have surpassed the Beast in its struggle to survive.
9. You experience uplifted feelings and new hope resulting from your commitment to abstinence.
10. You now go ahead with your life, wiser than before.

As you look back, your years of addiction will soon seem like another lifetime in which you were a different person. You were. Just ask anyone who knew you. Now, you know what it was that got the better of you—*a part of you that is part of being human but not the essence of being human. Not a human being.*

As a person who no longer drinks or uses drugs, you will save yourself and society a great deal of time, trouble, and money. Enjoy your new freedom from addiction, and enjoy your freedom from the lingering identity that often accompanies recovery. The dos and don'ts listed in Chapter 3 are still good advice.

You may notice occasional discrimination from other people, the kind that is easily passed off as social prejudice.

For example:

- Others who know about your difficulties may think you are vulnerable to strange influences. They may hide liquor from you and apologize to you for inadvertently placing alcoholic beverages within your reach. Tease these people good-naturedly, and they will probably laugh.
- If you tell your doctor you quit drinking, he or she may think you are still in need of "treatment" in the belief that you will drink again. If you cannot correct your doctor and he or she persists, consider getting a new one.
- Some people may not like you drunk *or* sober. This has nothing to do with your former addiction. That's just the way life is.
- Some people may want you to attend recovery group meetings, "to meet others of your own kind." Politely refuse, and

seek new relationships based on mutual interests, desires, and passion.

- If you are required or mandated to participate in addiction treatment or recovery meetings, remember that there are two parts to recovery—playing the recovery game and getting better—and the two often have little to do with each other.

These attitudes are short-term nuisances and will be forgotten as your abstinent life takes form. Congratulations. You have survived substance addiction in America, where the difficulties of addiction are compounded by our well-meaning but misguided society.

The Beast

It nearly destroyed my life, but I caught it in the act. I saw that it would kill me, so I defended myself against it. When I found it out, it was angered and attacked me in many ways. It used all means to convince me that I had no life without drink, but I saw I had no life with it. I had met a worthy opponent, and I feared for my life. But I believed in my own ability to defeat my adversary, the Beast.

I studied the Beast and learned its nature and its ways. Then I attacked it with all of my intelligence. I finally learned that to defeat the Beast, I would first expose it, and then become like it. I have matched its ways in every respect.

The Beast has one goal, to drink *forever.*
So I shall have the opposite goal, *never* to drink.
The Beast is *immortal* and looks forward to an *eternity* of intoxicated "nows."
So I became *timeless* and made a Big Plan for *eternal* abstinence.
The Beast is not capable of change.
Nor am I susceptible to change my decision never to drink.
The Beast has access to all that I am.
But it is not me, and I am always in control.
The Beast is undeterred by pain.
So I will endure as much pain as necessary and never drink.
The Beast has no memory of pain.

So I may forget why I never drink.
The Beast is unreasoning in its quest for drink.
So I do not reason with it, or explain to it why I never drink.
The Beast will kill me in its quest for drink.
So I am perfectly willing to feel it dying.
The Beast is a tyrant, demanding its stuff.
So I will be a tyrant, and feel it cringe.

I have hunkered down to meet the Beast on its own turf, and by equaling it I have won.

Am I now a Beast?

It would have me think so, but I am now free of the Beast that has ruled my life. I lived in its prison; now it lives in mine. I am a human being, freed from the chains of addiction, free to be myself, free to meet life on my own terms.

PART III

A Rational Recovery World

17

How to Help an Addicted Family Member

I don't have a problem with drinking. You do.

—Your loved one's Beast

Chemical dependence often starts in the home and grows into the family horror of addiction. Addicted people frequently struggle and suffer with their families in their homes, leave home to drink or use freely, and then start new families where the addiction may continue. Chemical dependence takes a high toll on family life, and traditional approaches are more often than not unsuccessful.

Nevertheless, more hope exists for many families than may appear. AVRT is a means for families beset with an addicted member to zero in on the problem and apply family values in a way that finally produces results. Although AVRT may not be used by one person upon an unwilling other, its simplicity and potency offer hope for families and encouragement for the addicted member. Here are some basic concepts to help you get your bearings so AVRT can work in your family:

- Regardless of what you do, the one you care about may not change. Some heavy drinkers and drug users are chemically dependent and not really interested in quitting. If this is true, that's that.
- If the one you care about desires to quit drinking or using,

even just some of the time, then he or she is addicted. In that case, the possibility of recovery certainly exists. Remember, most, but not all, chemically dependent people are also addicted, and any addicted person can abruptly quit drinking or using for good.

- Chemical dependency usually brings on bad consequences that create motivation to quit. One of the bad consequences of chemical dependence is that it ruins relationships with persons like you. Many unfettered chemically dependent people finally acknowledge that they are addicted when significant others, such as yourself, will not tolerate any further drinking or using. Once addiction is recognized or acknowledged, recovery is not far off.
- Drinking alcohol and using drugs are voluntary behaviors for the purpose of gaining physical pleasure from the substance. Anyone can quit an addiction, immediately, and for good.
- Your original perceptions of your loved one's changed behavior are probably correct, that he or she is behaving irresponsibly, is fully in control of the decision to drink or use, and is personally responsible for all of the consequences.
- Addiction is a state of chemically enhanced stupidity that can be overcome by abstinence. Your loved one does not suffer from a disease that causes him or her to drink or use drugs, or that prevents him or her from immediately quitting altogether.
- You carry no burden of change. You do not have a parallel disease called "codependency." No one does. You may be dependent on that person for love or approval or something else, so dependent that your own well-being is overshadowed. But that is not a disease.
- You are not an "enabler," even if you pour the drinks for your loved one. You cannot "enable" what someone is going to do anyhow.
- If the one you care about takes advantage of your better side, your trust, and your generosity, you might experiment with the expression "sucker" to describe your role.
- If you understand that you are being taken advantage of so your loved one can experience the pleasure of drinking alco-

hol or using drugs, your options may become more obvious and clear. You might, for example, treat your loved one's addictive behavior for what it is, the ultimate self-indulgence, and give an ultimatum that you would follow through with. You may be less cooperative with your loved one's manipulations and more independent overall. Or, you may stop searching for meaning where there is none and accept the status quo.

- Hope is essential to recovery, for it means the possibility exists.
- If your loved one refuses to get help, it may be because he or she is not suited for recovery group participation and would do much better to quit independently.
- If he or she has gotten some help and continues to drink or use drugs, this does not mean that you are failing in any way or enabling. Nor does it mean that the addiction is more "severe." It merely means that some desire to quit probably exists, but the knowledge of how to abstain does not.
- In either case, tell your loved one that you have learned about Rational Recovery, which is entirely different from 12-step or psychological approaches to recovery. Tell him or her that RR specializes in helping people who have tried recovery groups and addiction treatment, but have been unsuccessful in remaining sober.
- If the one you care about undertakes AVRT studies, you may expect some erratic ways for a time. Irritability, remoteness, and restlessness are common, but this is a natural reaction to giving up something that was very important. It doesn't mean drinking or using will resume. Remember that quitting addictions does not make people into ideal personalities.
- Do not be intimidated by suggestions that if you do so-and-so, you will "trigger a relapse." You are incapable of doing this.
- Call the Rational Recovery office to see if the Rational Recovery Self-Help Network (RRSN) has meetings in your area. Some people learn best with individual instruction in AVRT. Inquire to see if there is a Rational Recovery Center in your community by calling the number listed in Appendix C.

- Whatever your hopes are to help yourself, your family, or an addicted family member, drop all labels such as "in denial," "diseased," "sick," "codependent," "scapegoat," or "peacemaker." One label, however, may shed some light, as discussed in the next section.

Enabler or Sucker?

"Enabling," meaning the opposite of "prohibiting," is a key concept in addictions theory, as well as in social policies that are reminiscent of the Prohibition Era. The word *enabler* entered the vocabularies of professional people about twenty-five or thirty years ago, when the recovery group movement was in its infancy. Since then, the term has evolved to symbolize the inverted logic of current addiction care, and has become a paler version of "pusher." Originally, and for many years, "enabler" was a clinical expression used to describe someone who actively or passively made it possible for an addicted person to drink or use drugs. Many people, for example, believe that bartenders or hosts of parties where alcoholic beverages are dispensed are not only responsible for the amount the patrons or guests drink, but also for any harm or damage that results from their subsequent drunken behavior. A bartender who allows heavy drinkers to run up tabs, a policeman who smells alcohol on a driver but issues only a verbal warning, a wealthy uncle who sends regular checks to his drunken, unemployed nephew, a boss who winks at three-martini lunches, *and a spouse who passively tolerates endless drinking* are thought of as enablers who are somehow responsible for the behavior of diseased people—who are themselves powerless to act more responsibly on their own.

"Enabler" can be an intriguing term for people discussing the theory and dynamics of addiction and recovery, but in recent years it has begun to obscure basic questions of personal responsibility. "Enabler" now conveys the idea that chemically dependent people, because of a mysterious disease process, are powerless over their behavior and therefore *dependent on others* to manage their lives. This misunderstanding has caused unnecessary grief among family members who are counseled that they have been an active part or even a cause of the problem all along and are now contributing to the relative's addiction by not taking some strong, prescribed course of action, such as abandoning the person, cutting off all financial or other support, forcing the person into an addiction treatment program, or otherwise taking action designed to coerce the addicted person into shaping up.

Family members often face a serious burden of guilt based on the notion that they are partly responsible for the problem. Then, the self-described enablers face a dilemma of being advised to take some strong action that goes against intuition or better judgment. It is called "tough love," and tough it is. While strong action may get good results for some, it may aggravate the problem for others. Many who remain enablers by failing to take ill-advised strong action often experience feelings of guilt and self-doubt. Because they love their addicted ones, they play a waiting game, hoping that other influences will come along to cause them to pull out of the downward spiral.

The addicted family member may pick up on this pernicious concept and perceive that anyone who doesn't crack a whip over him or her must be an enabler. One man who had relapsed stated he was angry at certain people who didn't do anything to deter him when he appeared for work intoxicated in a disheveled state. He sincerely believed that others were somehow obligated to help or deter "alcoholics" who are in the early stages of relapse and that if they fail in this very important duty they are enablers who share in the responsibility for the downfall. "They *knew* I was an alcoholic," he said. "They should have stopped me, but instead, they enabled me." He later admitted that he knew they knew he was drinking, and that he had continued to drink because they didn't say anything. Some elementary AVRT would probably have helped here.

There is a cure for the skewed logic of enablement. Let us consider the experience of a distraught family member, Marge, who is married to an alcohol-dependent man named Brian. Brian drinks daily and is unable to keep a job for longer than six months. He sometimes ends up in jail, and when Marge invariably bails him out, she pleads for him to quit drinking or get help, and they have fights that sometimes become ugly. She struggles with a full-time job in order to pay the rent and meet the immediate needs of their two young children, but a good part of her earnings is spent on beer for Brian. In public, Marge apologizes for Brian's rudeness, and she even contacts his employers to tell them he has been called out of town when he is only suffering another hangover. When asked why she puts up with Brian's craziness, she explains that she loves Brian and hopes he will stop drinking so the family can remain intact.

It would be tempting to conclude that Brian is an alcoholic who is pretty sick and that long-suffering, codependent, enabling Marge is, in effect, keeping him that way.

Let's look at the situation from Brian's viewpoint. He married Marge before the trouble started, and his drinking increased along with the family's mounting problems. He knows that not all of the family's problems are caused by drinking. To him, Marge isn't the same person he married, either, but an insufferable, haranguing woman attempting to deprive him of the only thing he finds genuinely enjoyable. He loves her in the sense that he remembers the way it once was between them, and he sees himself as the family's strength, if only Marge would let up on him and respect him and his wishes. He perceives her antidrinking attitude as picking on him, and he resents it. Among his drinking partners he finds others like himself who laugh off their domestic problems sitcom style. He is determined that he will drink, regardless of Marge's overblown feelings, and if she decides to leave, then so be it. In that case, he will have tried his hardest to reason with her, but she just couldn't cut it.

Exactly what is Marge enabling? How can she enable Brian to do what he is hell-bent on doing? A codependency counselor might look at this picture and imagine an ideal outcome, that Brian would get into recovery; but for that to happen, something would have to disrupt the status quo, something that would force the issue. Marge is vulnerable, and she knows it. She has witnessed her lover transform from an energetic, caring, hopeful man into a self-centered drunk, and she has wondered all along why it happened. She wonders if she has failed in some subtle way, driving him away from her with only drink to satisfy his desire. She feels betrayed, sure enough, but she also feels self-doubt.

"Enabler" is the branding iron that marks everyone in contact with an addicted person. It says, "You are part of the problem. There's something fundamentally wrong with you that sets up and perpetuates your loved one's addiction. Your enabling is subtle beyond your ability to see it, and you will need help in order to change."

This is not only needless and false, but grossly unfair to Marge. Why make Marge into a sick person? Marge is the *healthy* partner in the relationship, the source of stability and hope for the future. When she apologizes for Brian's behavior or covers up his floundering, is she enabling him to drink or enabling him to bring home the next paycheck? She has artfully engineered a workable status quo out of a chaotic mess. Her thinking is not impaired by substance use. Enabler? It sounds like Dr. Beast came up with this. Don't addicted people usually say that others are driving them to drink, that so-and-so had better shape up?

Codependency counseling presumes that Marge should withdraw from Brian, let him sink or swim, and get spirituality to compensate for the loss of the love of her life. If he should come to his senses, he may join her in her new, compensated lifestyle. Life can never be the same for either of them.

This prescription has side effects, while AVRT has none. There is a great deal that Marge can do to help Brian and restore the family to harmony without feeling part of Brian's problem.

For example, Marge might confront Brian with an ultimatum. An effective message would say, "Listen, Brian, I don't know if you're sick or stupid, but I'm not going to take this anymore. I'm giving you notice right now that I will not live with a drunk. If you want to drink yourself to death, do it out of my sight." Would Brian back off and quit drinking? Certainly many do when reality finally sinks in. AVRT is a natural ability that some people discover on their own when sufficient adversity exists.

"I Can Quit Anytime I Want"

This is a famous quote, not of the Beast, but of addicted people who are telling the truth. Behind the strivings of the Beast can usually be heard the true self, saying, "I can take it or leave it. I'll quit when I'm ready. I just don't choose to quit now, and I'm not going to do it to please you." Don't laugh. It's true. Addicted people do quit, and quite often there is a happy ending when they do. So Marge might use a more supportive approach than an ultimatum, perhaps like this: "Can you really quit drinking, Brian? You say you can, but can you?"

Marge has got Brian either way he answers. If he says no, he can't, then she can continue, "Brian, you've absolutely got to read something. It's a book about a *new cure* for substance addiction. It is written by a man who was just like you, really in the bag, and didn't know how to quit. But he did quit, and now he says, 'If you want it done right, do it yourself.' It has started a new movement in the addictions field, Rational Recovery, and it's revolutionary."

If Brian says, "Yes, I can quit anytime I want," Marge can say, "I believe you, Brian. I really do. The reason I asked is that I just read something you've absolutely got to read for yourself. It's about a new cure for substance addiction called AVRT."

Conveying your enthusiasm for something new conveys hope to someone who in all likelihood feels hopeless.

One woman, Betty, called the Rational Recovery office with the story of how her entire family was held hostage by addiction treatment counselors who demanded that she and her children attend Al-Anon, Alateen, and Codependency Anonymous meetings as part of her husband's treatment for alcoholism. Her teenage children returned after their first meeting very upset, saying, "Those people are really scary. All they talk about is booze and God, booze and God. And they scare me because their language is so filthy and they smoke, and they keep telling us we have to believe the way they do." Betty felt conflicted about her children's report because she was attending an adults' Codependents Anonymous group in which the people were friendly enough, but she, too, had reservations about the message of the meetings. The children begged Betty not to send them back to the 12-step group, so Betty compromised and had her oldest daughter, an adult, accompany the younger siblings to the next meeting of Alateen.

The daughter went with her brother and sister, but did not sit with them, appearing as an unrelated newcomer. She came home from the meeting and reported that conditions in the meeting were just as the younger children had described. When Betty confronted her counselor with this, she was told that her family absolutely must attend all meetings because there was no chance their father could remain sober unless the entire family was involved in 12-step meetings. This was a serious threat because Betty's husband was a physician and would lose his medical license unless the family complied with addiction treatment. Over the next few months, the children were intimidated in the group and harassed by other students at school, and they became withdrawn and depressed. They were particularly confused because they didn't perceive that their father had a drinking problem in the first place, and this was seen as "denial" by the group. Betty felt that her children were being taken out of their childhood by aggressive, often bullying, personalities who were unconcerned about the family cohesion and family values. She felt exploited by the guilt of being implicated as a cause of her husband's excessive drinking, and she became increasingly anxious as she attempted to assume vaguely defined responsibilities aimed at keeping her husband sober.

Interventions

You may have heard of "interventions," in which a surprise party is arranged for the purpose of pressuring an addicted person to enter a treatment center voluntarily. An intervention is staged by people who disagree with someone else's use of alcohol or drugs. A professional counselor, sometimes called an "interventionist," usually instigates this radical, marginally legal, and often unethical arrangement. The object is to create the most emotionally stressful moment possible for the addicted person and then have him or her go directly to the admissions office of a local treatment center. In some cases, a van provided by the treatment center is nearby, waiting for its reluctant passenger. Sometimes the meeting is in the home, where the addicted person enters to find a roomful of friends, associates, long-lost relatives, the immediate family, and, yes, a chemical dependency counselor. Like on a rerun of the TV program *This Is Your Life,* each person begins by saying how much he or she loves the addicted person, and then tells about some incident of rudeness or inconsiderate behavior from the past. Some describe how much he or she used to love the addicted person and now sees only a crumpled shell. Tears flow, and the interventionist plays the agenda skillfully, asking if the addicted person will produce a health insurance card "as an act of love." When it is over, the friends and family have a warm session sharing their feelings of hope for their loved one.

Interventions are less frequent these days because insurance companies won't pay for extended inpatient care. Very few people manipulated this way are later grateful to their captors, in spite of those shown on TV talk shows who say they are; and of the small number who abstain for long following addiction treatment, those forced into it this way resent it the most and fare the worst. Wouldn't you?

When we hear "Alcoholism is a family disease" or "The whole family needs outside help" or "He/she is an enabler," we are hearing a skewed logic that systematically absolves addicted people of responsibility for acquiring, maintaining, or recovering from their addictions and that shifts responsibility onto those associated with the addicted person. Some notable parallels are the ideas that scantily clad women and pornography enable rapists and that windows without bars enable burglars. Replacing the sterile, clinical expression "enabler" with the earthy, tell-it-like-it-is term "sucker" reframes the dynamics of relationships affected by substance abuse, clarifies what is really going on, and, in many cases, suggests appropriate action by all involved parties.

Getting Started in Home-Based Recovery

Be sure you understand the difference between a chemically dependent person and an addicted person by reviewing the discussion of these terms in Chapter 4. If your loved one is simply chemically dependent and intends to remain that way, then there is little that you can do to help. Don't think for a minute that he or she is "in denial," blissfully unaware of what he or she is doing, and blind to the consequences of drinking or drugging. One might say that your loved one is "all Beast" in the sense that the Addictive Voice has embraced his or her sense of self. But it doesn't change anything for you to recognize someone else's Addictive Voice. "Addiction" exists in the presence of one's own desire to stop using the substance, not dependent on a family member's judgment. It is only when your loved one wants to change and recognizes the Addictive Voice that change for the better may occur.

Your Family Values: Trust Them

When you've given some thought to your role in helping your addicted loved one, you may feel more confident in moving ahead. Just as addiction can begin and thrive in the home, so can recovery. Every family has its own approach to fulfilling the American promise of "life, liberty, and the pursuit of happiness." Every family is the product of an earlier family and has within itself a unique capacity to define its purpose, seek its goals, and cope with adversity. When addiction threatens the family, coping mechanisms emerge that are based on the desire for happiness and the wisdom of previous generations. These may be innocent and ineffective in themselves, but they show the direction for future growth.

For example, the most common responses to the awareness of increased alcohol dependence are statements like these:

- "I will cut back."
- "I'll drink less."
- "I will only drink at parties, or on weekends."
- "I will quit drinking hard stuff and only drink beer."

It is true that many people who come to the attention of professionals are unsuccessful in their attempts to drink moderately and responsibly, but those efforts reflect an awareness of a problem, a desire to solve the problem, a willingness to take personal responsibility, and, probably most importantly, common sense. When one is drinking too much, it is good common sense to decide to drink moderately. Millions of people who do drink too much for a period of time under stress, or in college, or in the military, are quite successful in avoiding alcohol excess later on when irresponsible indulgence is inappropriate. Using common sense, intelligence, and determination, many people "recover" this way; they struggle with the problem for a while, and before long the addiction is over. Most importantly, they do it as an expression of values and concepts that they learned in their homes, and they credit themselves instead of others with solving the problem. This is what Rational Recovery is all about.

All addicted people, by our definition, are aware that they have problems stemming from self-intoxication, and they wish it weren't so. They begin working on the problem of alcohol dependence with reasonable, logical efforts that usually involve promises to themselves and others to drink less, or to drink less frequently, only at certain times, or to quit for a period of time and then drink only moderately. There is nothing wrong with this, and some people, however few, succeed in achieving the goal of moderate drinking. This simple approach to addiction or substance abuse often produces results and costs nothing.

But very often plans for moderation fail, and that is where a home-based Rational Recovery plan may begin. By making a commitment to abstinence, using the concepts of Addictive Voice Recognition Technique (AVRT), and developing a Big Plan, many people have overcome their addictions, thus restoring the family to well-being.

Each family with a substance-abusing member faces a crisis that threatens its survival and the future of its members. Rational Recovery helps the entire family, including the substance abuser, become aware of the state of addiction, so that constructive action may be taken. The following is a general, flexible plan for approaching the problem.

ACTION

Identify the Problem

Let the addicted one know that you know what the problem really is. Say, "The *real* problem is that (you, dad, mom) drink(s) alcohol."

Identifying the problem is just that simple. But the drinker's or user's Beast will place the blame on anything other than on the drinking. Most families troubled with addiction have difficulty identifying the problem—seeing the obvious can take years. When ready, a family member, usually a parent but often a child, may simply say,

- "Your booze cost $320 last month, and the children need shoes. This must stop."
- "I miss you when you're out drinking. Please come home sober."
- "You're ruining everything with your drinking. I want you to quit."
- "You're ugly and boring when you've been drinking. I like you better sober."
- "You have a problem with alcohol, and you had better take care of it."

ACTION

Confront the Addiction

When identifying the problem doesn't work to solve it, taking action is the next progressive approach. Action serves four general purposes: to protect yourself and your future, to protect the children's future, to avoid participating in an addiction that is harmful to the entire family, and to educate the addicted person. State that you will take specific actions, for example:

- "I am taking out a separate bank account because of your drinking expenses."
- "I am sending the children to Aunt Alice's so they won't be around your drinking."
- "I have moved your things to the attic room. I won't sleep with you because you are always drunk."
- "I won't visit the Johnsons because you always get drunk there."
- "I won't come to bail you out of jail this time. It's time you take care of yourself."

When confronting the drinker or user, always refer to specific consequences of self-intoxication rather than general disappointments in the relationship. Tell your loved one that he or she may be addicted and explain that only he or she can know for sure. Explain that addiction is when one continues to drink or use drugs *against one's own better judgment.* Ask if he or she believes him or herself to be addicted. If the answer is "yes," tell him or her that defeating an addiction is not a big deal, that it can be learned by reading *Rational Recovery,* by going to an RR meeting, or by obtaining skilled AVRT instruction.

ACTION

The Ultimatum

Finally, when lesser means have failed, it is time to tell your self-intoxicating loved one what you will do if the drinking or drugging doesn't stop. Don't bluff. Carry through on everything you say you will do. For example, say:

- "If you continue to drink after today, I will leave."
- "If you continue to drink after today, I will put you out of the house."
- "If you don't get some help for your addiction within twenty-four hours, I will file for divorce."
- "I have filed for divorce. If you stop drinking, I will consider whether to proceed with it or not. If you don't stop drinking, we are finished."

Ultimatums are big guns, but addiction is also a big gun. You are telling your loved one to choose between you and the substance of choice. You win either way.

Give your loved one this book, and give him or her information on local RR groups and information on AVRT: The Course. It may be very helpful for your alcohol-dependent family member to meet others with similar problems who are actively involved in RR. For information, he or she may call the national office of the Rational Recovery Self-Help Network listed in Appendix C.

Self-Recovery Is Commonplace

The progression of chemical dependence is a painful and sometimes damaging experience for the family. But human beings are quite often able to manage and solve problems of addiction in this setting. When a chemically dependent person begins getting negative feedback, then finds the family withdrawing, and finally is expelled because of the addiction, change is viewed as not only possible, but also desirable and realistic. By confronting the problem, you may play a part in helping a chemically dependent person, who does not want to quit, become an addicted person who does. Remember, addiction exists only against one's own better judgment, not against the family's judgment. Millions of people quit their addictions when the consequences finally become unacceptable. This is a human ability, and self-recovery is commonplace.

RR emphasizes human strengths and competencies. Participants are discouraged from thinking they are suffering from an inherited disease that causes them to be powerless over the desire to intoxicate themselves. The American addiction treatment industry is based entirely on the experiences of people who *didn't know how* to recover in a natural, unassisted way and who were then actively *discouraged* from doing so. So, if your loved one has resisted getting help, it may not be so much a problem with motivation as with his or her rejection of the *kind* of help that has been available. If you or your loved one has attempted to get help without success, it is entirely possible that your family would do much better to go it alone, using common sense, self-reliance, and AVRT.

AVRT consists of simple logic that provides a well-marked path out of the seemingly endless maze of addiction. This technique has been compiled from the actual experiences of thousands of people who have quit their addictions on their own, without attending meetings, getting sponsors, working a 12-step program, or seeking medical or other professional help.

It is essential that people struggling against their addictions not be discredited for the sincere efforts they are making to control or stop drinking. You may expect a lot of irritability, low moods, and social withdrawal for a while. This should not be used as evidence that there is something wrong with your loved one and that he or she needs "treatment." Depending on the substance used, withdrawal can take weeks or many months, during which time there is a natural healing process under way. Anyone who says, "I can handle my own problems" is on the right track and can learn from others who have been down that track.

RRSN Self-Help Groups

If the home-based Rational Recovery plan fails, the time has come to act decisively and use outside resources. The Rational Recovery Self-Help Network (RRSN) is a division of Rational Recovery Systems, Inc., that manages free-of-charge self-help groups in most communities in the United States, plus many foreign countries. Just call the main Rational Recovery office listed in Appendix C to find the nearest group in your area.

People who attend meetings are reminded that the meetings are self-help, not support groups that encourage new dependencies and feelings of belonging. The groups are confidential, and the leaders are usually people who stopped drinking on their own using AVRT-style methods.

The meetings are group discussions that usually start with a question like "Who's been thinking of drinking?" or "Who has a problem or a trouble they would like to work on?" Self-help principles are sometimes applied to problems *directly related to addiction,* but most meeting time is used to learn AVRT to *defeat the addiction itself.* Group members are encouraged to consider permanent abstinence and shown some of the basics of AVRT, and they are expected to leave the group when they are confident that there will be no future drinking. Some people attend only a few meetings, with good results, while others decide to put off their decision to quit altogether until a later time. RRSN groups are not places for fellowship, social support, solving personal hang-ups, or roundtable discussion of philosophy or psychology. They are highly focused on learning the skill of abstinence.

Professional Help

Many people who attend RR groups will also seek professional consultation for personal problems including marriage and family counseling, individual psychotherapy, and treatment of psychiatric disorders. Again, the original Rational Recovery plan need not be altered. Many health care professionals are Certified Rational Recovery Specialists who do not treat addictions or refer people to 12-step support groups. Instead, they assign complete responsibility to their addicted clients to become abstinent, and then make information on AVRT available. They provide excellent services for other problems, including those related to addiction, but will not suggest that by solving those other problems they are in effect treating addiction or making self-intoxication any less likely.

AVRT: The Course is a brief, intensive program available by calling the national RRS office. These sessions are available in a growing number of cities. In the last several years, insurance and managed care agencies have begun to require client participation in planning treatment. When the economy and effectiveness of AVRT is compared to addiction treatment, AVRT will become available in more communities. Rational Recovery is keeping up with the times by providing each person a real choice in the means to defeat addiction.

ACTION

Using AVRT on Your Addicted Family Member

Can't be done. Addicted people, however, can use you as a sounding board, a coach, to catch the Addicted Voice when it surfaces in daily family life. If your addicted family member decides on AVRT-based abstinence, it is possible that you might be of some help with your own knowledge of AVRT.

Here are a few guidelines and pointers before attempting to help your loved one with AVRT.

1. Address the matter clearly. For example, say, "I've read up on AVRT, and if you are willing to use me as kind of a sounding board, like a coach, I may be able help you spot your Addictive Voice. Is this interesting to you?"

   If you are rebuffed at this point, *drop the subject.* You may raise the subject later or drop it altogether. But don't forget the other concerns you have about the family. Show you mean business by describing what you will or won't do if your loved one continues the addiction. Your loved one may have to choose between you and the bottle. If, however, you get a serious show of interest, you and your loved one are on your way to a fascinating journey into AVRT. It is quite likely that your loved one will defeat the addiction—for good.
2. It is essential that you both read this entire book and keep rereading it from time to time.
3. Remember that with AVRT, addicted people don't need help; they need only information. Some can learn from others; some can't.
4. Remember that your loved one's addiction is not your addiction, and you aren't responsible for creating it or defeating it.
5. Be certain that your loved one clearly agrees to have you discuss AVRT. You might even have him or her formally ask that you offer some AVRT feedback when you think you have heard or observed the AV.
6. Both of you should acknowledge beforehand that the Beast operates in secrecy and cannot tolerate exposure. Accordingly, anyone who exposes the Beast may feel the heat of resentment, at least until the addicted person recognizes the AV. Never push the issue; just comment, "Sounds like the Beast from here."
7. Make sure you don't expand the AV concept to serve purposes other than abstinence from specific substances. If you are quarreling over something, don't scapegoat your spouse's arguments as Beast activity. The AV, once again, is substance specific.
8. If you have discussions on AVRT for a while and encounter serious objections, repeated lapses, or continuous drinking by your

loved one, promptly throw in the towel. He or she will have to go it alone or get help in RR meetings, at an RR Center, or from other community resources.

In the larger sense, you can't really make a mistake in dealing with your addicted loved one as long as you are willing to try anything, including divorce, putting your loved one out of the house, cutting off the money, or using any other legal means. Whatever you do, your loved one may continue to drink or use drugs. If your loved one defeats his or her addiction with a little input from you, you may benefit from having a happy, sober person again, but you get no "credit."

Trying to help an adult family member, however, is risky. Although you can't really make things worse than the addiction itself would, trying to help can backfire. Remember, the Beast will do anything to survive, and it perceives persons who threaten the supply of alcohol as enemies. Beasts do not have lovers; they have only partners. Many addicted people confronted with change will leave their families to drink unrestrained. These are choices that addicted people may make and are entirely their own. Counselors and family members who confront or try to help addicted people are not responsible for the decisions made by such people. Addiction is a condition that often results in death, so it is crucial that you understand that *you have no responsibility whatsoever should that occur, regardless of what you have or have not done.*

AVRT with Juvenile Substance Abuse

Children begin using alcohol and drugs and become dependent upon them for the same reasons as adults. Curiosity, experimentation, social expectation, and family values play into the onset of alcohol and drug use, and persistent use is motivated by the pleasure effect. Dependency on alcohol and other drugs often develops, and addiction, in which there is a motivation to quit, has become common.

AVRT, as described in *Rational Recovery*, is designed for

adults, and its effectiveness may be attributed to concepts that do not apply to children. For example, AVRT describes chemical dependence as an individual liberty, addiction as the persistent use of substances against one's own better judgment, and recovery as an individual responsibility. Substance abuse (note the title of this section) is simply other people's opinions about one's use of intoxicating substances.

The term *substance abuser* best describes children who drink and use drugs because of their status as minors. Any juvenile substance use in our society is *substance abuse* because prohibition applies to all minors. Further, juveniles are not responsible, in the usual sense of the word, for their behavior; their parents are. If caught violating the law, they are most often exempted from prosecution that would follow for an adult. When parents fail in their responsibility for the behavior of their children, the state will take over as a substitute parent with final authority. Childhood is a time of *becoming* a responsible adult, not being one.

The media [probably more than reality] have made drug abuse the worst nightmare of family life. Adult suspicions and tensions reign in most discussions pertaining to the drug menace. Uniformed police officers enter classrooms speaking of exotic, forbidden substances and daring students to inform on peers or relatives who may use them, while star athletes whose careers seem a series of outstanding games, drug busts, and treatment programs appear regularly in the news. Children readily perceive the mystery of drug and alcohol use and understand that in American society, using drugs is possibly the worst thing they can do.

It is normal and healthy for adolescents to challenge adult authority, to test forbidden waters when their peers are doing so. When children do experiment with drugs and find the experience pleasurable and socially appropriate, it is predictable that they will experience a sudden sense of alienation from adult authority, parental or not. In the same way that sexual awakening transforms adolescent personality, the intense sensory pleasure of alcohol or drugs gives life to the desire for more, long before other life fulfillments are understood or attainable. A Beast is born that easily defines life as an extended party, and the seemingly boundless energy and creativity of adolescence is there to fulfill that agenda. The stage is set for serious conflict with adult authority and social sanction, and those who would interfere are regarded as the enemy. The developmental process toward autonomy is radically accelerated, and the child is thrust prematurely into an independent state predicated on obtaining the substance of choice. Early adulthood ensues, complete with a supportive, antisocial subculture. Retrieving a child from the influence of alcohol or drugs is often a major struggle that can destroy a family, unless the child makes an independent decision to abstain from alcohol and drugs.

Existing substance abuse programs for children, including addiction treatment programs for juveniles, borrow their authority from parents and sometimes from the state in order to exert influence and control over children who drink or use drugs. Children in existing programs, therefore, are being subjected to adult authority that prohibits the use of substances, regardless of the child's viewpoint or motivations.

Twelve-step treatment programs go against what is known about adolescent developmental psychology. Adolescence is a time to become differentiated from the peer group, with a unique identity as a competent person, not to become assimilated into a contrived subculture that instills dependence, powerlessness, humble servitude, and a spirituality prescribed for disease victims.

Adolescents typically resent forced indoctrinations of any kind. They intuitively don't like the 12-step program because it is condescending to their healthy motivations, and it is recognizably religious. The unproved disease concept creates a serious identity crisis during adolescent vulnerability. When coerced into participation, as is most often the case, adolescents struggle against the group pressure to conform, but often give in to the awful perception that they are congenitally defective, suffering a disease that will define their lives henceforth. They often feel segregated from the social mainstream into groups of their own kind, separated and distinct from "normies." It is not surprising that so many prefer the life of substance addiction when offered a second-rate lifestyle anchored in parental authority and government sponsorship. If the 12 steps are inappropriate for adolescents, this can be more true for their families, who are also considered diseased on account of their child's misbehavior, and in need of a substitute religion.

Guidelines for AVRT with Minors

The structural model of AVRT is an excellent way to present chemical dependence to youth. It is free of the disease stigma, and it allows adolescents to take personal responsibility for acquiring, maintaining, and ending substance dependencies. It releases adolescents from peer pressure so that they may predictably refuse alcohol and drugs under all conditions. It respects the challenges of growth and maturation by stressing autonomy, self-reliance, and individual responsibility in the matter of self-intoxication.

Owning the Decision

Childhood involves a crisis of authority conflict throughout, and adulthood poses authority conflicts as well. The key to successful addiction care for children and adolescents is in helping an addicted child make an autonomous commitment to abstinence. The alternative is shackling the child, either physically or through indoctrinations that paralyze autonomy and free will.

It is unrealistic to expect that an adult will live by decisions made as a child. Nevertheless, a child may make a sincere decision to abstain forever from alcohol and drugs and learn to stick to that decision under all conditions. AVRT obtains its potency from its unyielding stance on total abstinence. To preserve this strength, a Big Plan suggested to minors may be presented as an option, in effect until one's twenty-first birthday. The child will agree to voluntarily obey the law until he or she comes of age, at which time the Big Plan may be converted into a plan for lifetime abstinence, or abandoned in favor of flexible decision making. Many adolescents, however, will reject this option, preferring the adult-style Big Plan.

This is not to say that AVRT for adolescents encourages them to have a twenty-first birthday celebration with alcohol or drugs. A Big Plan for adolescents says, "I will not drink alcohol or take any other nonprescribed drug at least until my twenty-first birthday. At that time, I may decide to make a lifetime commitment never to drink or use. Or, I may reserve that decision until I have evidence that drinking or using drugs is detrimental or causing me personal problems."

The Big Plan for minors has enormous implications for growth and development. It is quite likely that for adolescents the Abstinence Commitment Effect will far surpass hoped-for outcomes of addiction treatment. When psychosocial treatments are indicated or required, they will be for problems other than substance abuse and will have a much better chance of success.

AVRT with minors will bring forth common adolescent issues such as self-esteem, social acceptance, and sexual and personal identity, but this is part of being a child, and they should be encouraged to see they have what it takes to grow and endure, rather than assume they are congenitally defective or inherently deficient. When problems persist with continued abstinence, or when significant developmental problems are known to exist, continued care is available in a wide variety of settings.

Let's help young people quit their addictions without making them sick. Let's tell them what their grandmothers might tell them: "That's an adult pleasure, and it's not for kids! You'd better decide to stop that altogether, or you'll get into even more trouble. It isn't hard to quit, but when you do, you'll feel strange for a while. But that's okay, because you can take it, and you don't have to do everything you feel like doing. Pretty soon, your mind will be on other things, and you can grow up and enjoy life without all the trouble of being hooked on drugs."

18

AVRT for Gamblers

Family life can be disrupted by behaviors other than drinking and drugging. Although gambling is not an addiction in the sense that drinking and drugging are, AVRT may be applied with similar expectations of success. *Rational Recovery* may be read by a problem gambler and applied by substituting the words *gambling, wagering,* and *betting* for *drinking, drugging,* and *using.*

Gambling is a growing industry in America, spurred by the popularity of state lotteries and Native American interests. For some people, the allure and excitement of gambling overrides their better judgment, resulting in serious damage to their financial security and default on responsibilities to family and creditors.

Rational Recovery does not discourage people from wagering as they please, but offers persistent losers a means to end their gambling careers. Addictive Voice Recognition Technique (AVRT), well known for its success with substance addiction, is also an appropriate means to defeat persistent behavior patterns, including gambling. We sometimes refer to the undesired behavior as "wagering," or "betting," because the word *gambling* has a broader meaning that includes simply taking risks that may have little bearing on the negative outcomes of betting or wagering.

Wagering, for the purpose of AVRT, means placing bets of money or material value on games or events with uncertain outcome, including casino games, private games, state lotteries, raffles, races, sports, or chain letters. Whether skill or chance is involved is not relevant. We may also refer to persons with gambling problems as "losers," because it is most unlikely that people who do well at gambling—those who win, break even, or know how to cut losses—will have the incentive to adopt the stringency of AVRT. Do not be concerned about using this expression, because losers always know that they are losing and always desperately want to do something about it.

It is unnecessary to speculate on why a gambling problem exists in order to cease and desist from betting and wagering. The decision to abstain from wagering may be difficult when substantial debt has accumulated and the promise of jackpot redemption beckons. In recent years, the recovery group movement has convinced many people, including problem gamblers themselves, that habitual losing is a symptom of some inner deficiency, and that in order to quit gambling they must get outside help. Many have become convinced that the "big loser" syndrome has mysterious origins and that persons who lose more than they can afford are not entirely responsible for their financial losses. Several lawsuits brought against casinos by sore losers have failed to convince juries that losers are inherently different from winners and therefore are to be exempted from legitimate debts. Compulsive gambling is widely believed to be a disease that afflicts victims until they hit bottom and admit that they are helpless, asking to be stopped before they lose again. This reflects how much the radical disease/treatment philosophy of the recovery group movement has overtaken traditional American values during the last few decades.

AVRT for losers suggests that some people cannot handle the action of wagering and betting because they get too excited about winning and too upset about losing. Some people become intellectually entangled in gaming strategies that create the illusion of probable success when a high probability of loss actually exists. Very likely, superstitious or magical thinking contributes significantly to the "big loser" syndrome. These and other contributing factors summarily result in gross impairment of judgment that is probably limited to wagering and betting activities and strongly suggest that one abandon those activities in favor of other recreation or other gainful activity.

AVRT for losers focuses on the difficulties of quitting:

1. The promise of easy money has made gambling an activity of great interest and concern for millennia. Wagering is romantic, alluring, exciting, entertaining, and sometimes profitable. The noisy din of casinos and the quietness of formal poker games arouse the desire to wager in many people, not just problem gamblers.
2. Wagering in spite of substantial losses seems to make sense because, according to some calculations of probability, it would seem that one's luck will eventually change for the better. Redoubling bets is a common casino tragedy that is prevented to some degree by casinos' limiting the size of bets. Naturally, the casino also benefits from this protection because whatever is lost by this point cannot be won back with a doubled bet. But other tables are available. . . .
3. Losing often results in self-damnation and a "loser" identity. Jackpot redemption means reclaiming self-respect more than recouping losses; the emotional payoff is larger than the monetary payoff. This helps establish a long-term losing trend that increases both emotional investment as well as financial investment and intensifies loss in both columns.
4. The loser syndrome is often accompanied by the use of alcohol or other drugs. Casinos shrewdly distribute free alcoholic beverages, understanding that betting usually increases along with blood alcohol content. Occasionally, some wagerers may manage their problem by abstaining from alcohol, but most often a plan to refrain permanently from wagering, *planned abstinence,* is the most effective remedy.

5. It is impossible to prohibit anyone from gambling. Strangers on the street can flip for a quarter, children can toss coins in the rest rooms at school, and Ed McMahon will always have his "free" sweepstakes. Social and political changes are bringing us many new gaming establishments, and even the state governments now depend on income from gambling losses. It is important these days to know when, and most importantly *how*, to cut one's losses from wagering and betting.

One particularly harmful misconception is that gamblers are actually chemically dependent and in need of outside help patterned after programs for alcohol and drug addiction. This usually means attending meetings of Gambler's Anonymous, where people talk about their problems and endorse the panacea-like 12-step program of Alcoholics Anonymous. Gamblers, however, are not addicted to a substance, despite the addictive-disease argument that identifies adrenaline or seratonin as the cause of gamblers' problems. As this argument goes, each time a gambler pulls the handle of the slot machine, he or she receives a hit of adrenaline that gives a rush of intense, excited feelings. This kind of sophistry creates the illusions that gamblers are somehow less responsible or less able to quit wagering and that our bodies manufacture illicit substances that are "addictive." This, of course, is nonsense. Anyone can quit betting and wagering for the rest of their lives by deciding to do so and then learn to stick to that decision under all conditions. A Big Plan for problem gamblers is the ultimate way to cut one's losses, build a new financial security, and grow personally by squarely facing life's problems and individual responsibilities.

Knowing When to Run

Successful gambling, according to gambling experts, means limiting wagers to specific amounts, never betting more than one can afford to lose comfortably, understanding the approximate odds of any wager, understanding the rules of the game, and most importantly, according to Kenny Rogers, knowing when to walk away, and knowing when to run. The latter, "knowing when to run," is what AVRT for losers is about. *Running* means running away from all forms of betting and wagering and staying away for the rest of one's life.

A Big Plan to refrain from betting and wagering may be proposed to problem gamblers, and their objections to this idea may be identified as the Addictive Voice. The structural model of addiction has somewhat less relevance, since, unless one is also dependent upon alcohol or drugs, gambling problems do not result from functional impairment caused by the presence of a foreign substance in the body. The Beast concept of AVRT, therefore, is best used in its metaphorical sense, without strong ties to the structural model. The Lapse Reconstruction Sheet (in Chapter 13) may be used with the same caution.

A Big Plan to refrain from betting and wagering should be as specific as possible in order to make compliance as simple and automatic as possible. Various betting or wagering formats should be identified, starting with one's favorite game, whether it be keno or slots, and then all other formats that one has ever played, such as craps, canasta, flipping coins for money, penny-toss, office pools, sports bets, boys'-night-out poker, and so on. It is desirable to acknowledge the fun, excitement, and enjoyment of wagering activities as a prelude to making the Big Plan, so that it is fully understood what is being sacrificed.

Wagering is a way of life for most problem gamblers. The rewards are intense, and the pain of loss compels one to continue the quest for satisfaction. The idea of never wagering or betting again may be extremely threatening, just as with substance addiction. Visions of depression, personal inadequacy, poverty, and unending boredom may accompany the idea of abandoning the tables for good. Wagering becomes transformed from long-odds recreation to a vital source of money and personal gratification, although it is not well suited for either purpose.

Some intelligent participants will undoubtedly point out that making a Big Plan is in itself an enormous wager because it fits our working definition of *wagering* as "placing bets of money or material value on games or events with uncertain outcome." A

Big Plan is a guarantee that there will be no more gambling losses; but there is no guarantee—only a probability—that one's life will improve by abstinence from wagering. By transcending the necessity of winning, by making a single, final bet based on the gambler's finest intuition, problem gamblers may really hit the jackpot and win a more rewarding life.

19

Professionals in the Post-Treatment Era

Substance addiction is a treatable disease.

—The Collective Addictive Voice

AVRT is a prescriptive technique based on the experiences of people who have quit their own addictions without treatment or any other kind of help. Our observation is that defeating an addiction is actually relatively easy compared to the difficulty of remaining addicted and that complete recovery is easily accomplished for most AVRT participants within a matter of months or sooner. We pose no obstacles to people who want to quit for good, encourage them to do just that, and immediately provide them with the necessities for getting the job done.

By reading this book, you may be able to share your understanding of AVRT with your addicted clients, but *Rational Recovery* is not a training manual. For all its simplicity, teaching AVRT requires skills and techniques that go beyond theoretical understanding. AVRT is a protected service mark that describes certain skills possessed by trained AVRTechs. Although you may not offer AVRT as a professional service, you may refer substance-addicted clients to Rational Recovery, in the same way you might refer them for addiction treatment. Before you refer anyone for addiction treatment, give them a chance to quit!

Addiction treatment and the values at the core of the recovery group movement conflict sharply with the values and philosophy of the counseling profession. The counseling professions have traditionally valued independence, self-reliance, self-determination, self-acceptance, confidentiality, and individual differences. In addiction treatment, your client will be required to form a dependent relationship with a virtual stranger and divulge highly confidential information in an unsupervised group setting. Your client will be admonished to relinquish personal responsibility and self-determination in favor of group norms and to practice the 12 steps that focus on immorality, confession, and repentance. Instead of being the active agent in personal growth, your client will learn to expect God to remove character defects. If these are the values you want your client to learn, you might instead consider referring him or her to a pastor or inviting him or her to accompany you to church.

The presence of substance abuse is a major barrier to therapeutic goals you may have for your substance-abusing clients. Sending them for AVRT is *pretreatment*, which can produce the abstinence that is critical to your ongoing work. As your clients become abstinent, you may resume important work on the problems that originally brought them to you. Because addiction treatment requires extensive commitments and is a major medical expense, referral for addiction treatment is tantamount to closing your case for good. AVRT will keep the door of your office open for uninterrupted continuing care.

Very often, addicted people will have to unlearn what they have been taught in their previous programs. They may suffer iatrogenic problems that I have described as *recovery group disorders* and *addiction treatment disorders*. Just as "denial" cancels the self as a viable entity in the struggle against addiction, AVRT cancels addiction treatment as a viable entity in the struggle against addiction.

As throughout the CD (chemical dependency) field, AVRT favors practitioners who have a personal history of addiction, but some without that history have become quite talented in AVRT. They have shown that they are educable and are able to communicate the AVRT format effectively. Most never-addicted professionals, however, have proved to be "ineducable," persisting in the traditional idea that chemically dependent people "cope" with life's problems by escaping into the bottle. Well trained in particular schools of thought, they are unwilling to surrender their credentials and theories at the threshold of addiction, enter that world with an open mind, and listen to those who have been there and recovered on their own.

In your counseling role, you are sensitive to your addicted clients' pain and suffering. Their explanations of why they drink are heartfelt and sincere. They describe emotional problems that appear to be reasons for intoxicating themselves, problems that you are well trained to help them overcome. It is logical to undertake therapy aimed at these problems. You may observe improvements in their feelings and functioning, and they may report that they drink less or use drugs not at all as a result of therapeutic gains. But they will rarely articulate the mentality that underlies their addictions. Because of that, gains are illusory, tainted by the user's underlying plan to return to the pleasure of substance intoxication.

If you are interested in entering the post-treatment era of addiction care, AVRT can help you augment your skills and modify your personal and professional orientations toward addictions. There is a desperate need for efficient, cost-effective addiction care in every community. Individuals, agencies, and hospitals that become licensed Rational Recovery providers may offer AVRT in a variety of formats including AVRT: The Course. Formerly addicted lay persons may also become certified in AVRT.

I have conducted many AVRT sessions over the years. Here, the subject, "Richard," is addicted to alcohol and has trouble with depressed moods. This lengthy transcript will show some common techniques of AVRT instruction and some predictable patterns of learning. The transcript demonstrates a session with a subject.

The Case of Richard

ME: What substance are you having trouble with?

RICHARD: I want to quit drinking.

ME: What stops you from just quitting?

RICHARD: I can't stay away from it. When I quit, I know I will drink sometime later. It's ruining my life, so I want to quit.

ME: If you want to quit, you can. Are you going to drink anymore?

RICHARD: No. I don't want to drink anymore.

ME: Supposing you did want to drink?

RICHARD: That's the problem. I might change my mind. I've quit a thousand times, just like right now, and I'm usually serious about it, but . . .

ME: You quit and then change your mind. Why do you choose to drink when you have decided to quit?

RICHARD: To cope with my bad feelings, like guilt and depression. Boredom, too.

ME: How do you feel about the idea of quitting for good?

RICHARD: Great. That would be wonderful.

ME: Would it? You say you drink to cope with life's problems. You seem to have a very good reason to drink.

RICHARD: Not drinking will prevent more troubles and bad feelings.

Richard's illogic doesn't phase him. As yet, he perceives no contradictions.

ME: But you said you drink to *cope* with problems and bad feelings. Now you say you feel good that you will not drink. You drink to cope with depression, but feel good about giving it up?

RICHARD: No, my drinking *caused* troubles and bad feelings. I will quit and have fewer problems. That feels good.

ME: You must really like to drink, to go through all the trouble you do.

RICHARD: No, I don't like it at all. I hate it.

ME: You hate coping with depression?

RICHARD: I drink to relieve depression, but it doesn't help.

Richard—actually, his Beast—is carefully concealing the pleasure that motivates drinking alcohol. He frames his drinking as if it were medicine for treating problems and depression. He has attended many recovery group meetings where people tell what an awful experience it was to drink and never discuss the real reasons they drank. I will now draw his Beast out so he can recognize it.

ME: What's your favorite drink?

RICHARD: Malt liquor. After a few of those, sometimes I have a few shots of whiskey. That puts me out of it.

ME: What kind of whiskey? *(I mention my own favorite brand here.)*

RICHARD: Old Rhinehard.

ME: Is that a rye whiskey? *A fellow drinker, I'm hooking his Beast. It cannot resist and takes the bait.*

RICHARD: It's a blend, but a better bottle than Kissoff vodka. That Kissoff is death, really bad hangovers.

ME: So you like Rhinehard with some beer. Do you mix Rhinehard?

RICHARD: It goes beautifully with hot coffee.

ME: Probably late in the evening. Ever try that in the morning?

RICHARD: You bet. Hey, you must like to drink yourself.

ME: Part of me does, just like you. So we both know the deep pleasure of drinking. Let me ask you once again, Richard, what is your plan for the future use of alcohol?

It may seem cruel to excite Richard's Beast and then expose it to his critical judgment, but AVRT is a no-holds-barred attack on Richard's addiction—his Beast.

RICHARD: *(He is unable to speak.)*

ME: Why do you drink, Richard?

RICHARD: I guess I drink to feel good.

ME: Do you mean to say you *like* to drink?

RICHARD: I *love* to drink. *(Smiles.)*

This telling smile is part of Richard's Addictive Voice, an expression of the desire for pleasure produced by alcohol. I sometimes call it "the limbic smile," because of its obvious subcortical origins.

ME: This is making more sense, now. You love to drink whether you feel good or bad.

RICHARD: Yes. I love to drink. I drink because I love the way it makes me feel.

ME: This is quite a different statement from saying you drink to cope with depression.

Now, Richard is speaking from his "right mind," telling the truth about alcohol addiction. As yet, he has not acknowledged that never drinking again is actually a terrifying idea. His Beast operates in secrecy, conveying bravado about not drinking, while concealing its covert intention to resume drinking at the earliest moment. It is critical that people who initially report good feelings about the idea of abstinence recognize that there are also concealed negative feelings—ambivalence—about that course of action.

RICHARD: If I continue to drink, it will cause me more problems.

ME: Is that a plan?

RICHARD: No. I really should stop drinking.

ME: Is that a plan?

RICHARD: Well, you don't just decide you won't ever drink again.

ME: Why not?

RICHARD: That's not the way it is. I meant I would never get drunk again.

The Beast has taken control of language here, using sophisticated shifts of phrasing to preserve its freedom to drink. This is a highly developed language skill in addicted people.

ME: How do you feel right now?

RICHARD: Anxious, uptight.

The Beast senses danger. This conversation is not going its way, so I will now address Richard directly in order to help him separate his own perceptions from his Beast's. It helps to imagine that you are talking with two people, attached like Siamese twins, both of whom hear and struggle for control. My role is to teach the underdog how to become top dog.

ME: Does it seem like I'm trying to get you to stop drinking?

RICHARD: Sure does.

ME: How does that feel?

RICHARD: It bothers me. I don't trust you. You are jerking me around.

ME: Richard *(I address him by name)*, it seems like I'm talking to two people. When you sat down, you said you felt very good that you would never drink again, and now you seem to feel very bad about that same idea. Do you see this, too, Richard?

RICHARD: I feel confused about this. It's like you're twisting words.

ME: I have no interest in whether you drink or not. Drinking is a liberty with some risks, and you are free to continue or quit. Either you will drink some more, or you won't. It's entirely up to you, but you could decide to quit for good. People do it all the time, when they've had enough for one lifetime. Part of you likes that idea, but part of you is scared to death of it.

RICHARD: Yes, I feel both ways. I really do want to quit, but I can't think about really doing it. It doesn't seem like me.

ME: How would it be to say there really are two of you? You, Richard, are the one who sincerely wants to quit drinking, once and for all, but this other thing in you that wants to drink, drink, drink, is your Addictive Voice. Does that make sense?

RICHARD: This is really strange, because I have often thought that myself. Like there are two of me, duking it out over drinking. This really helps.

ME: Your Addictive Voice is just an expression of your huge appetite for alcohol. It's part of your animal nature to love pleasure, like a party animal. *(He laughs.)* That's why we sometimes call it the Beast.

RICHARD: I used to call it Louie. It would sit on my shoulder sometimes, listen to my troubles, tell me to drink them away.

All addicted people hear the Addictive Voice, and a good many form a talking relationship with it. Few recognize it, but many externalize it in the form of "shoulder people," imaginary imp-like characters that, perched on one's shoulder, harrass and pester one to drink alcohol.

ME: It's the same with practically everyone who is addicted—a voice that keeps saying, *"Drink."* We move it from your shoulder to inside your head, where it actually resides. (Here I show the structural model of addiction diagram and discuss its workings.)

RICHARD: This helps me understand why I keep it up in spite of the trouble. It makes sense. I thought I had a disease or something.

Very important! He is relieved to feel "normal," and he is ready to move ahead to feel competent.

ME: I actually do not care if you continue to drink. But isn't it interesting that although you have severe problems caused by your habitual drunkenness, you have no plan to stop it?

RICHARD: Well, if you put it that way. I can see how it looks to you, but . . .

ME: How do you feel about the question?

RICHARD: Anxious.

ME: You are feeling your addiction. Addictions often feel anxious.

RICHARD: I thought my addiction was my love for alcohol.

ME: Beasts have feelings, Richard. When you think of quitting for good, you are threatening it with death. Your Beast behaves like an animal in the jungle. It exists only to obtain alcohol, and it will do anything to get it. To the Beast, booze is the equivalent of oxygen or food. It becomes desperate when the supply is threatened. To demonstrate the point, let's try an experiment. Just play with the idea of never drinking any alcohol for the rest of your life, right now. Close your eyes and think of never drinking again. How does that feel?

RICHARD: This is bad. I feel bad, *depressed.*

I am educating Richard on the emotional component of the Addictive Voice, so that he may recognize certain emotions as pertaining only *to the use or nonuse of alcohol.*

ME: Is this a familiar feeling?

RICHARD: Yes. I often drink when I get that feeling.

ME: What does your Beast say when you feel that way?

RICHARD: Life's a bummer. Life sucks. Only one thing matters—being able to drink.

Here is the fork in the road between AVRT and addiction treatment. Trained counselors reflexively lunge at this kind of thinking and delve into why one would conclude that life is meaningless or dissatisfying. They would presume Richard's depression would respond to an opening-up approach, searching for past trauma, disappointment, or conflicts. My advice: Resist temptation. Do not become hooked by your client's Beast, which wants you to believe that he drinks because he is depressed, and that when he resolves his depression he will not drink as much or at all.

ME: Maybe life does suck, and maybe it doesn't, but your Beast will have you drink either way. But I can understand that life does suck when you're strung out on booze half the time. What does your Beast think you should do because life sucks?

RICHARD: Drink. It'll feel better. It does for a while, but then I feel worse.

ME: How depressed do you get?

RICHARD: Real bad. Sometimes I think of killing myself.

ME: And what does your Beast say to do about that?

RICHARD: Same thing. Drink some more.

ME: Dr. Beast says drink, and you take your medicine.

This is the addicto-depressive condition, for which abstinence is the best treatment. If he is medicated, he will continue to drink even though the medication helps. He does not want to feel less depressed, but rather, high.

RICHARD: It works better than Prozac.

ME: Isn't that because Prozac can't do what Old Rhinehard does? *(Here, I smile, hooking his Beast.)*

RICHARD: *(Also smiling.)* There's no substitute.

ME: So your Beast uses depression as a reason to drink. Do you think it really cares if you're depressed?

RICHARD: I doubt it. Maybe that's why I drink on top of the meds.

ME: Maybe?

Listen for qualifiers like "possibly," "maybe," "a little," "I think," and "somewhat" in response to questions pertaining to the use of alcohol and other drugs. These aid the Beast in its haven.

RICHARD: *(He smiles, but this time it is* he, *not his Beast, who smiles.)* For sure. When I drink, I even hear myself thinking, "Who cares if you're depressed if you can drink it away? The pills only get you back to reality, and reality sucks anyhow."

Notice the use of the second-person "you."

ME: That's a major statement, Richard. You have broken through to your Beast. You see how it is controlling you. How does that feel?

RICHARD: Hey, terrific. It does feel good to get that out.

ME: It's not "getting it out" but *recognizing* it that feels good. Can you illustrate how you drink to get rid of depression? Tell me about a time you drank to get rid of depression.

RICHARD: The last time is a good example, when I relapsed and finally ended up here with you. I was out of work, living in an apartment, and had been sober for fourteen months. I felt the depression coming on a month before, and it kept getting worse. I lost my job for being late in the mornings, and then my money got low, and my friends didn't want to be around me, and I didn't want to be around them. I would lie in my room, staring at the TV day after day, and the place got like a pigpen with dishes and garbage all over. I felt so low, depressed, no energy, like I weighed a thousand pounds. I would think about how hopeless life really is, how futile. But I refused to drink.

ME: Sounds like you were thinking of drinking.

RICHARD: Sometimes. Yes, I would think about running down to the liquor store and getting a bottle and downing it in the parking lot. I knew I would feel better, but only temporarily.

ME: Think back carefully, and see if you can recall how you felt at those times you were thinking of drinking.

RICHARD: Depressed. I knew I shouldn't drink. I knew my problems are caused by drinking in the first place, and drinking would only make things worse.

ME: So you are telling me that when you would decide not to drink, you would feel depressed. But I'm asking how you felt at the moment you actually were considering going down to the liquor store and downing a bottle of booze in the parking lot. What feeling did you have when you thought about actually drinking?

RICHARD: Nothing except depression. One time I actually got up and started toward the door, but then I stopped myself. I thought, "No way am I going to do that," and I lay back down, more depressed than before.

The Beast operates in secrecy, and Richard is convinced that (1) he experienced only depressive feelings prior to drinking, and that (2) his reason for drinking was to medicate his depression. Addictive Voice Recognition Technique often requires persistent, patient questioning to expose the fact that alcohol-dependent people drink simply because they love to drink.

ME: Let's backtrack for a second. You had isolated yourself in your apartment and felt depressed. You felt like you weighed a thousand pounds. What happened to the fatigued, heavy feeling when you got to your feet, headed for the liquor store?

RICHARD: *(Pause.)* I guess it faded.

ME: Now think very carefully. Do you remember thinking about getting up from your bed before you actually got up?

RICHARD: Yes. I was thinking about the liquor store and a bottle of Rhinehard. I was thinking about where my wallet was, and I got up to find it.

ME: How did you feel inside, as you got up to look for your wallet?

RICHARD: Oh, I see. I guess I felt better. I forgot about being depressed. Actually, I felt a little excited. *(Smiles.)*

ME: Where is that smile coming from?

RICHARD: *(Stops smiling.)* The Beast?

He knows, but the Beast restricts his answer to a passive question, "The Beast?"

ME: You're asking me? I would also wager that you were smiling as you got up from your bed. Where did your depression go?

RICHARD: Hmm. I see what you mean. For that moment, I didn't really feel depressed. But then I decided I wouldn't drink.

ME: Then, *how did you feel?*

RICHARD: It all came back, only worse. I had to lie down again.

This dialogue demonstrates relapse anxiety. When Richard thinks of drinking, he feels guilty and depressed, but there is a corresponding arousal of energy and excitement. When he thinks of not drinking, he feels fatigued, depressed, forlorn. AVRT will help him to sense the positive feeling of being in control and the hope for a better life through planned abstinence.

ME: You felt much better walking toward the door than you did when you were walking back to the bed. You weren't depressed the entire time before you drank. Then what happened?

RICHARD: I felt hopeless. I thought I may as well be dead. I had suicidal thoughts. I thought about jumping into the river, where the water's real fast—no chance to escape. But I'm terrified of water. So I thought about shooting myself. And then I remembered there is a gun shop a few doors from the liquor store. And I thought about getting a gun and blowing my brains out. I thought about this real seriously. And for a while I thought I would really go ahead and do it. Get rid of myself once and for all. I kept thinking, "Life sucks. Life really sucks. Get it over with. Kill yourself. You may as well be dead."

ME: So did you actually kill yourself?

RICHARD: *(Laughs.)* I guess not.

ME: So what did you do instead of killing yourself?

RICHARD: I went ahead and got up again and went to the liquor store and got the bottle of booze, drank some in the parking lot, and took the rest home and drank the rest of the evening. And I stayed drunk for five weeks, working up from a pint to a liter and a half of whiskey a day. I finally fell on the steps to my apartment, passed out, and the ambulance took me to the hospital, and then I came here to the Rational Recovery Center.

ME: Back up a little. Do you remember getting up from your bed the second time? Did you still feel depressed?

RICHARD: I felt numb more than depressed. I knew if I didn't drink, I would kill myself.

ME: Some Beast you've got.

RICHARD: This is the Beast?

ME: Pure Beast. It was saying, "Drink or die. Get booze or die."

RICHARD: Hey, I didn't hear that.

ME: In effect, that was precisely the message. But here's what you probably did hear, just like thousands of others who think they are medicating depression: "Life is no good. You may as well be dead. Go ahead kill yourself. Use a gun, wreck your car or something. But wait a minute. That's so messy and scary. You don't really have to do *that*. There's something *else* you can do that will help you with your depression, and that is to have a little drink. That is far better than killing yourself. So drink up. It's better than being dead."

RICHARD: That fits me to a tee.

ME: How long have you been doing this?

RICHARD: For about eight years. I saw a psychiatrist who started me on antidepressants three years ago. The pills don't help, so I drink anyhow.

ME: There it is again. You are telling me you drink to relieve depression. Now, let's get back to how you decided to relapse, this time around, and find out if it is really true that you drink to relieve depression. You went back to bed after deciding you wouldn't drink, and you felt much more depressed. You heard your Beast telling you that you may as well be dead, and it even suggested ways for you to kill yourself. Then what?

RICHARD: I got up, and . . .

ME: As you got up, how did you feel? Think back carefully.

RICHARD: Well, I didn't feel too heavy to get up. I guess I was thinking more about drinking than being depressed. But I was still very depressed and scared. I mean, I was suicidal at that point.

ME: **Just because you are thinking of suicide doesn't mean you are suicidal.** Then what did you do?

RICHARD: I got my wallet and keys, and drove to the store, and bought the bottle of Old Rhinehard.

ME: Where was the bottle you wanted?

RICHARD: On the shelf directly behind the cashier.

ME: So you glanced around and spotted it. When you spotted it, how did you feel?

RICHARD: Relieved. Help is at hand.

ME: What happened to your depression?

RICHARD: I knew I was depressed enough to kill myself, and I was glad to see the bottle.

ME: You are saying you felt less depressed when you saw the bottle.

RICHARD: Yes, but as I left the store, I felt really bad. Guilty, because I knew what I was doing was stupid.

ME: So now your depression centered around what a dummy you are instead of how hopeless life is. Right?

RICHARD: Well, I guess.

ME: So your Beast shifted gears as you left the store. Instead of a victim of the cosmos, you became a stupid shit. Then what happened?

RICHARD: I got in the car and drank.

ME: Do you remember opening the bottle?

RICHARD: No. *(Pause.)* Yes. It was still in the bag. I twisted the bag around the neck and unscrewed the cap all in one motion. A piece of the bag tore off and fell to my lap.

ME: Then, what did you think?

RICHARD: "Cheers." *(Pause, and then a sly smile at the corner of his lips.)*

ME: I see you smiling.

RICHARD: *(Avoids eye contact, smile broadens.)*

ME: I think you smiled just before you drank.

RICHARD: I don't remember.

ME: I think you felt like smiling just before taking the first sip. Your smiling right now is the same feeling you had when you opened the bottle, right?

RICHARD: *(Pause.)* Maybe.

ME: This is important for you to know. Maybe this is your chance to recognize your Beast.

RICHARD: Okay. I did smile. I thought, "Cheers," and I felt really excited. I remember.

ME: Now here is the key question. What happened to your depression?

RICHARD: I see what you're driving at. My depression went out the window.

ME: Your depression also went out the window at least twice, back when your Beast got up to go to the store. Your depression faded when your Beast spotted the bottle and when your Beast twisted the cap off. It also said "cheers," only minutes after it told you you may as well kill yourself.

RICHARD: Some Beast I've got. This is weird, I mean, really crazy.

ME: The Beast plays by no rules and will use any warped logic to get alcohol into your blood. Now let me ask you again, and think this thing through. Do you drink to relieve depression?

RICHARD: No. I don't. I get depressed to justify drinking. By the time I take the drink, my depression is entirely gone. I drink because I love to drink. This is amazing, now that I think of it.

ME: You have an addicto-depressive disorder that is not a true depressive illness. Large numbers of addicted people who are not mentally ill are called "dually diagnosed" and given pills for depression. But they drink against advice because the Beast knows that alcohol isn't to treat depression, but to get pleasure. When people discover that their depression is only a well-worn path to the bottle and make a Big Plan, they find that it is hard to take their depression seriously. AVRT can ruin your depression by removing the alcohol payoff for the Beast. Supposing you had a Big Plan and knew that you would *never* drink again.

RICHARD: Wow. That's a tough one.

ME: Go ahead and experiment with this idea. See how it *feels*.

The Beast has no conception or perception of time and only understands the concepts of "now" and "never." "No" only means "later," no matter how much later, and "later" means "Anytime I feel like it." The Beast will threaten a life of hell while promising heaven on earth. In the addicto-depressive disorder, the Beast resists a Big Plan by promising hellish depression under which one must yield in order to escape death by suicide. Therefore, making a Big Plan arouses fears akin to facing imminent death. The fear of its own death, of course, is the Beast's great fear, rather than the death of the person.

RICHARD: *(Pause.)* This is scary. How do I know I won't kill myself?

ME: Do you want to kill yourself?

RICHARD: No.

ME: So a better question might be, "How long are you willing to feel intense depression before you cave in and drink?"

RICHARD: Well, my depression is pretty bad.

ME: Is it intolerable?

RICHARD: Well, no.

ME: So, how long are you willing to tolerate it to smoke out your Beast?

RICHARD: *(Pause, anxiety-laden body language.)* As long as it takes, I guess.

ME: How does that feel?

RICHARD: Good. *(He becomes tearful, cries for a minute or so.)*

Although strong emotions often accompany the insights into the workings of the Beast, this is not always so. Others may work through to a solid Big Plan with much less emotional turmoil. But these emotional experiences are clear clinical signs to watch for in AVRT.

ME: I know it feels good. You are defeating the greatest enemy you will ever face. It has ruined most of what you love, and it won't give up until you're dead. But now you've got its number, and you are on top of your addiction. You have seen the enemy, how it operates, and you recognize its ruthlessness, its persistence, its cleverness, and its secretiveness. But you've also seen that your Beast is weaker than you, less intelligent, and you understand that it must appeal to you to get what it wants. When it is exposed it is destroyed, and it collapses under a Big Plan.

RICHARD: This thing—this Beast—has been working me like that for years. Now I know what's going on in my head and why I've continued to relapse. I really think it's over, coming to a rapid end. I won't be drinking anymore no matter how I feel. And just knowing that is a good feeling in itself, a feeling that replaces my depression. This is good stuff. This is the first time I've felt like I'm really in recovery and getting better. I can feel it all over.

ME: Can you imagine what your life might be like without drinking?

RICHARD: It's hard to imagine not drinking, like it's impossible.

ME: I'm hearing your Beast, loud and clear. The sound of your voice right now is the sound of your Addictive Voice.

RICHARD: I see. It says, "It can't be any other way," so I'm powerless to change.

ME: That's it. You just recognized your Addictive Voice again.

You've heard it for a long time, but now you are *recognizing* it. Is it speaking the truth?

RICHARD: No. I probably can stop drinking if I decide to do it.

ME: Probably?

RICHARD: Okay, I know I can. It's simple. I just won't drink anymore.

Fine. So what's your plan?

RICHARD: You keep asking that question. I can't seem to answer it.

ME: I hear your Beast saying, "You can't answer that question. It's a stupid question."

RICHARD: Um-hmm.

ME: How do you feel?

RICHARD: Irritated.

ME: What is your Beast angry about?

RICHARD: I don't like these questions. You're messing with my head.

ME: What do you feel like doing?

RICHARD: Something else. I'll think this over.

ME: Your Beast is getting desperate. It wants to run.

RICHARD: I feel uptight.

ME: *It* feels uptight! But you are choosing to remain seated, even though it wants you to get the hell out of here. Do you see, it's like there are two of you. There are two parties to your addiction—the Beast that wants to keep drinking, and the person who wants to get better.

RICHARD: I'm starting to see. I am of two minds about it. This is a real struggle.

ME: I know. It's tough. But if you follow the simple logic of AVRT, like we are right now, and decide to put up with some tough feelings, you can get your addiction behind you and live a normal, happy life. Do you want to go on?

RICHARD: *(Pause.)* Yes.

ME: Your Beast wanted you to say no.

RICHARD: Yes, it did.

ME: How does that feel, to say, "It feels uptight and wants to get the hell out of here?"

RICHARD: Better. Like I'm in control again.

ME: So what's your plan?

RICHARD: Quit—pretty much forever.

ME: Where did "pretty much" come from?

RICHARD: My Beast? No, I'm not asking. It *was* my Beast.

ME: You got it again. This is very typical of the Beast. It plays word games, like getting you to say, "pretty much forever," which means absolutely nothing. Look, can you think of "never"?

RICHARD: That's irrational. I can make that choice when the time comes.

ME: What time?

RICHARD: Anytime I feel like drinking.

ME: Why not decide now?

RICHARD: I can't predict the future. How can I know for sure?

ME: You can't, but why can't you make a plan for lifetime abstinence?

RICHARD: I might fail.

ME: So what?

RICHARD: I'd feel terrible about myself, like a complete failure.

Here is another fork between AVRT and counseling. We could explore Richard's guilt complex and possibly help him to become more self-accepting, but that would play into his Beast's agenda, which is to talk about anything *rather than a plan to quit drinking for good.*

ME: Are you aware that your fear of feeling guilty is based on the prediction that you will drink? Is this really a reason *not* to quit?

RICHARD: Now that I think of it, it is more of a reason to quit absolutely for good. That way I won't have the downfall I am afraid will happen.

ME: You're catching on to AVRT logic, which is potent stuff. Instead of cowering to the Beast you are confronting it, tit for tat, matching its every move. "Never" scares it to death, Richard, and your Beast wouldn't be scared if it didn't know full well that you are capable of succeeding.

RICHARD: Yeah. That's crazy, isn't it?

ME: Recognizing that means you sure aren't crazy. Think about the idea of never drinking again. How does it feel?

RICHARD: Sad.

ME: What do you feel like doing?

RICHARD: Crying. *(Tears well up.)*

ME: Where are the tears coming from?

RICHARD: *(Snaps out of it.)* Is my Beast crying? That's it. It's upset and crying!

ME: How do you feel?

RICHARD: Pissed at it. That son of a bitch has practically ruined my life. Now it's crying like a baby when I threaten to cut off its alcohol.

ME: What do you feel like doing?

RICHARD: Killing it.

ME: Sounds reasonable, since it is a deadly enemy. How can you kill it?

RICHARD: Cut off all the booze, forever.

ME: We know your Beast can't imagine life without drinking. But can you think of how your life might be if you didn't drink?

RICHARD: I would be myself. I would get a better job, maybe start school, maybe marry someone.

ME: How does it feel to think of that?

RICHARD: It's a good feeling, more than I should really hope for.

ME: I hear both of you. You have hope; your Beast hates it when you have hope for a better life by not drinking. Trust your feelings, Richard. Hope is very important.

It helps to draw out the contrast between the hopes of the Beast, which are for drinking in many situations, and the hope of the self for authentic pleasures and fulfillment. When this is clear, a Big Plan is more realistic.

ME: So what is your plan for the future use of alcohol?

RICHARD: I will never drink again.

ME: How do you know?

RICHARD: I don't know, but I know what I'm dealing with now, and I can recognize what my Beast is. I recognize its feelings, and I'm ready to do whatever is required to defeat it. *(Looks puzzled.)*

ME: *How do you feel?*

RICHARD: I can't express it. Something is changed inside me, and it seems that for the first time I know what's going on in my head. I feel something deep, like there's real hope for me. I feel like I'm in control but not in control. I'm getting goose pimples.

ME: This is a very important breakthrough, and it is understandable that you have these feelings. AVRT affects many others the same way, and now you're having some good feelings for a change. *Trust your feelings.*

RICHARD: I could cry. *(Tears.)* I am crying. I know what I'm crying about.

ME: What are your tears saying?

RICHARD: Like I'm getting my life back. I can see that I will be able to win, no, that I am winning. I know there are two things I won't do. I won't kill myself, and I will never drink again. It's like I'm getting my self back, the person I used to be when I believed in myself. It's a relief, a release from something. That's why I'm crying. It's good. Very good.

ME: I can understand how you feel. Congratulations.

This emotional display is the Abstinence Commitment Effect (ACE), a common, predictable experience in AVRT. The ACE experience signifies a significant breakthrough. The ACE experience is not to be interpreted as false hope, a pink cloud, a flight into health, or superficial confidence, because it is a pivotal experience for future AVRT.

20

The Politics of Recovery

In the last decade, I have devoted my full time to two activities—creating a discipline for independent recovery from substance addictions, and facing off against the 12-step recovery community. To me, both activities blend into one because it is impossible for me to speak to a chemically dependent person without addressing the social context of the problem. I have gained a well-earned reputation as a foremost detractor of the 12-step program, as well as an unearned reputation as an angry contrarian. So be it.

I have seen some rewarding results from this work, particularly the response of addicted people to AVRT and the growth of the Rational Recovery Self-Help Network. We have entered the commercial mainstream by establishing Rational Recovery Centers that can compete on critical economic turf. Mass addiction, however, continues to plague our society, fed by a politicized social movement dedicated to the proposition that we are all created diseased and in need of a Good Program. In spite of widespread abuses and improprieties that directly affect a large segment of society, Rational Recovery remains the only voice directly opposing the recovery group movement.

I have pointed out that AA is an ancient ruse in modern

guise, and that it has the ability to mutate into any form that opportunity or its survival dictates. The recovery group movement delivers a potent, transforming experience that profoundly affects participants and their families. Like a chain letter, the recovery group movement spreads itself to every receptive being it can reach and then uses that niche to advance to others. It expands for its own sake, becoming an end in itself for its adherents.

I never expected my stand against the recovery group movement to be popular. Indeed, the movement flourishes on popular good will gained by plucking the heartstrings of mainstream America. But more than that, the recovery group movement banks on the acquiescence of a large majority who look askance upon it rather than speak out against it. By *looking askance,* I refer to the intuitive first impression most people get when they observe recovery group movement concepts and activities. By acquiescence, I refer to the way people *accept* the explanations and justifications for what is going on. People who see through the 12-step philosophy often assume that the benefits of 12-step activities to some people probably outweigh its drawbacks for others. To speak out against a highly visible movement based on God, sincerity, and altruism might make one appear insensitive, ghoulish, uninformed, or, heaven forbid, angry. The sum effect is that the end has come to justify the means—the oldest, most repeated, and most tragic error in human affairs. Unfortunately, the beneficial "end" is far from what it appears to be, and the means is corrosive to American society.

It is difficult for people to believe that the recovery group movement poses a problem of any kind. Newspapers are entirely uninterested in the fact that a secret society has infiltrated the government—that billions of tax dollars are released into an industry created by and staffed almost entirely by members of Alcoholics Anonymous. Elected officials, finger-to-the-wind, ignore complaints from citizens on institutional AA, and the American Civil Liberties Union gives low priority to known instances of 12-step incarceration and other widespread systematic violations of the First, Fifth, Eighth, and Fourteenth Amendments of the U.S. Constitution. Even conservatives in the Republican Party believe that prescribing religion for addicted people makes sense, and they have difficulty seeing that AA's 12-step program is causing the problem they are mandated to stamp out.

Despite its eloquent defenses, in spite of its size, and in spite of its use of social authority to intimidate the vulnerable and the heretic, institutional AA is easily taken down. It cannot stand to be called what it is—to be exposed as a manipulative mind-set, a bullying mentality. The 12-step program, with origins in religious fundamentalism, cannot coexist with other forms of addiction recovery. It loses in every debate because it is largely a set of slogans, mottoes, and overlearned explanations supporting articles of faith. So it carefully avoids controversy and debate.

Few people will see the underside of addiction treatment unless they are directly involved. Fewer still are those who will talk about it. Rational Recovery has become an organization people often call when they become entangled with the addiction treatment system. Their stories will bring much-needed change to the field of addictions.

The American Treatment Tragedy

In *Webster's Collegiate Dictionary*, the word *treat* is defined as meaning "to care for or deal with medically or surgically" and "to regard and deal with in a specified manner." The word *treatment* is then defined as "the act or manner of treating someone," and "the techniques or actions customarily applied in a specified situation."

According to these definitions, "treatment" might just as accurately describe AVRT. Indeed, insurance companies pay for health education, and many health insurers will happily pay for AVRT "treatment," knowing that it is educational and recognizing its abstinence outcome.

But the prevailing concept of addiction treatment is the first and most obvious one listed in *Webster's Dictionary*, "to care for . . . medically or surgically." From the medical/disease model, "treatment" has seeped into the other health professions and finally into subprofessional enclaves.

There is a pecking order among the professions, with medicine on top holding the most power and prestige and receiving the most compensation. Several others (nursing, social work, psychology, and some others) are subordinate to medicine in power, prestige, and compensation and vie for second, third, and lower ranks on the ladder. As a way to gain credibility, each of them has formed a trade guild around special knowledge and training, and in recent years each of them has emulated medicine as one way to enhance professional status.

When I was in graduate school, I did not hear the word *treatment* used to describe my activities. "Treatment" was the exclusive domain of physicians. I was being trained in a method called social casework, in which I would provide individual counseling, family therapy, and group psychotherapy. A few years later, my counseling and casework came to be called treatment, and my casework plan became a treatment plan. I felt a little odd, borrowing so conspicuously from medical traditions. I had a nagging suspicion that I was misrepresenting my counseling by calling it treatment, because it sounded so medical and conveyed that my clients were sick instead of troubled. I got over this before long, however, when my wife, Lois, an English teacher, came home from work and told me she would soon be expected to do "clinical teaching." We laughed, and she joked about wearing a stethoscope during class and requesting that desks be replaced with gurneys.

Clinical teaching, however, is now taken very seriously by school administrations who insist that the classroom is like a clinic, structured around psychological principles and learning theory, where teachers diagnose educational deficiencies and prescribe sterile remedies according to an individual educational plan. The quest for status—and funding—has led to progressive medicalization of human services in America and has spawned practices that offend common sense, produce little, and very often create new problems worse than the original.

The addiction treatment field is an example of an enclave of *laypersons* who unified and endowed themselves with "professional" status as "chemical dependency counselors," "substance abuse counselors," and "drug and alcohol abuse counselors." This began in the 1970s when people having no qualifications other than working a good 12-step program began certifying themselves as experts.

Few professionals of that time objected that a new group was making an exlcusive claim on an unattractive clientele, probably because substance abusers often have little money and don't respond well to professional services, anyhow. Since then, however, substance abuse counselors have made a deliberate attempt to restrict options available to addicted people through a certification program that amounts to a guild. More recently they have gained academic status by creating university departments where they promulgate disease-treatment concepts without rigorous outside scrutiny. These self-credentialed experts have since convinced many state legislatures to accept that (1) the hypothesis that addiction is a disease is a fact, (2) this hypothetical disease can be "treated," (3) addiction treatment is a highly specialized form of counseling that falls outside existing curricula, (4) addicted persons are entitled to addiction treatment provided only by persons trained and certified in the specialized methods, (5) persons and organizations that help addicted people to quit drinking or using drugs are providing treatment, (6) treatment must be licensed and subject to state-imposed regulations, and (7) persons not trained and certified in the treatment of the disease of addiction are breaking the law or are not qualified for employment working with addicted persons—in effect, practicing medicine without a license. Consequently, every organization that helps people with their addictions is under considerable pressure to offer services that are congruent with the concepts of the 12-step program of AA.

Addiction care today can be viewed as a political outcome of social unrest of the 1960s and early 1970s. The Vietnam war was over, the hippies had retreated or gotten jobs, and the flower children had gone to seed with New Age spirituality and a proclivity for self-involvement. AA, still on the fringes as a voluntary, self-supporting fellowship, became home for idealistic, chemically dependent young adults with a vision to change the world to their liking. Support groups proliferated, and soon AA became a front-burner item in communities around the land. The message of the 12 steps was heard in high places, and increasing numbers of health professionals, civil servants, and elected officials found that AA helped with their own substance addictions. It seemed a healthy enough trend, away from drugs, toward human interaction, growth, and spirituality. I believe that during those years AA was a positive force in American society.

But then something happened that would change America's destiny. In the early 1980s, Congress passed legislation cutting community mental health services to the bone, followed by substantial federal block grants for addiction treatment to fight the much-hyped epidemic of addictive disease. Mentally unstable clients of mental health centers were set adrift, to be caught in the safety net of volunteerism and now identified as alcoholics and addicts. Suddenly government social service programs were in bed with, and financially dependent upon, the recovery group movement. The event that would create the American addiction tragedy was the passage of laws requiring states to require insurance companies to pay for services called "addiction treatment."

No treatment existed, of course, but throughout America the 12 steps became the twelve rungs of a career ladder that began in church basements and ended as state director of drug and alcohol services. Although money created a demand for something that didn't exist, the 12-step program literally moved in to fill the well-funded, imagined need. Wings of hospitals throughout the land were converted for use by AA professionals, and tens of thousands of addiction treatment programs sprouted wherever federal dollars fell. American had turned its problems over to an unknown power, one that now influences social policy on all levels. Common sense and wisdom were lost in a cacophony of victimhood spawned by the recovery group movement.

Who, even twenty years ago, would have sued a restaurant after spilling coffee on oneself? Who, then, would have believed that tens of thousands of young and not-so-young women—and men—would "recall" terrors at the hands of Satanists who conducted rituals of torture, sexual depravity, and baby-eating? Could anyone twenty years ago have believed that the courts of the land would assume that these stories merited the dignity of due process?

A lynch mentality developed in the 1980s when federal funds

were released for child abuse investigation. This energized a cadre of militant professionals on the fringe of the recovery group movement who created a new specialty, recovered memory therapy, which combined the grisly stress syndrome of military combat, post-traumatic stress disorder, with Freudian concepts of repression and denial. The resulting hybrid launched an activist campaign unmatched since the Salem witch trials. Laws were passed allowing adults with decades-delayed recollections of memories of sexual abuse to prosecute their parents. Divorce courts were transformed into arenas of conflict enlivened by estranged spouses waging nuclear war with accusations of child molestation. The assumption of childhood sexual abuse was applied indiscriminately, and many who could recall no such problem were told that they were "in denial," suffering post-traumatic stress disorder, and in need of intensive, expensive care. "Truth serums" were administered in hospital settings to "enhance memory recall," and people entering 12-step addiction treatment began learning that they must have been sexually abused by their parents, otherwise they would not be troubled. Victim-support groups such as Adult Children of Alcoholics, Codependents Anonymous, and Incest Survivors Anonymous, guided from the fringe by professional therapists, proliferated and found many receptive members who could pin their adult troubles on suddenly remembered memories of childhood trauma. Celebrities broadcast their own victimhood and talk show hosts found guest victims with tales dramatic or bizarre enough to compete in the short-attention-span theater of television. Other public figures became the accused—always treatment-bound. Our government, energized by a new, exciting opportunity for social engineering, took victims of sexual harassment into a long—much too long—embrace, and wrote new, politically correct regulations governing American sexual conduct and referring victims and perpetrators alike for treatment of their symptoms.

The molestation craze has subsided somewhat since the falsely accused have gone to bat for the newly accused. The False Memory Syndrome Foundation, an association of accused families, joined with respected scholars and clinicians to create a scientific and legal foundation to strike back against ignorance, intimidation, and injustice. They exposed a society-wide cadre of poorly educated charlatans, with strong ties to the recovery group movement, who systematically incited memories of abuse among suggestible, often troubled, individuals. Thousands of families, destroyed by false accusations of incest and satanic ritual abuse, came forth with the same stories of persecution, prosecution, and conviction by juries blown aloft by the furious winds of molestation mania.

The winds have mercifully changed, and complaints of recovered memories of childhood sexual abuse are now being considered more objectively and in the light of common sense. Suits against accusers and their therapists are bringing belated justice, and just as in the Salem witch-hunt, recantations are pouring in from former accusers who are mortified that they were sucked into the bad dreams of their dirty-minded therapists. Juries may be getting the message that victimhood is no excuse, such as with the recent conviction of the Menendez brothers, whose attorneys argued that because the boys were molested they were justified in blasting their parents with a shotgun a decade later. The second (some say third, including the McCarthy hysteria of the 1950s) American witch-hunt may be winding down, but the victim-of-disease mentality continues as an enticement to those who are substance addicted or have other behavioral problems.

The recovery group movement, however, remains an engine of disturbance. It still incites a ripping undercurrent of disease-victim sentiment across the land. At the time of this writing, an excited media is announcing a new, previously undetected, widespread disease, attention deficit disorder (ADD), that explains the daily-living problems experienced by vast multitudes of victims. Professionals speaking in refined scientific language tell about how people suffer needlessly from it and what may be done to help them. Getting help to see if you or someone you love has attention deficit disorder involves reading books, seeing a professional who specializes in it, and going to a free support group that you can find by calling an 800 number. If you go to a support group for people suffering from a vague, newly discovered malady, one for which no laboratory protocol exists, your chances of "having it" are extraordinarily high. If you don't keep coming back, you'd better watch out.

Stepping on America

Beginning conspicuously with the drunk-driver diversion program, courts have expanded the role of forced 12-step treatment for a wider range of offenders. Addiction treatment funding is now attached to grants for corrections and law enforcement, in spite of the lack of evidence that treatment works. Schools promote the disease concept as fact without a balancing viewpoint, such as with the creationism-evolution issue. The Social Security Disability program pays people to remain addicted but justifies this by requiring intermittent, expensive, unwanted treatment, in order for one to remain "entitled" to benefits. The Americans with Disabilities Act prevents appropriate disciplinary action against substance abusers and requires employers to pay for treatment. The federal bureaucracy might do better to allow chemical dependency to be the unattractive lifestyle it is, rather than one protected by law, by victimhood status, by politically correct euphemisms, and by entitlement programs.

Employees with alcohol problems are required to attend 12-step meetings as a condition of employment. Often, parents are denied custody of their children unless they participate in 12-step meetings. Servicemen may be discharged from the military for refusing AA participation. Professional people are forced to participate in 12-step meetings and very expensive addiction treatment programs under intimidation of losing their licenses, and applicants for organ transplant are increasingly required to attend AA meetings to qualify to receive a vital organ. In all of these examples, abstinence is the desired and reasonably expected outcome, yet services called "addiction treatment" do not typically result in secure abstinence.

Twelve-Step Incarceration in America

Many people are imprisoned or refused parole because they conscientiously object to the 12-step philosophy and refuse to attend 12-step meetings. One woman, convicted of drunk driving in 1994, writes occasionally to the Rational Recovery office. She has chosen to serve her full sentence of several years in an Arizona prison rather than submit to 12-step participation in prison. AA is offered as a "voluntary" program, even though the group meetings are coordinated by prison staff and attendance is counted favorably toward early release on parole. She could have been released on parole long ago by pretending to be interested in the 12-step program. Indeed, insiders often say, "Fake it 'til you make it."

This woman did attend some meetings at first, but decided that the content went against her religious beliefs. She believed that she was responsible for quitting her addiction and that it would be inappropriate for her to shift responsibility for lifetime abstinence to God or any other Higher Power. She also wanted to avoid social entanglements with ex-convicts and substance abusers following release from prison and objected to being inducted into the 12-step fellowship while in prison. She was portrayed as angry and resistant, although her letters to Rational Recovery reflect sincerity and a commitment to permanent abstinence that exceeds expectations in any 12-step program. Oddly, neither the sentencing judge nor any prison personnel have ever asked her what her plan is for the future use of alcohol or drugs. Instead, it is assumed that she is *not responsible* to make and hold to any decision to abstain. By refusing treatment, she was classified as "high risk" and in need of more severe punishment. Drunk driver diversion programs nationwide are based on similar concepts of "treatment as punishment." Proponents of 12-step incarceration cite meager statistics in support of this unconstitutional, counterproductive approach to highway safety. We still hear from her, and her letters have become a regular feature in *The Journal of Rational Recovery.*

Twelve-step incarceration has become common in the United States, yet there is little outcry that our society is taking on the characteristics of theocratic and totalitarian regimes we have traditionally held in contempt.

For example, I recently spotted on the Internet a list of bills before the 104th Congress. At the top of the list was SB 171, the

Medicaid Substance Abuse Treatment Act, introduced by Senators Daschle, Simon, Kennedy, Kerrey, Reid, and Akaka. It authorized continued funding of addiction treatment as a condition of Medicaid benefits, which amounts for forced 12-step participation. The bill generously guarantees "an *opportunity* for exposure to Alcoholics Anonymous and Narcotics Anonymous." I do not know if the senators introducing or voting on this bill have any concept of what they are perpetrating upon the public, if they understand what "exposure to AA" is really like, if they know how abysmally unsuccessful the 12-step program is at achieving the objective of abstinence, or if they are themselves members of AA. I also do not know how long AA has been written into the law of the land in this top-level, blatantly unconstitutional fashion. But I am aware that AA meetings for members of Congress are held under the Capitol Dome every morning and that some judges in our highest courts are members of Alcoholics Anonymous.

A Humble Program of Coercion

The recovery group movement is rapidly making 12-step participation *a precondition for health care.* During the last week of 1995, Lois received two calls for help, one from Texas and one from Ohio, from people who are being required to attend AA meetings. These two particular calls stood apart from the usual 12-step abuses because both callers were suffering from terminal liver disease. To be considered for organ transplant, they must join an AA group, identify their sponsor, and report that they are attending at least four meetings per week—whether they want to or not.

Before one liver candidate died, I spoke with his family. They said he was fatigued due to medical complication of liver disease and was spending nearly all of his energy on the meeting attendance routine. His initial outrage at being inducted into AA as his life was slipping away gradually disappeared. He became depressed and died.

The other AA inductee is doing better medically but nevertheless headed rapidly toward a crisis requiring organ transplant.

A physician who is more sensitive to alcohol than others, he writes a regular column using a pseudonym called "Dr. X-Ray's Recovery Chronicles" for *The Journal of Rational Recovery*. His indomitable wit and humor under oppressive conditions delight thousands of readers. Dr. X-Ray describes his mandatory AA experiences in graphic detail, including the political intrigue surrounding his Big Plan. He describes the counselors and group leaders as familiar stereotypes easily recognizable to anyone who has been subjected to involuntary 12-step indoctrination. One priceless quote from Dr. X-Ray goes, "I told him (the group leader) the truth, that I am a teetotaler, that I never drink, and that I never will again. That *really* gets them!" The reader soon realizes that the writer is risking the death penalty for resisting the insipid teachings of his captors.

These American citizens, both in midlife, with families and successful careers, developed terminal liver disease—yes, they both drank excessively—and faced the excruciating choice between AA and death. Prior to the rise of the recovery group movement, people faced simpler decisions, such as between quitting drinking and dying of liver failure. Then as now, many summarily quit drinking in order to extend their lives. Today, that heritage of human competency has been forgotten. Heavy drinkers are presumed to be powerless to abstain from alcohol, unfit for organ transplant—unless, of course, they seek privilege by joining AA.

What's the Big Deal?

From a practical viewpoint, one might ask, "So what's the big deal if an organ consignment committee tries to make the very best use of precious human tissues? At least AA is an answer to alcoholism, and we don't want to waste a precious liver on someone who will continue drinking."

This line of thinking is riddled with problems too numerous and too complex to address here in full. Some salient points are:

1. AA doesn't work! Abstinence rates for people in the recovery group movement are astonishingly low, under 10%.

2. AA is intensely religious. It is a violation of the U.S. Constitution and subsequent civil rights law to discriminate against someone on the basis of religion.
3. AA activity *forbids* their participants from permanently quitting their addictions. No reasonable person would object to being taught how to quit drinking if that was wanted.
4. Only those willing to die for certain principles of freedom will object to forced AA membership. The hideous implications of reserving health care for members of Alcoholics Anonymous cannot be whitewashed with talk about "proper motivation," "noncompliant attitudes," and "reasoned distribution of scarce tissues."

How Could This Happen in America?

Not long ago I half-joked to an audience, "Knowing what I know about the nature of the 12-step movement, it won't be long before organ transplants will be reserved for AA members."

I was only half-joking, because I know "how it works." Few people, if any, sit as I do—in a position to hear daily from the "constitutionally incapables" who do not fit the rigors of AA discipline. Indeed, it appears that very few *are* capable of fitting the 12-step mold. Lately, not fitting the 12-step mold can be a dangerous limitation.

Anyone who doubts the intent of the American recovery group movement or is puzzled about its routine use of intimidation to gain new members may find out most of what they want to know by reading its two chief references, *The Big Book* and *Twelve Steps and Twelve Traditions,* the former published just prior to World War II and the latter published the year after. Here is a sampling from *Twelve Steps,* which may illuminate the phenomenon that has overtaken America:

> Tradition One: Our *common* welfare should come first; personal recovery depends upon AA unity.

The unity of AA is the most cherished quality *our society* has. Our lives, the lives of all to come, depend squarely on

> it. Without unity, AA dies. The AA *has to* conform to the principles of recovery. *His life actually depends upon obedience to spiritual principles. If he deviates too far, the penalty is sure and swift; he sickens and dies. At first, he goes along because he must, but later he discovers a way of life he really wants to live.* Moreover, he finds he cannot keep this priceless gift unless he gives it away. Neither he nor anybody else can survive unless he carries the 12-step message. Most individuals find that they cannot recover without an AA group. Realization dawns that he is but a small part of a great whole; that *no personal sacrifice is too great for the preservation of the fellowship.* He learns that the clamor and ambitions within him must be silenced whenever these could damage the group. It becomes plain that *the group must survive if he is to survive.* [emphasis added]

Therein lies a serious problem: People in AA place a greater value on their program than upon those who come seeking help. It is only a short step from there to representing the 12-step program as infallible and universal and then predicting that people who do not accept the program, or who object to it, will naturally come to a bad end. For many years, this has been happening at practically every meeting. This is no innocent support group. It is a hard-core, secret society of zealots. Their brash, grandiose confidence in the program, embedded in disarming rhetoric, has directly affected public administrators who must solve vexing problems in an expedient, socially acceptable way. Here is more dreaming by the early architects of AA:

> Here are some of the things we dreamed. *Hospitals don't like alcoholics,* so we thought *we'd build a hospital chain of our own.* People needed to be told what alcoholism was, so we'd educate the public, *even rewrite school and medical textbooks.* We'd gather up derelicts from skid rows, sort out those who could get well, and make it possible for the rest to earn their livelihoods in a kind of *quarantined confinement.* Maybe *those places would make large sums of money* to carry on our other good works. *We seriously thought of rewriting the laws of the*

> *land,* and have it declared that *alcoholics are sick people.* No more would they be jailed; *judges would parole them into our custody.* We'd spill AA into the dark regions of dope addiction and criminality. We'd form groups of depressive and paranoid folks, the deeper the neurosis the better we'd like it. It stood to reason that *if alcholism could be licked, so could any problem.* It occurred to us that *we could take what we had into the factories* and cause laborers and capitalists to love each other. Our uncompromising honesty might soon *clean up politics.* With one arm around the shoulder of *religion* and the other around *medicine,* we'd resolve their differences. Having learned to live so happily, we'd show everybody else how. We thought our society of Alcoholics Anonymous might be *the spearhead of a new spiritual advance! We might transform the world.* [Emphasis added.]

This paragraph is under Tradition Six: "An AA group ought never endorse, finance, or lend the AA name to any related facility or outside enterprise, lest problems of money, property, and prestige divert us from our primary purpose." Tradition Six is lost in the tens of thousands of hospitals and addiction treatment centers that are based solely and rigidly upon the 12 steps, with staffs entirely made up of AA members trained in 12-step counseling methods. Those who would compete ideologically or economically with the 12-step community are intimidated by economic reprisal or regulatory interference.

The dreams above were listed ostensibly as examples of unreasonable optimism. The fact that they were even listed, and when listed not denounced, is open to interpretation, but *each one of the dreams of the early AAers has come true,* and the scope of the movement's ambition has soared beyond those initial dreams. Medical textbooks have been rewritten around the myth of addictive disease and its treatment, which is quarantined consignment to AA. The laws of the land have been rewritten, and not only are alcoholics considered sick people, but they cannot be fired because of their disability. AA has cleaned up on politics and has powerful lobbies for the nonprofit treatment industry.

There has been a spiritual movement, and other countries are also turning it over to the American-made Higher Power.

Very recently I spoke to a group of addiction treatment specialists who work with impaired professionals. They were aghast that I would recommend a simple prescription of abstinence in lieu of mandated 12-step indoctrination and asserted that alcoholism is a disease that must be aggressively treated if people are to function adequately. Sparks flew in the meeting room, and afterward one disgruntled medical doctor approached me and said, "What will you have to say when the human genome is unraveled? You know that's coming." He was referring to the rapid advances in genetic research that will soon unlock the genetic code for the human organism, including a marker for the disposition to drink excessively. He seemed jubilant that a blood test might identify people at risk. I answered that science can be used for good or bad ends, and I hope the day will never come when a child can be diagnosed alcoholic before the first drink and anyone can be funneled into the AA fellowship based on a blood test.

Coerced 12-step participation in the workplace is becoming more common, particularly in the managed health care industry. Hospitals suffering from recent cutbacks in health care funding by managed care organizations present employees with management-supported spiritual indoctrinations aimed at absorbing legitimate complaints that would ordinarily come to union attention, creating a climate of emotional dependency upon management.

The recovery group movement expansion into the workplace includes problems unrelated to substance abuse. As reforms in health care continue, the suspicious, recently coined expression "behavioral health" is gaining widespread use. What is the opposite of behavioral health? You got it: behavioral disease. And the treatment for behavioral disease? Right again.

In the San Francisco Bay Area, managed care cutbacks are accompanied by support groups for nurses under stress from increased workloads. The support groups are by no means spontaneous, but programs focused on sensitivity, spiritual awareness, and "getting it together." In my own area, physicians and employees have been required to attend a hospital staff development program offered by management. In less than two years, about $1.5 million has been spent on a psychologist guru who conducts intensive training sessions. As usual, the required program is "voluntary," but the consequences of not participating include job discrimination and economic reprisal. The program's newsletter carries testimonials on how the program changed employees' lives and provided a spiritual awareness they can take to patients, particularly in wards where death is imminent. "A program to die for," gushed one nurse initiate. But some who complained that the management-sponsored program was cult-like were suddenly without jobs.

A medical-legal behemoth has emerged that affects every social and business organization in the nation, with ever-constricting regulations on liberty and civil rights. In my opinion, America is at peril of losing its heritage as a result of a chain of unfortunate circumstances and unintended consequences.

The Place to Call

Rational Recovery is known as the place to call by people who have been harmed, mistreated, or had their rights violated by forced AA attendance or while receiving addiction treatment. RRS, Inc., a small family-held business, has tried to help those people in a number of ways, including AVRT, moral support, circulating a petition for the abolition of addiction treatment, appealing to the American Civil Liberties Union (ACLU), working with attorneys who would represent cases in federal court, direct services and advocacy for a number of persons victimized by the addiction treatment industry, attempts to recruit attorneys to represent people who call, and publication of the list of suggestions for chemically dependent persons that appears early in this book.

The problem has grown considerably worse in spite of what we have done so far. The number of calls and letters from people who have been abused by the recovery group movement and addiction treatment programs is increasing, and the types of abuse are getting more serious. The story is always similar. The callers are too intimidated by the 12-step fellowship or financially vulnerable to the addiction treatment providers' whims to take a stand. Something more is needed to encourage people to challenge forced 12-step participation.

The Rational Recovery Political and Legal Action Network (RR-PLAN)

RR-PLAN is an international association of people who want to see change in addiction care and are willing to do something about it. Sometimes people join because of their own experiences in addiction treatment or the recovery group movement, but others get involved because they are concerned about the impact of the disease concept on American society. The purpose of RR-PLAN is to bring to an end the coercive and deceptive tactics commonly used by the chemical dependency counseling professions and an end to mandated participation in the recovery group movement and its business arm, the addiction treatment industry. In effect, the purpose of RR-PLAN is to put AA out of business—the addiction treatment business they say they aren't in, the business of politics they shouldn't be in, and the daily business of health professionals, educators, civil servants, and elected officials who make a claim to the public trust. These ends should not conflict with members who accept AA traditions at face value, traditions that state it is a program of attraction rather than promotion, that AA should remain forever nonprofessional, and that AA should not lend its name to any facility or outside enterprise.

RR-PLAN groups are starting up alongside the regular RRSN groups, and they are a logical place for people to get together following the brief period required for AVRT-based recovery. At this stage of our history, most who come to Rational Recovery for help have tried AA without success, and many of them are angry that they were forced by expectation, mandate, and lack of choice to persist in that program long after it was clear it wasn't working. The result has been unproductive venting of pent-up frustration at meetings designed for more constructive purposes. RR-PLAN is the appropriate place for expressing those feelings and taking constructive action.

One initial task is to make our presence known to our elected representatives so that they can take a second, hard look at the dubious assumptions that have driven their law-making and funding policies. Then they may turn away from the tangled web of agencies they have created in the struggle against the will of chemically dependent people. The next task is to reach the helping professions and encourage them to lay down their credentials at the doorstep of addiction recovery and refuse to enter an area in which they are unprepared to serve. The health professions, especially medicine, psychology, social work, and certified substance abuse counselors, have failed at great expense to "treat" substance addiction. Instead of promoting programs devised by those who say they are powerless, they may seek advice and counsel from *capable* people who have quit on their own, people who have *priceless* knowledge about addiction and recovery. In post-treatment society, new policies may be based on human strength and resiliency instead of powerlessness, dependence, and gratitude.

The next task is to reach those who still suffer from substance addiction and inform them of their capabilities and responsibilities in ending their addictions. With that knowledge, they will be more able to assert their rights to refuse treatment and avoid unwholesome involvements with the recovery group movement.

A final task is to reach the general public, many of whom may already suspect that the concepts underlying AVRT and Rational Recovery are the proper foundation for any nation's addiction care program. RR-PLAN activists have begun distributing a petition for the abolition of publicly funded addiction treatment. If you support the concepts and values in the petition printed on the next page, please copy and sign it and send it to RRS, Inc., Box 800, Lotus, CA 95651.

PETITION FOR THE ABOLITION
OF PUBLICLY FUNDED ADDICTION TREATMENT

Whereas:

Quitting an addiction is a natural, human ability that may be learned,

Whereas:

There is no known disease that causes or constitutes addiction to alcohol or drugs,

Whereas:

There is no known treatment for substance addiction,

Whereas:

Addiction treatment is not a professional competency,

Whereas:

Programs claiming to provide treatment are based on values that are objectionable to large numbers of people,

Whereas:

The philosophy used in practically all addiction treatment programs, because of its religious nature, has been ruled unconstitutional in many state and federal courts,

Whereas:

Addiction treatment, by its nature, forecasts further substance abuse and in many cases aggravates addiction,

Whereas:

Addiction treatment does not work, producing abstinence rates no greater than no treatment,

Whereas:

The cost of addiction treatment in America is billions of dollars annually,

Whereas:

Services now called "addiction treatment" may be renamed to describe accurately the actual services that are being provided,

Whereas:

Drinking alcohol and using drugs are voluntary behaviors for the purpose of pleasure,

Whereas:

Most people who quit serious substance addictions do so independently,

Whereas:

Anyone who wants to quit an addiction may do so by discontinuing the use of the product,

Whereas:

Recovery from addiction is the responsibility of an individual and not society,

Whereas:

The savings to taxpayers from abolishing addiction need not be applied to any other social ill,

Therefore,

let it be known to the Legislature of the State of __________ that my signature below voices my desire that from this time forward, no further public funds be used for the following items:

1. Public education promoting the disease concept of addiction, including public schools.
2. Programs that claim to, or are licensed to, provide "treatment" for substance addiction.
3. State agencies that currently develop, support, monitor, and license programs, or certify individuals that claim to provide treatment for substance addiction.
4. Programs that divert drunk drivers from lawful sentences and punishments into programs that promote the disease concept of addiction.
5. Any program based upon, or requiring attention to, the 12-step program of Alcoholics Anonymous.
6. Programs in the prison and corrections system that promote the disease model of addiction or provide treatment for "addictive disease."

Signed: ____________________ Date________________

Address:______________________________________

The RR-PLAN Class Action Effort

Like AVRT, the RR Class Action Effort is a simple and obvious solution to a severe, worsening problem. We will continue assisting individuals with problems as they arise, but we ask that they register as potential litigants in the future. RR-PLAN manages a registry of potential plaintiffs in future class-action litigation. Although Rational Recovery is a tiny organization, we can be the mouse that roared.

The eventual class action effort will directly affect every addiction care service provider in America, public and private, including: inpatient and outpatient hospital treatment programs; services by licensed professionals in private practice; services by nonprofit organizations providing professional or volunteer services; and public institutions that offer or require participation in the recovery group movement and its business arm, the addiction treatment industry. These include jails, prisons, detention facilities, social welfare agencies, courts, military organizations and their health facilities, third-party payers for addiction treatment such as insurance companies and managed care organizations, and employers whose personnel policies include referrals, direct or indirect, into employee benefit and health care programs that provide addiction treatment and expect participation in the recovery group movement. When we have a critical mass of potential plaintiffs in any jurisdiction, anywhere, or against any service provider, anywhere, we will identify proper legal representation and file.

How many is a critical mass? We receive at least one unsolicited call every day—often several—telling of some mistreatment, abuse, deception, or violation of constitutional rights. The American treatment tragedy may come to an end in a pile of legal briefs.

Following is a list of common reports of abuse and mistreatment we receive at our main office. If you have experienced any of them or others, contact RR-PLAN for further information on the class action effort.

1. You were told by a licensed, professional person that the reason you use drugs or drink alcohol excessively is be-

cause you have a progressive, inherited, physical disease called "alcoholism" or "addiction."

2. You were told that you could not learn to abstain from alcohol or drugs relying on your own abilities, or that you were powerless to abstain on your own.
3. You were told that Alcoholics Anonymous is the only program or approach that is effective with the problems of alcoholism and addiction.
4. You were told that the 12-step spiritual healing program of Alcoholics Anonymous is not religious.
5. You were told that in order to remain sober and/or have a meaningful life you must adhere to or accept the belief system presented in the 12-step program of Alcoholics Anonymous or Narcotics Anonymous.
6. You were told that you would inevitably drink alcohol or use drugs if you did not conscientiously believe the 12-step program.
7. You were told that even if you abstained from alcohol you would nevertheless be a "dry drunk," seriously ill with the progressive disease of alcoholism.
8. You were depressed as a result of incoherent 12-step indoctrinations and told that you were suffering symptoms of alcoholism such as "dry drunk" or "denial."
9. You were warned against leaving the recovery group or treatment program because you would inevitably drink or use again.
10. You were told that your objections to or questions about the 12-step program or addiction treatment program were in themselves symptoms of the fatal disease, alcoholism or addiction.
11. You were required to attend AA meetings as a result of violating any law, including drunk driving.
12. You were required by a court of law to attend recovery group meetings as an alternative to other sentencing or imprisonment.
13. You were required by a parole board, probation officer, or parole officer to attend 12-step meetings as an alternative to imprisonment.

14. You were imprisoned as a direct result of refusing to participate in 12-step activities.
15. You were required to attend 12-step meetings in a jail or prison as a condition of early release or "good time served."
16. You were ever coerced in a jail or prison to take the fourth step or fifth step, in which you are expected, under group pressure and with prison personnel present, to admit personal guilt for offenses against other persons that you were not charged with at the time.
17. Your reputation with your family, employer, or the public was ever harmed by the release of information you divulged in mandated 12-step meetings by your sponsor or other members of Alcoholics Anonymous.
18. You were admitted to a hospital with the understanding that you would not be exposed to the 12-step program but were switched to that program once admitted.
19. You attempted to leave an addiction treatment program because it was disagreeable but were discouraged from leaving against medical advice because the insurance company would not pay your bill, and you could not afford to pay it yourself.
20. You were denied services without a referral to an alternative program when you refused to participate in the 12-step program that was offered.
21. You were admitted to more than one medically supervised 12-step addiction treatment program.
22. You were ever the subject of an "intervention," in which professional persons orchestrated a surprise confrontation by your family, employer, neighbors, or friends, and which resulted in admission to a for-fee addiction treatment program.
23. You were required to participate in 12-step recovery groups or an addiction treatment program even though you had been abstinent, or nearly so, for over a month.
24. You were told, even though you do not have a drinking or drugging problem, that, because your relative or close associate suffers from the disease of "alcoholism" or sub-

stance addiction, you therefore suffer from a parallel disease called "codependency," and, in order for your relative or associate to abstain from alcohol or drugs, you must participate in 12-step recovery groups.

25. You were told by your employer or a hired agent of your employer that as a condition of employment you must participate in a 12-step program.
26. You were ever refused employment or terminated from employment because you were not a member of Alcoholics Anonymous or you disagreed in principle with the disease/treatment concept or the 12-step program.
27. You were threatened with revocation of your professional license pending your participation in 12-step activities.
28. You were threatened with discharge from military service because you refused to attend 12-step recovery groups.
29. A court took custody or changed custody of your children pending your participation in the 12-step program.
30. You were denied any health care because you refused 12-step participation.
31. Any health care, including organ transplants, was provided to you with the stipulation that you participate in 12-step activities.
32. You were denied health insurance because your medical record contained the diagnosis "alcoholism," or because you failed to report information concerning your use of alcohol.
33. You are a resident of California and were required by any state agency since June, 1994, to attend recovery groups of any kind by any court or social agency and were not advised of your right to refuse AA, NA, or other 12-step participation.

If any of these or similar conditions exist, call or write a letter to RRS, Inc., stating your experiences. If you are presently facing mandated participation in the spiritual healing program of Alcoholics Anonymous, here are some suggestions:

- Get everything you can in writing, especially documents stating that you are required to attend AA or other 12-step meetings in order to avoid penalties or punishments.
- Go to the mats with AA bullies; this may produce a win because their positions fail to meet basic concepts of legality, fairness, decency, and common sense. They are unaccustomed to being held accountable for their pronouncements and practices.
- Write letters to the persons immediately responsible for your treatment, with copies to their superiors. Express concern about the diagnosis "alcoholism." Ask how it is decided that certain persons suffer from the disease, and ask for scientific evidence that there is a disease called "alcoholism." Ask exactly what the treatment for the disease consists of.
- Ask specifically for written responses to these letters.

Simply doing these few things may deter further intimidation, but may also excite the system into more aggressive actions against you. You are the judge of whether you think resistance is worth it.

21

A Rational Recovery System

Those RR people are just in it for the money.

—The Collective Addictive Voice

You may have guessed by now that AVRT is bound to stir up a fuss wherever it is discussed, just as it does within addicted people. Just as AVRT scares the hell out of the Beast, it also threatens those with vested interests in the status quo.

AVRT is like a contagious virus that attacks substance abuse by identifying the infinite variety of concepts, philosophies, and policies that justify any further use. When you discuss Rational Recovery with others, notice how their initial objections seem to support continued substance use by the addicted. "Treatment works," they say. "People can't just summarily quit." Or, "There are many roads to recovery," which can lead one to ask, "Just how many ways are there to quit doing something?" AVRT is a pristine insight that results in major changes in the way people think about substance abuse.

RR-PLAN calls for the abolition of addiction treatment. How's that for black-or-white thinking? All or nothing. From billions of tax dollars invested annually in addiction treatment—to zero. Could this be a responsible position, or is it a radical, militant stance?

Many would respond to our proposal with images of rampant crime, roads filled with swerving cars, domestic violence, and new heights of suffering. They may hold up statistics showing the "impact" of treatment on those tragic conditions. The "savings," they say, are in the billions not spent on crimes and sufferings that have not happened. But there is another picture that does not predict catastrophe, but a more humane and effective approach for the problem of mass addiction.

If every treatment center in America shuts its doors, what would happen? Nothing at all. Hardly anyone would notice, except those who intended to drink or use while they obtained public services. It would be like going back to the 1970s, prior to the cutbacks in community mental health services and the lavish funding that gave birth to the addiction treatment industry. Remember, there were very few addiction treatment centers until fairly recently.

It might be better to ask what addicted and chemically dependent people would do if there were no treatment centers. Would they stop wanting to quit their addictions? Would they stop recovering on their own? Very likely, many, many more would do so. But what about the hopeless ones, the desperate and the vulnerable who cannot stop, cannot stay stopped, cannot function, and who have multiple personal problems? Would they be turned away in the night, to suffer, die, or commit mayhem on others? Hardly.

The United States of America has a fine health care system, offering some of the finest mental health services available on the planet. They would receive excellent care, not only in existing facilities, but in an *expanded* human service system that can finally focus on legitimate health and social problems rather than the human will to self-intoxicate.

In this *rational* recovery system, chemically dependent people are given the choice to continue drinking or using, with eligibility for some services contingent on a commitment to permanent abstinence. Why waste everybody's time and money on treating the untreatable when addicted people can recover more frequently without treatment? If people are serious about solving their addictions, then it would seem that they would begin to view their substance dependence as a liability rather than a pleasurable asset and consider abstinence as a reasonable exchange for public services. For them, *the state of ambivalence essential to recovery is produced by public policy* rather than through exhortations and disease indoctrination.

No services for legitimate health, mental health, or other social problems would be withheld if every addiction treatment service disappeared. Drunks would still be detoxed, the homeless would still be housed—abstinent or not, junkies could still get methadone, psychiatric patients could still get the finest services available, and newly abstinent people with substantial mental health and social problems would still receive excellent professional care. But none of these services would be called addiction treatment! They would be reserved, not for people in recovery, but for formerly addicted, recently addicted, abstinent people. Any clinician will notice that this is already a standard in the professions, in that it is well known an actively addicted person benefits little from services.

But what about the chronic relapsers who either won't quit or cannot seem to stay clean or sober for more than a few months or possibly years? Would services be denied because of a slip or a relapse? No way, but the range of services would be narrowed considerably, just as is the case now. Instead of addiction treatment, however, chronic users and relapsers could receive a hefty dose of AVRT in order to qualify for an extended range of services. No addiction treatment would be necessary, but for some, placement in a recovery house might be appropriate as long as their freedom of conscience was observed. Some might *choose* to attend AA or NA meetings because they were attracted to that philosophy or lifestyle.

American society has accepted undue responsibility for the problems of chemically dependent people. An AVRT-based addiction care system shifts responsibility for recovery back onto addicted people who do want to quit, greatly reducing the obligation of society to chemically dependent people who have no serious desire to quit.

It is proper for a government to assist its free citizens. That is one reason democracies are created. AVRT separates the addicted, to whom we can give immediate assistance, from the chemically dependent, who are at liberty to continue to their substance use until, if ever, they are ready to quit. The inherent sorting process of AVRT opens the door for recovery to anyone who wants to quit for good. With AVRT, very inexpensive means will provide the very best approach, and consequently it has enormous economic implications. As information on AVRT becomes more widely available, we may expect that people who have been reluctant to enter treatment programs will finally find recovery from addiction within their reach, and we will have stopped a financial hemorrhage that has bled America for too long.

The Rational Recovery Centers

RR Centers are places where addicted people go to quit their addictions to alcohol and other drugs. They attend a series of AVRT sessions taught by formerly addicted people who have recovered using AVRT or similar methods. The sessions are instructional, covering material presented in this book, with individualized instruction on AVRT in small groups. No records are kept of personal or background information, other than confidential identifying information for business purposes. The services are brief, always voluntary, less expensive than any form of addiction treatment, and require no follow-up or aftercare. At last, there is a no-nonsense program, available to every community, that gives exactly what addicted people want—information on how to quit a substance addiction for good.

Already RR Centers are springing up throughout the United States and Canada, and we hope soon there will be an RR Center conveniently located in every population center.

Employee Abstinence Programs

Employers, in particular, may be intensely interested in what AVRT has to offer. Employee Assistance Programs (EAPs), which began in the late 1960s as an alcoholism detection and diversion concept, have ridden the wave of disease/treatment into escalating costs and managerial paralysis. Salaried EAP personnel, most often members of AA, function in roles traditionally reserved for management and personnel offices, bringing their disease thinking and spiritual remedies into the workplace. Unable to fire "diseased" employees who appear for work intoxicated, they work under regulations that require them to refer suspected substance abusers, through their in-house EAPs, for expensive 12-step treatment, with pay. Large corporations have permitted 12-step meetings on the work premises and "invested" in mandated drug awareness programs that go far beyond their legitimate business interests and produce an atmosphere of unwholesome vigilance for signs of "disease" among employees. The cost of the investment is promised to be made up in productivity, but in reality EAPs are less effective and more expensive than progressive discipline alone. The phrase "behavioral health" is used to disguise its opposite, "behavioral disease," and as the range of "disease behavior" grows, management is pulled away from making logical, businesslike decisions about common workplace problems, including employee alcohol and drug abuse. Rational Recovery, respecting the boundaries between businesses, offers AVRT as a direct, contractual service for employees identified as impaired by the use of alcohol or drugs by their supervisors and management.

Where EAPs exist, we suggest eliminating them and creating a *direct management function* called an RR Employee Abstinence Program (RREAP). American businesses have no legitimate interest in the personal lives of employees, much less their spiritual or religious leanings. But they do have a vital interest in curbing factors that relate to job performance and retaining valued employees who have become addicted to a substance. RREAPs show employers a way out of the treatment era, when government regulations enforced disease hysteria in the workplace. In the post-treatment era, RREAPs will continue to stress abstinence as the only reasonable solution to performance problems once progressive discipline has failed, but they will draw the line between legitimate business concerns and the expensive, inappropriate agenda of the recovery group movement.

APPENDIX A

The Rational Recovery Dictionary

Below are some glossary definitions of terms used in the Rational Recovery program. From the beginning, Rational Recovery has struggled to devise help using the tortured language of the recovery group movement. One by one, nearly all expressions and concepts in the field of addictions have been found to be inverted, misused, or, all too often, frankly pathogenic. In order to facilitate clear, helpful communication, the RR Dictionary attempts to bring order to linguistic chaos. Many of these definitions have come from Coordinators and correspondents to *The Journal of Rational Recovery.* Your suggestions are welcome. An understanding of AVRT is helpful in formulating definitions that will be included in this expanding reference. The purpose of the RR Dictionary is to aid people with planned abstinence, not to satisfy the rigors of science or lexicography.

RR is a new approach to addiction recovery with different concepts from the traditional ones, and realistic language. For example, we do not speak of being "in recovery," but of being *recovered.* To us, the concept of "denial" and "relapse" are perfectly nonsensical. Likewise, terms like "codependency" and "enabler" have no meaning in RR. We have language that is better, we think, because it is based on common sense rather than recovery group movement jargon. Following are a few definitions, to get you started on AVRT-based recovery.

Abstain, abstinence. 1. To forego or refrain from the use of mind or mood-altering substances.

Abstinence Commitment Effect (ACE). 1. The ambivalent or mixed feelings associated with the prospect of lifetime abstinence. 2. The fundamental dilemma faced by addicted people. 3. Most often used in the positive sense, e.g., the pleasant, uplifted feelings resulting from sensing control and return of hope.

Abuse. An overused, much-abused expression of the recovery group movement that heightens the perception of victimhood.

Addiction. 1. Addiction is chemical dependency that exists against one's own better judgment and persists in spite of efforts to control or eliminate the use of the substance. Logically, since addiction is known only to the individual, it may not be "diagnosed" except by asking the individual. 2. Addicted people are not out of control in the usual sense of the word, but have reversals of intent that lead back to drinking or drugging. 3. Addiction exists only in a state of ambivalence, in which one strongly wants to continue drinking alcohol or using other drugs, but also wants to quit or at least reduce the painful consequences. With AVRT, recovery from addiction is a simple, mercifully brief undertaking. (See **chemical dependence** and **substance abuse**.)

Addiction Diction. Using changes in grammar to force the Addictive Voice into a defensive, submissive posture.

Addiction treatment disorder. 1. The psychosocial aftermath of intense, repeated exposure to 12-step-based counseling, especially under coercion. Prominent symptoms include intellectual disorientation, guilt associated with failure to remain abstinent, resignation to endless substance addiction, depression stemming from hopelessness. 2. The belief that addiction is a disease or condition that may be "treated." (See **recovery group disorder.**)

Addictive Voice. Any thinking or feeling that supports one's future use of alcohol or drugs. An expression of the Beast.

Addictive Voice Recognition Technique®. 1. A summary of the subjective experience of self-recovery from substance addiction, described in useful detail by Jack Trimpey, founder of

Rational Recovery. 2. An easily learned thinking skill that defeats any substance addiction within a short period of time, usually a month or so. Permits total recovery through planned abstinence.

Addicto-depressive condition. The depression that arises from and universally coexists with dependence on alcohol, stimulants, hallucinogens, and mood-altering drugs. The addicto-depressive condition mimics major depressive illness in several ways: low mood, sleep disorders, loss of interest, loss of appetite, interpersonal conflict, social isolation, and morbid suicidal ideas. Usually mistaken by physicians for inherent depressive illnesses, the addicto-depressive condition is often medicated with substances that provide relief from depression. Because addicted people seek pleasure and not relief, they typically continue to use alcohol or drugs while taking the medication. The therapeutic effect of medication is usually not achieved, and even when it is, the addiction is likely to continue. Such therapies rarely succeed.

Agnostic, atheist, skeptic, humanist, disbeliever. Words sometimes used to classify people who are resistant to or criticize the spiritual teachings of AA. According to AA founder Bill Wilson, these people do not have a ghost of a chance to survive the ravages of substance addiction unless they come to believe in a Higher Power.

Alcoholic. 1. Person thought to be suffering from the hypothetical disease "alcoholism." 2. Self-description required for addicted persons seeking help from AA. 3. *adj.* Having to do with or containing alcohol. 4. *syn.* Heavy drinker.

Alcoholics Anonymous. 1. A group of formerly addicted people who desire to help others quit drinking or using. 2. A recovery club for people who have not made a personal commitment to lifetime abstinence. 3. A self-supporting, altruistic, nonprofit organization that scorns the profit motive yet uses public resources to channel vast sums of public money to its members and supporters. 4. An intensely religious, secret organization with a creed that states it is not a religion.

Alcoholism. 1. A folk expression for alcohol dependence and alcohol addiction that does not distinguish the two. 2. Mistakenly thought by many to be an inherited, incurable disease that renders one powerless over the decision to drink or not and requires divine intervention for one so afflicted to achieve tentative abstinence.

Anger. 1. A normal, healthy emotion that has nothing to do with drinking alcohol, using drugs, or recovery from addiction. 2. When one is deprived of or refuses alcohol or drugs, the AV. 3. An emotion mistakenly assumed to characterize persons critical of 12-step programs. 4. An unwholesome feeling sometimes experienced by defenders of the 12-step program toward 12-step critics.

Antabuse®. 1. Disulfiram, a substance used in the process of vulcanizing rubber for automobile tires. When some workers at a Swedish tire factory became ill and others did not, it was discovered that those becoming ill were also the ones who stopped to drink at a local tavern after work. Workers who did not drink after work showed no ill effects, although long-term studies were not conducted. Creative addiction treatment professionals saw in this a means to declare chemical warfare upon persons who drank irresponsibly, and they marketed this potentially poisonous substance as antihedonic medicine for the hypothetical disease of "alcoholism." It rarely works for long, because the Addictive Voice that directs one to drink alcohol also directs one to avoid the use of Antabuse. Even so, many Americans are mandated to take a chemical that, if mixed with alcohol, produces a medical emergency, often with deadly results.

AVRT®. The acronym for Addictive Voice Recognition Technique. AVRT is an educational approach to addiction that nullifies the approaches of American addiction treatment industry and recovery movement. It is a cybernetic device that, once learned, quickly renders one incapable of drinking or using drugs. As old as the hills and as common as the sunrise, the concepts of AVRT are alien to mainstream American thought. We owe this omission to the health professions and the bureaucrats who permitted a frankly religious organization to infiltrate their homespun nonsense into the public human service system.

Beast. Ofted used synonymously with "Addictive Voice," but more accurately, the appetite or desire for substance-induced pleasure.

Big Plan. A transcending personal commitment to unconditional, permanent abstinence.

Chemical dependence. 1. The use of any substance for any purpose. For example, "I use salt to make my food tast good. I *depend* upon salt to make food taste better." Or, "I breathe oxygen to stay alive. I *depend* upon oxygen to survive." Or, "I take asapirin for headaches. I *depend* on aspirin to relieve pain." Or, "I drink vodka to feel different. I *depend* on vodka to produce certain feelings." Or, "I drink beer to have a good time. I *depend* on beer to enjoy a party." 2. *Chemical dependence* (especially upon drugs and alcohol) is an individual liberty with known health risks and known personal disadvantages including regrettable behavior, social ostracism, relationship problems, divorce, unemployment, and imprisonment. If one is willing to accept the risks, *chemical dependence* is a "legitimate" option. Regardless of the content of prohibition laws and the best efforts of law enforcement and others who oppose *chemical dependence,* using alcohol and drugs for pleasure is a personal liberty that cannot realistically be controlled by others. (See **substance abuse.**)

Codependency. A hypothetical disease thought to affect persons associated with another person who is suffering from the hypothetical disease "alcoholism."

Denial. 1. A relatively rare condition noted in the probably never-addicted, experimental subjects of psychoanalyst Sigmund Freud. 2. Purposeful lying, expecially to sustain an addiction, as in, "I drink socially, just like anyone else." 3. An alleged symptom of the hypothetical disease of alcoholism, in which an addicted person is presumed to be blithely unaware of the connection between drinking or drugging and the painful consequences. It is assumed that addicted people are pathetic dumbbells who do not know that they are addicted. In connection with drugs and alcohol, the phenomenon *denial* has never been reported or observed outside the recovery group movement, or in its business arm, the addiction treatment industry. 4. Used to denote disagreement with chemically dependent people, as in, "He has a problem, but doesn't know it. He's in *denial.*" 5. Archaic: Unpardonable sin of heresy or blasphemy, as in, "The heretic *denied* God and must burn at the stake."

Enabler. 1. In the recovery group movement, used to describe a person taken advantage of by an addicted person in order to continue drinking or using drugs. *syn., slang,* sucker. 2. A person thought to suffer from the hypothetical disease of codependency. (See **codependency.**)

Freud, Sigmund. Founder of psychoanalysis in the early 1900s who introduced the word *denial* as part of his theory and therapy. He used "denial" to describe unusual defense mechanisms, mainly as an expression of unconscious wish-fulfillment. His outmoded, pseudoscientific work has been hybridized, along with New Age transpersonal psychology, to fortify the religio-spiritual philosophy of the 12-step recovery movement. Denial, as it is used in the addictions field, has no connection to the phenomena observed by Dr. Freud. Dr. Freud was dependent on nicotine and cocaine during most of his later years, and he died of drug-related causes.

God, a loving. 1. An ineffable presence around which 12-step groups gather. 2. The ostensible authority behind AA, endlessly invoked but not defined by AA. 3. The source of strength, sobriety, sanity, and good fortune among alcoholics who meditate and pray to Him.

HALT. 1. The first letters of *hungry, angry, lonely,* and *tired,* four inevitable experiences of daily living when it is believed that persons afflicted with the hypothetical disease of alcoholism or substance addiction are vulnerable to an undefined, superior force that results in self-intoxication. Protection is afforded disease victims by avoiding those conditions or, when that is not possible, to summon, call upon, meditate upon, or otherwise relate to one's Higher Power.

Higher Power. 1. A euphemism for a Supreme Being, Allah, God Almighty, described in considerable detail in the Talmud, Koran, and New Testament. 2. A flexible expression that suggests the use of experimental, training deities that may later be replaced by a more appropriate deity, as in, "Anything can be your *Higher Power.*" 3. Belief in a *Higher Power* is a condition of abstinence, personal well-being, and good fortune in 12-step programs.

Incapable. 1. Powerless. 2. Used within the recovery movement to describe persons who disagree with the 12-step program, as in, "They are constitutionally *incapable* of being honest." Persons thus described most often are refusing the first "step," admitting that one is powerless, that is, *incapable* of independently quitting an addiction. The founder of AA, Bill Wilson, after many relapses, concluded that he was *incapable* of resisting his own desire for the pleasure produced by alcohol and subsequently found a religious solution for himself, which became the foundation of AA.

Issues. 1. In the recovery movement, a euphemism for *reality*, or for personal problems, as in, "The meeting really dealt with some good *issues*." 2. That with which recovering people "deal" or "cope," as in, "I'm dealing with many issues." 3. Used to describe another's diseased condition, as in, "I can see you have some real *issues* to cope with."

Jung, Carl. A psychologist of the early 1900s who, knowing that there is no treatment for alcohol addiction, was glad to learn that "alcoholics" could go to 12-step meetings rather than to his office. Never addicted himself, he thought that getting drunk must be a variety of religious experience like speaking with God or going to heaven. Often cited as an endorser of AA.

Lois. 1. Wife of Bill Wilson. 2. Wife of Jack Trimpey. No relation. Just coincidence.

Moderation. 1. The passionate wish and death-defying goal of all addicted people. 2. The unrecognized expression of the Addictive Voice. 3. A euphemism for getting drunk without suffering negative consequences, as in, "I just want to learn how to drink *moderately*."

National Council on Alcoholism. A nonprofit organization with the sole purpose of disseminating propaganda supporting the disease concept of alcoholism, founded by Marty Mann in 1950s, when the large majority of AA members were securely abstinent. Not a governmental or scientific institution in spite of its pretentious name. Renamed in 1993 as The National Council on Alcohol Dependence and Drug Abuse.

Neurotransmitters. 1. Chemicals that facilitate electrical activity within the brain, especially at synapses. Serotonin, epinephrine, and dopamine are *neurotransmitters.* 2. Naturally occurring substances found in the brain that produce emotional tone and pleasure. Because variations in neurotransmitters affect mood, they are of intense interest to addicted people and those who purport to treat addiction, as in, "I drink because my *neurotransmitters* are out of whack," or, "You drink because your neurotransmitters make you feel bad." 3. In the arcane language of 12-step disease thinking, a substance secreted by the brain to which one may become addicted or unwholesomely dependent upon, as in, "Codependents are really serotonin junkies."

Newtotaler. A neologism (from **teetotaler**) desribing newly abstinent people with a Big Plan. Contrast with "baby," or "pigeon," which are terms used in recovery fellowships. *Newtotalers* are indistinguishable from others except they have had a recent personal history of substance addiction. Most newtotalers experience more Beast activity than persons with longer periods of abstinence, a condition that fades with time. Within months, newtotalers recognize this and become common teetotalers. (See **teetotaler.**)

Planned abstinence. 1. A style of recovery based on individual responsibility, native intelligence, self-determination, and self-reliance. 2. The essence of AVRT. 3. Contrasted with "harm reduction," which presumes continued substance abuse, *planned abstinence* aims at harm avoidance or harm elimination.

Rational. 1. Having to do with conscious thought processes. 2. The use of intelligence and reason to solve problems, as in, "*Rational* Recovery teaches the skill of planned abstinence."

Rational-emotive behavior therapy (REBT). 1. A comprehensive system of psychotherapy and self-help based on a psychological theory devised by Albert Ellis, Ph.D. Helps people gain control over emotions and behavior through self-disputation. 2. Suggested in Rational Recovery as one of many alternatives to the religio-spiritual teachings and lifestyle of AA, none of which are direct or efficient means to achieve permanent abstinence.

Rational Recovery (RR). 1. A service mark registered with the United States Patent and Trademark Office, owned by Rational Recovery Systems, Inc., a California corporation. 2. The concept of self-recovery from substance addiction through planned abstinence.

Rational Recovery Licenses, Inc. 1. A California corporation approved by the California Department of Corporations to engage in interstate licensing of Rational Recovery Centers, owned and operated by franchisees.

Rational Recovery Self-Help Network (RRSN). 1. A division of Rational Recovery Systems, Inc. 2. An association of volunteers who promote Rational Recovery and facilitate free self-help meetings in their communities.

Recognition (of the Addictive Voice). 1. Immediate recollection with comprehension. 2. A natural, inherited function of the human brain notably absent in lower creatures. 3. A function of short-term memory, in which the prevailing AV is consciously recalled, apprehended, and classified primarily as a violation of an earlier, well-made commitment to abstinence, and secondarily as a likely instigator of hardship and pain, that is, an "enemy." 4. The ability to observe one's own thoughts and feelings related to the use of alcohol and drugs. *Recognition* nullifies desire and fosters conditioned avoidance. Extremely easy for addicted people to learn because of the significance of alcohol and drugs and the conspicuousness of related thoughts.

Recovery (from addiction). 1. The state of enduring, planned abstinence from alcohol and other drugs, typically followed by gradually improving functioning and emotional tone. 2. A planned event, rather than a lengthy process of psychological and transpersonal self-discovery, as in the commonly voiced procrastination, "I'm in recovery."

Recovery group disorder. 1. A common, well-known outcome of involvement in 12-step recovery, in which group members remain dependent on the group in spite of not being helped or not wanting to be there. Follows the general pattern of addiction. (See **addiction.**) 2. The belief that attending support groups, self-help groups, and other gatherings where addiction issues are discussed are vital to recovery from addiction. 3. A syndrome of associated symptoms resembling addiction treatment disorder, but resulting from excessive meeting attendance, and including preoccupation with self, compulsive meeting attendance, fear of the Addictive Voice, and preoccupation with philosophical riddles, mystical and occult phenomena, and bodily functions, particularly one's own neurotransmitters. (See **addiction treatment disorder** and **neurotransmitters.**)

Recovery group movement. 1. A subculture centered around indirect means, both spiritual and psychological, to defeat addictions, as in, "Rational Recovery is not part of the recovery group movement because its discussion groups practice AVRT." 2. A religious movement based on the 12-step program of Alcoholics Anonymous, with various denominations centered around different sacramental substances. 3. Together, the nonprofit organizations that field volunteers to coordinate support and self-help groups that use indirect, palliative means to help addicted people. 4. The social trends arising from the disease/treatment philosophy of the recovery group movement. A set of assumptions that dilute traditional values of self-sufficiency, self-reliance, and individual responsibility, as in, "I wasn't late for work. I have chronic lateness syndrome, and I was attending a recovery group for people with that condition," or "He will get a lighter sentence because he was abused as a child and is getting treatment for his problem." 5. The spread of the recovery group's victim philosophy into social programs, as in, "That was a very bad earthquake. The government should send in some psychologists and social workers to set up support groups and counsel the victims."

Relapse. 1. In the recovery group movement, something that happens to an individual who does not acknowledge a conscious decision to drink alcohol or use drugs, as in, "I don't know what I was thinking. I just had a relapse." 2. An expression to convey that decisions to drink or use happen to people, and that people themselves are not responsible for that decision.

3. Relapses do not occur in Rational Recovery, although anyone may decide to drink or use alcohol. 4. A synonym for "lapse," as in, "He had a lapse of good judgment and got drunk again." The prefix "re-" obscures the voluntary, willful, and purposeful nature of returning to the use of pleasure-producing substances. 5. Borrowed from medical vocabulary to convey that symptoms of a latent, mysterious disease have resurfaced, as in, "Her multiple sclerosis was in remission, but she has had a *relapse* and now she cannot walk." 6. A simple reversal of intent, wherein one has earlier decided not to drink, but then changed one's mind in order to experience the transient pleasure of self-intoxication. Lapses/relapses are normally shrouded in circumstancial internal dialogue, the unrecognized Addictive Voice, explaining why self-intoxication is appropriate or proper. (See **slip**.)

Religion. 1. A personal set or institutional system of religious attitudes, beliefs, and practices.

Revia®. 1. Naltrexone. 2. An antihedonic substance taken to block the pleasure-producing action of alcohol, prescribed as treatment for the hypothetical disease of alcoholism. Its proponents claim it relieves one's immediate desire for the easily recalled pleasure produced by drinking alcohol. Said by its proponents to be ineffective without other treatment for the hypothetical disease of alcoholism. Used originally for the treatment of heroin addiction, with disappointing results, but achieved popularity when its promises were advertised by the media to the much larger population of alcohol users, their families, and their remaining friends. Not explained is an addicted person's reasoning process in deciding to take a pleasure-blocking substance. The cost of naltrexone is about $200 for a week's supply, as contrasted to the cost of alcohol, which in most cases is less. 3. Sometimes confused with Relive®, a nutritional supplement that enhances vitality and health.

Silkworth, Robert; "Dr. Bob." A physician who applied religious teachings to his drinking problem, which he thought was a disease. He believed he was incapable of resisting his desire for the pleasure produced by drinking alcohol and found reassurance in his relationship with like-minded Bill Wilson. Together, they ministered religion to others who drank too much and found that their ideas of shifting responsibility for abstinence onto God and other people were popular among drunks.

Slip. 1. A willful choice to intoxicate oneself with alcohol or drugs for the purpose of experiencing physical pleasure. 2. An expression to convey that such decisions are accidental.

Slippery places. 1. Places or situations that allegedly increase the probability that one would accidentally choose to drink alcohol for the pleasure it produces. These may include drinking establishments, planes, trains, automobiles, foreign countries, anyplace out of town, anyplace in town, parties, celebrations, funerals, being in a crowd, being alone, becoming hungry, angry, lonely or tired, etc. (See **relapse**.)

Spiritual. 1. *adj.* Concerned with or attached to religious values; ecclesiastical rather than lay or temporal; things of a religious, ecclesiastical nature; something that in ecclesiastical law belongs to the churgh or to a cleric. 2. A musical form created in America during the 1800s by people held lifelong in slavery. To east their torment and enhance social cohesion under oppressive conditions, the slaves sang inspirational songs expressing reliance on God for deliverance from bondage. These songs came to be called *spirituals*. 3. A descriptive term applied to the 12-step recovery movement, as in "AA is not religious; it is *spiritual*."

Substance abuse. 1. Abnormal, aberrant, or excessive use of alcohol or drugs. 2. Someone else's opinion about an individual's use of certain substances, as in, "*Substance abuse* does not presume addiction."

Supply-side. 1. From *supply and demand*, the economic principle in which the supply of a commodity or service tends to offset demand for it, and demand for it tends to increase the supply. A vital force in capitalist societies that creates wealth and opportunity. 2. Focusing on the supply or presence of something rather than its meaning to human beings. 3. An economic principle favoring the suppliers of commodities and services, often justified by the "trickle-down" theory, in which consumers indirectly benefit from the accumulating wealth of suppliers. 4. The American addiction-care system is supply-side thinking, focused on the availability and properties of the supply of alcohol and drugs. Users of those substances are presumed to have a disease that makes them incompetent to refuse them; thus, laws are enacted for the purpose of limiting access to the supply. Believing that, unsupervised, they might decide to intoxicate themselves, persons recovering from addictive disease often prefer the company of persons similarly afflicted and structure their lives around avoidance of the supply.

Teetotaler. One who for any reason or no reason never drinks or uses nonprescribed drugs. Once thought to be rigid, uptight, and rare, teetotalers are actually commonplace and unremarkable. Teetotalers find no difficulty in not drinking. (See **newtotaler.**)

Treatment. 1. A method applied to solve psychological, medical and other clinical problems. 2. With addictions, an effort by one person to dissuade another from drinking or drugging, often using the most tangential means, and then to claim responsibility for an abstinent outcome. Assumes that drinking is a symptom of underlying, hidden causes rooted in genetics, brain chemistry, childhood miseries, adult disappointments, and separation from God. Always based on the assumption that addicted people are incapable of immediately and permanently quitting the addiction. 3. An agreement between a counselor and client that the client will continue to drink or use drugs for an indefinite time, at least until certain for-a-fee, therapeutic exercises are performed. 4. Addiction *treatment* is a historic curiosity of the middle-to-late twentieth century.

Trickle-down. The sensation produced by drinking a cold alcoholic beverage.

Triggers. Familiar or novel circumstances, sometimes charged with emotion, that provide possible excuses for drinking or drugging that would result in physical pleasure, such as getting high. These boozing or buzz opportunities are quickly seized upon by the Beast and described by the AV as *triggers*. Some scientists offer *triggers* as an explanation for why people self-intoxicate. (See **slippery places.**)

12 Steps. 1. A Christian-oriented religious creed centered around a homogenized deity, substituting "addiction" and "disease" for sin. 2. Neo-Buchmanism. 3. The state-endorsed religion of the United States of America, exported to other countries along with democracy and capitalism. 4. A career ladder for former drunks. 5. A moral betterment program to arrest the sin-disease of alcoholism, with specific elements to forestall commitment to permanent abstinence. (See **Wilson, William.**)

War on Drugs. An outgrowth of disease thinking, which asserts that pleasure-producing substances, like aggressive microorganisms, actively infect people and threaten society. Addicted people are viewed as victims of a disease that renders them unable to refuse drugs, while society views itself as a victim of an imported epidemic. A national quarantine has been enacted, with the domestic production, distribution, and use of pleasure-producing drugs made criminal offenses, and with the military and police activated to enforce it. Diseased drug users, wiling to pay large sums of money, demand drugs and create an attractive market for domestic sales representatives of economically depressed countries willing to fill orders for drugs. The vibrant drug trade creates domestic and international tension, thus providing internal and external enemies to divert attention from the self-indulgent behavior of addicted people.

Wilson, William; "Bill W." A cofounder of Alcoholics Anonymous, now regarded as a saint in the recovery movement. Unable to recognize his Addictive Voice, he concluded that he was incapable of resisting his desire for the pleasure produced by drinking alcohol. His example of surrender is now forcefully taught to all addicted people in America. While under the influence of the hallucinogen belladonna, administered in a hospital as an aversion therapy, he had a profound beatific vision he later interpreted as a God-inspired, spiritual awakening. He joined a Christian fundamentalist sect called the Oxford Group, which suffered image problems in the 1930s when its founder, Frank Buchman, expressed agreement in principle with a rising European politician named Adolf Hitler. Wilson bowed out of the Oxford Group prior to its being renamed Moral Re-Armament and formed a nearly identical sect, based on the same ideology but catering only to problem drinkers, called Alcoholics Anonymous. He drafted some theological refinements to Buchman's theology, making it inclusive of a wider range of desperate people, thus creating the 12-step program in use today. To add credibility to his "religious solution," as AA was originally regarded by all, he gained endorsements from members of the medical profession and notable psychologists of the time who admitted they were powerless to persuade people to quit seeking the exquisite pleasure produced by drinking alcohol. Had they known that Mr. Wilson's organization would overtake society as it has, their support might have been more tempered with caution.

APPENDIX B

Give Us Some Feedback

Now that you have read *Rational Recovery* and presumably will intoxicate yourself no further, you have made your amends to society. Your behavior will naturally be more ethical, moral, and pro-social, and no more will be spent from public or health care funds on your addiction problem.

Beginning on page 341 is a questionnaire. If *Rational Recovery* has helped you, there is one thing you can give back. We would like to hear from you. Your voice is important because we live in a democracy.

If you believe you have been harmed by the disease/treatment model of addiction, say so in the comments section. By completing the questionnaire, you will not become an experimental subject but a political citizen. Mountains of research have shown us little useful information about addiction. Science doesn't really dictate public policy; democracy does. You will be doing your part to help others avoid becoming lost in the recovery hall of mirrors.

You can fill out the questionnaire and mail it to Rational Recovery Systems, Box 800, Lotus, CA 95651.

I will tabulate the questionnaire results to produce documents for *political* purposes. The information may be of some scientific interest, insofar as the AVRT hypothesis may be investigated further in the future.

THE CONFIDENTIAL QUESTIONNAIRE

Rational Recovery Systems, Inc., is experienced in protecting your confidentiality. Your name and other identifying information are entirely optional. If you provide your name, it will be added to the general mailing list of Rational Recovery Systems. If your questionnaire is used for scientific research by an independent organization, all identifying information will be blacked out and your response will be identified by a serial number. With your permission only, you may be contacted at intervals for follow-up information. Many people will want to see if you remain abstinent using the concepts of AVRT. Don't fear that you would be embarrassed if you are contacted and not perfectly abstinent. (That fear, of course, is a residual of your Beast, easily recognizable by now.)

Feel free to offer criticism of *Rational Recovery.* AVRT is a product of what I have learned from people. My job is to incorporate feedback into AVRT.

Use a separate paper for your responses, following the outline guides, or photocopy the pages, or tear them out. Your answers may be brief or as long as you like.

CONFIDENTIAL QUESTIONNAIRE

Return to: Rational Recovery Systems
Box 800
Lotus, CA 95651

Optional Information (see previous pages)

Name ____________________

Address: ____________________

City ____________ State ________ ZIP ____________

Telephone ____________________

THE QUESTIONS

1. In a sentence or two, what did you think about *Rational Recovery?* Feel free to write in more detail on another paper.

2. What kind of addiction have you been trying to solve? What substance or substances?

3. How many years were you addicted when you got this book?

   ____

4. What have you done in the past to help yourself with your addiction? (Be specific about how many meetings, programs, rehabs, DUI/DWI programs, etc. you participated in, whether voluntarily or involuntarily.)

5. What was most helpful about *Rational Recovery?*

6. What was the chief weakness?

7. Were you drinking/using up until reading *Rational Recovery?* ___ Yes ___ No
8. Have you continued to drink or use drugs since reading *Rational Recovery?* ___ Yes ___ No
4. Did you quit your addiction as a result of reading this book? ___ Not Applicable ___ No ___ Yes
9. Do you plan to attend any self-help or support group meetings? ___ Yes ___ No
10. Have you seen any psychologists or counselors since reading the book? ___ Yes ___ No
11. If you answered "yes" to the above, what was your counselor's response to your Big Plan?
12. What is your plan for the future use of alcohol or drugs?
13. Has your life improved since reading *Rational Recovery?* ___ Yes ___ No
14. How much? ___ Very much ___ Somewhat ___ Not at all ___ Worse
15. If you have a Big Plan and still have significant personal problems, describe them in a sentence or two.

    Will their presence result in drinking or drugging?

    What is your plan for those problems?

If you have further comments, they are welcome (use additional sheets of paper), or you may call the Rational Recovery office at 916-621-2667 and talk with any of us.
Thanking you in advance for your help,

Jack Trimpey

APPENDIX C

About Rational Recovery

Email: rr@rational.org
http.//www.rational.org/recovery/
916-621-2667 or 916-621-4374

PARTICIPATION

Rational Recovery is the *first* thing someone with a drinking or drug problem should explore, and the last thing to turn to when nothing else has helped. Building on your natural strengths and abilities, you learn simple mental skills for abstinence and independence. If you have not been helped by 12-step programs, or if you find it difficult to withdraw from meetings, Rational Recovery is a way out of addiction and "recovering." For information on groups in the United States and abroad, call 916-621-2667, Monday through Friday, 8:00 A.M. to 4:00 P.M., Pacific time. Anyone with an addiction to work on is welcome to attend RR meetings.

RATIONAL RECOVERY SELF-HELP NETWORK (RRSN)

RRSN is a division of Rational Recovery Systems, Inc., and meetings are free of charge. Our groups are places where people can get started in AVRT-based recovery. They are discussion groups led by an RR Coordinator who has recovered using AVRT. We teach people how to make a commitment to permanent abstinence and how to stick to it no matter what happens. Each meeting is an opportunity for anyone present to make a Big Plan for permanent abstinence, and there is open discussion and orientation to the structural model of addiction and Addictive Voice Recognition Technique. The Coordinator will listen to your problems and the circumstances in your life, but will make no effort to convince you to abstain from alcohol or drugs. Nor will the Coordinator attempt to guide you or counsel you on your personal problems. Groups don't keep you sober; you do.

An RR group is not a support group and offers no secrets for making life easier or more meaningful. You are a pioneer in your own life, carrying the same burden as others to answer life's great questions, unravel life's mysteries, and solve life's problems. An RR group is not a home or a social fellowship, but a staging area where you may take stock of your problems with drinking or using, learn about the survival skills we call AVRT, make some very important decisions about your use of substances, and then leave the group knowing that you have made an informed decision. A month of weekly meetings is enough to take hold of any substance addiction, but if you remain divided in your thinking about abstinence, you may go on to study AVRT in earnest with skilled instruction.

We know that very few people who come to any recovery meeting stay for long, that perhaps only one in twenty would come for more than a month. We know that many are greatly helped by their brief exposure to AVRT. We want to know what becomes of you, what are your successes and your difficulties, because we want to let it be known that addicted people are competent and whole, and most need only scant resources, if any, to end their addictions to alcohol and drugs. Rational Recovery volunteers have contributed their energies and expertise for a decade, and it is time that they receive the recognition they deserve for their generous contributions to their communities.

For the above reasons, we ask that you identify yourself by name and address, so that we may call on you down the line. Rational Recovery will add your name to a large, confidential list of our friends, and we will contact you by phone or mail from time to time. If you do not trust us to know your name and never to share it with any other person or organization, you are free to study our program in the quiet of your room. Your sincere efforts to recover will be rewarded no less than if you had attended our meetings.

LEADERSHIP

Bring Rational Recovery to your home community! It isn't difficult to start a local project of Rational Recovery Self-Help Network. If you like people and enjoy the excitement of social change, this could be a great opportunity. Some may find new career opportunities at Rational Recovery Centers and in workplaces as more employers seek out persons with a Rational Recovery background. To volunteer as a group Coordinator, call 916-621-2667.

CAREER

RR Certification

Certification is available to persons wishing to become part of the Rational Recovery service system. Coordinators (laypersons only) may apply for the Certified Rational Recovery Coordinator (CRRC) certificate. The AVRTech credential is available only through supervised internships in Addictive Voice Recognition Technique at Rational Recovery Centers. Training in AVRT is available through the Rational Recovery Training Institute.

LICENSURE

The Society for Licensed Rational Recovery Providers

Join the growing family of hospitals, agencies, and professionals in private practices who are licensed to make commercial use of the federally registered Rational Recovery and Addictive Voice Recognition Technique (AVRT) service marks. Licensure identifies your organization as a leader in the field of addictions, a vital community resource, and a hub of professional education. The Society of Licensed Rational Recovery Providers (SLRRP) welcomes new member organizations. Inquire at 916-621-4374.

FRANCHISE OPPORTUNITIES

Rational Recovery Licenses, Inc., was approved in 1995 by the California Department of Corporations to offer interstate franchise sales. Franchisees may operate and own Rational Recovery Service Centers, providing educational services on Addictive Voice Recognition Technique. This is a unique business opportunity for investors who understand the significance of AVRT, and a career opportunity for lay persons who desire a rewarding career as an Addictive Voice Recognition Technician (AVRTech) Specialist. For further information and the RRL, Inc. prospectus, call 916-621-2667.

RR ONLINE

A variety of RRS-approved activities take place online, including a page on the World Wide Web, discussion groups, chat lines, Email services, and newsgroups. The Email address for Rational Recovery online is rr@rational.org. We maintain an up-to-date page on the World Wide Web that you may visit at the URL http://www.rational.org/recovery/ See you there.

APPENDIX D

For Further Information: Reading and Tapes

BOOKS

Bufe, Chaz, *Alcoholics Anonymous: Cult or Cure?* See Sharp Press, 1991.

Ellis, Albert, and Robert Harper, *A New Guide to Rational Living.* Wilshire, 1975.

Katz, Stan, and Aimee Liu, *The Codependency Conspiracy: How to Break the Recovery Habit and Take Charge of Your Life.* Warner Books, 1991.

Trimpey, Jack, *The Small Book: A Revolutionary Alternative for Overcoming Alcohol and Drug Dependence.* Delacorte, 1992.

Trimpey, Jack and Lois, *Taming the Feast Beast.* Delacorte, 1994.

JOURNALS

The Journal of Rational Recovery, bimonthly since September 1988. Lotus Press (see following page), subscription $20 per year (in Canada $28 per year).

CATALOGUE

The Rational Recovery catalogue, available from Lotus Press.

AUDIO/VIDEO

Special Item: A set of three one-hour audiotapes, *The Final Fix Audiotapes,* has been developed for people who have read *Rational*

Recovery and who want to increase their understanding of AVRT. These tapes are strongly recommended for people who are serious about permanently abstaining from alcohol or other drugs. $39.95.

Addictive Voice Recognition Technique (VHS format), 40 minutes, Jack Trimpey, 1993, $39.95.

The Boston Talk Show Event, two 90-minute audiotapes, Jack Trimpey with Gene Burns on WRKO, Boston, 1991, $15.95.

Rational Recovery at Grand Rounds, Jack Trimpey presents AVRT to the medical staff at the Veterans Administration Hospital in Minneapolis, 1995, $9.95.

All materials are available from Lotus Press, P.O. Box 800, Lotus, CA 95651 (books also available at your bookstore or library). Order by telephone: weekdays from 8:00 A.M. to 4:00 P.M. Pacific time, 530-621-2667.

SOURCES

INTRODUCTION

On page 10, the reference to "spontaneous" recovery, estimated from 40% to 70%, is from Stanton Peele's *The Diseasing of America: Addiction Treatment Out of Control* (Lexington, MA: Lexington Books, 1989, pp. 67, 173–176). This was the first significant publication describing the American addiction treatment tragedy. Drawing on the works of Vaillant and others, Peele showed the irrelevancy of addiction treatment to therapeutic outcomes and identified the deleterious effects of addiction treatment. Peele's examination of Vaillant's unpulished data, which suggested the harmful effects of addiction treatment, stirred brief controversy in the field but was forgotten amid government-funded announcements, which said that treatment works.

On page 15, the discussion of the characteristics of those who do well in RR refers to Willis Ceane, et al., "Alternatives in Self-Help for Alcoholism: Reasons for Discontinuation of AA," Harvard Medical School, a 1993 paper presented at the 1993 annual convention of the Association for the Advancement of Behavioral Therapy. At the back of *The Small Book* is a confidential questionnaire for readers to fill out and send to Rational Recovery. It asks a few questions about one's philosophical orientation, drinking or using history, what attempts were made to help oneself prior to reading *The Small Book,* why those approaches didn't work, whether one is now abstinent, and what means were used to become abstinent. The study is flawed to the extent that respondents who were not helped by the book were probably less likely to fill out the questionnaire, but it is nevertheless remarkable that 89% had extensive exposure to AA and 91%

were abstinent along the lines of AVRT. The most common reasons for leaving AA were, in order of frequency, the religious component, the disease-powerlessness concept, endlessness of recovery, the social interactions within the recovery groups. Interestingly, fully 27% of the sample described themselves as "religious," more than those who described themselves as atheist, agnostic, or secular humanist.

The reference on page 15 to elements of RR effectiveness is from Marc Galanter et al., "Rational Recovery: Alternative to AA for Addiction," *American Journal of Drug & Alcohol Abuse,* 19 (4), 1993, pp. 499–510. This study produced sensational results unanimously ignored by the public addiction treatment bureaucracy. Galanter et al. sampled 10% of all of the 500 RRSN groups that existed in 1992. A questionnaire distributed to participants at selected groups found that 74% of those who had attended for four months were abstinent, far exceeding typical abstinence rates for the broader recovery group movement. But the most interesting statistic compared abstinence outcome between groups addicted to various substances. There was no significant difference between alcohol and the hard drugs. This came as no surprise within Rational Recovery, although it contradicts the popular notion that some substances are more "addictive" than others.

CHAPTER 2

On page 31, the comment that few people need medical attention for detoxification points out an exaggerated emphasis on the medical aspects of detoxification in mainstream discussions of chemical dependence. (Vincent Fox, *Addiction, Change, and Choice: The New View of Alcoholism.* See Sharp Press, Tucson, AZ, 1993, pp. 190–191. Provides a good common-sense discussion of detoxification, sans medical obfuscations.)

CHAPTER 3

On pages 46–47, the discussion of labeling oneself "alcoholic" refers to Ken Ragge, *More Revealed* (Henderson, NV: Alert! Publishing, 1992, p. 150). This out-of-print, self-published book fell by the wayside, as most self-published books do. At the time of its writing, Mr. Ragge was a blackjack dealer in Las Vegas, apparently recovering more from his immersion in the 12-step program than from a substance addiction that led him into the recovery group movement. The book describes the indoctrination techniques used within the recovery group movement to disarm newcomers and create profound psychological dependency on the recovery program. Self-labeling, he says, is the critical first step in an unfolding indoctrination that undermines one's personal identity and confidence in one's own thought processes. *More Revealed* is carefully researched to show the history of the 12-step program and its roots in the Oxford Movement, and discusses the implications of AA in society. It stands as a definitive work on the recovery group movement and has had a significant influence on the development of Rational Recovery.

CHAPTER 4

On page 70, I cite from *The Harvard Medical School Mental Health Review,* "Alcohol Abuse and Dependence," a special report on a series of articles, "The Treatment of Drug Abuse and Addiction," published in three parts in *The Harvard Mental Health Letter* from August to October 1995 (editors, Lester Grinspoon, M.D., and James Bakalar, J.D., p. 5.)

On pages 78–79, the statistics on self-recovery are cited from *The Harvard Mental Health Letter,* Vol. 12, No. 4, October 1995, p. 3. The article "The Treatment of Drug Abuse and Addiction, Part 3" is by the editor, Lester Grinspoon, M.D., who surveys cumulative research on addiction treatment. Worth mention here is an unnamed study showing that 80% of those who recover on their own for over a year, including those unsuccessfully treated, do so on their own. Although the meaning of these statistics is not discussed, the fact that the self-recovered subjects were interviewed is significant. Fifty-seven percent of them said they simply decided alcohol was bad for them, and 29% said health problems, accidents, blackouts, and other negative experiences persuaded them to quit. Others used such phrases as "Things were building up" or "I was sick and tired of it."

The discussion on page 78 of veterans who self-recovered refers to L. N. Robbins et al., "Drug Use by U.S. Enlisted Men in Viet Nam: A Followup of Their Return Home," *American Journal of Epidemiology*, 99, 1974, pp. 235–249. Oddly, the study of this population of veterans has been limited to reporting simply that they recovered independently from the addiction treatment industry. I can imagine the subjects could practically earn a living providing endless interviews with publicly funded researchers and the mass media.

The mention on page 79, Illusion #10, of recovery being more common among more seriously addicted people refers to George Vaillant, M.D., *The Natural History of Alcoholism* (Cambridge, Harvard University Press, 1983), and his more recent press releases to the news media, such as CNN. Dr. Vaillant's long-term study of a group of "alcoholics" is widely accepted as a definitive scientific study. His fence-sitting on the disease concept of addiction is overlooked in favor of the quality of his methodology and findings in an area that is virtually unresearched, the outcome of treatment versus no treatment. It seems to some, especially Stanton Peele, that Vaillant failed to notice in his own statistics the adverse effects of addiction treatment on abstinence outcome. Ken Ragge suggests that Vaillant's oversight might be attributed to his personal affinity for the 12-step program, expressed on p. 194. "By turning to recovering alcoholics (AAers) rather than Ph.D.s for lessons in breaking more or less involuntary habits, and by inexorably moving patients into the treatment system of AA, I was working for the most exciting alcohol program in the world." Vaillant's unpublished works later were found to contain evidence that AA-based subjects did less well than their non-AA counterparts.

CHAPTER 8

On page 97, I include some sloganeering typical of 12-step programs, discussed in more detail in Chaz Bufe's *AA: Cult or Cure?* (Tucson, AZ: See Sharp Press, 1991). This book provides an indepth discussion of cult-like practices in AA. Using a fourteen-point checklist, Bufe concludes that AA is not a cult. Others with personal experience in the recovery group movement who use the same checklist, however, may conclude without a doubt that AA is a cult.

On page 134, in the discussions of addiction treatment out of control, I refer particularly to Griffith Edwards et al., "Alcoholism: A Controlled Trial of 'Treatment' and Advice," *The Journal of Studies on Alcohol,* Vol. 38, no. 5, 1977, pp. 1004–1031. This study was performed twenty years ago, showing clearly that addiction treatment is irrelevant to abstinence outcome. Many studies duplicating its results published since have also been ignored by policy makers. For example, at a special symposium in 1992, the National Institute for Drug Abuse (NIDA) queried a panel of experts, including myself, "What is addiction treatment?" NIDA did not know and wanted to find out, since billions were being spent on treatment, and they also were trying to establish addiction as a disease. Two years later, no treatment has been identified by NIDA, but a book is being pulled together that will probably not present AVRT because it is not a treatment and identifies some pernicious aspects of addiction treatment.

CHAPTER 15

On pages 233–234, the statement that there is little relationship between how parents and children drink was reported in the *Milwaukee Sentinel* (Sept. 12, 1990, "Study Challenges Tradition on Adult Children of Alcoholics"). A study conducted by the University of Wisconsin showed few differences between the children of alcoholics and those of nonalcoholics. Reviewed in *The Journal of Rational Recovery,* Vol. 3, Issue 2, pp. 23–24. The expression "adult child" seems to sum up the findings of this study.

CHAPTER 20

In Chapter 20, I have referred to AA as America's unacknowledged state religion, alluding to the rise of AA as a world religion sponsored by the United States government. Gaetano Salamone, M.Div., has written an outstanding series of articles on the religious aspects of AA. In his "Theological Assessment of Twelve-Step Recovery,"

Journal of Rational Recovery, Vol. 6, Issue 2, Jan/Feb 1994, p. 12, Salamone points out that all of the world's great religions have emerged with the active assistance of a national government, often to produce theocracies. He highlights the extraordinary support given AA by the United States government and American social institutions, particularly in their support of the disease-treatment concept, which is analogous to that of original sin.

On page 303, the statistic concerning the high dropout rate in AA come from Alcoholics Anonymous itself, the 1989 Alcoholics Anonymous Membership Survey (New York: Alcoholics Anonymous World Services, 1990). Like most research on addiction recovery, this survey omits attrition (program dropouts) from calculations of outcome. Abstinence rates of from 34% to 54% are reported in this study for those who continue in the program past certain time milestones—e.g., one year, three years, five years. The absolute numbers concerning abstinence grow smaller as the percentage of abstinent participants increases. Interestingly, internal AA polls in the 1950s reported very high abstinence rates for members, around 85%. Since the publicly funded addiction treatment industry, symbiotically dependent on the recovery group movement, emerged, abstinence rates have plummeted to single-digit figures.

In Chapter 20, the meta-analysis referred to is from Chad Emrick, J. S. Tonigan, Henry Montgomery, Laura Little, "Alcoholics Anonymous: What Is Currently Known?", *Research on Alcoholics Anonymous,* edited by Barbara McCrady and William R. Miller, Rutger Center for Alcohol Studies. This was a study of studies, an exhaustive "meta-analysis" of numerous studies on addiction treatment over the years. Scarcely readable to nonacademics, this study shows what has been evident for decades—treatment doesn't work. Research like this is abundant, very convincing, and ignored by policy makers who fund the addiction treatment industry.

The Rational Recovery Dictionary

On page 336, the mention of the Oxford Group is from Gaetano Salomone, "Holiness Revivalism and Recovery Theology," *The Journal of Rational Recovery,* Vol. 6, Issue 2, Jan/Feb 1994, p. 24.